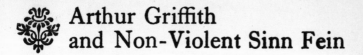

Arthur Griffith
and Non-Violent Sinn Fein

Arthur Griffith
and Non-Violent Sinn Fein

Richard P. Davis

Anvil Books Dublin

First Published 1974

Printed in the Republic of Ireland by
The Kerryman Ltd
Tralee, County Kerry

Contents

Illustrations

1917; 35—W. E. Shackleton; 36—John Sweetman; 37—Sean T. O'Kelly.

38—John O'Leary and Major John MacBride at Fontenoy, 1905; 39—P. S. O'Hegarty; 40—Jack O'Sheehan.

41—Bulmer Hobson; 42—Sean MacDermott; 43—Denis McCullough; 44—Patrick McCartan.

45—Anti-recruiting cartoon from *The Republic*, 1906.

46—C. J. Dolan; 47—Constance de Markievicz; 48—F. E. Meehan; 49—P. A. McHugh.

Between pages 186 and 187

50—Arthur Griffith—*from an early pencil sketch*; 51—Padraig Pearse; 52—James Connolly.

53—Sean Milroy; 54—Eamon Ceannt; 55—John Redmond; 56—W. T. Cosgrave; 57—Michael (The) O'Rahilly; 58—Eoin MacNeill.

59—Arthur Griffith with members of the O'Donovan Rossa funeral committee, 1915.

60—Arthur Griffith and Desmond Fitzgerald, 1918; 61—Arthur Griffith with (from left) J. J. Walsh, Mrs. Griffith and Mrs. Walsh, Croke Park, 1921.

62—Arthur Griffith and Eamon de Valera, London, July 1921.

63—Plenipotentiaries at Hans Place, London, December 1921; 64—Plenipotentiaries leaving London on their way to Dublin, December 1921.

65—Arthur Griffith arriving at University College, Dublin, for the Treaty debate, 14 December 1921.

66—Removal of the remains of Arthur Griffith from St. Vincent's private nursing home; 67—At Arthur Griffith's grave, Glasnevin, Dublin.

ACKNOWLEDGMENTS

National Library, Dublin (Nos. 1, 5, 6, 18, 19, 20, 21, 22, 25, 26, 27, 28, 29, 33, 34, 50, 51, 55, 56, 58, 59); National Gallery, Dublin (Nos. 2 and 7); Trinity College, Dublin (No. 4); Carden family, Dublin (No. 31); John O. Sweetman, BL, Castleknock, Dublin (No. 35); Vincent Colgan, Dublin (No. 36); George Shackleton, Lucan, Dublin (No. 37); Joe Keaney, Manorhamilton (No. 47); Sligo County Library and Museum, Sligo (No. 48); *Radio Times* Hulton Picture Library, London (Nos. 60, 62, 63, 64, 65, 66, 67).

Foreword

ARTHUR GRIFFITH gave Irish nationalism a coherent and rational philosophy. To any who had considered the road to Irish freedom only in terms like those of Mitchel's Ego to his engaging Doppelganger—"Go to, the revolutionary Leveller is your only architect" —he supplied the sane and necessary corrective that a progressive nation is fashioned from the energy and dedication of self-reliance. Sinn Fein, in its original and authentic meaning of self-reliance, could never fail, claimed Griffith, and to the motto 'no language, no nation' he would add as the essential complement 'no character, no nation'.

Arthur Griffith, whose ancestors came from Ireland's Presbyterian province, aimed to mould the Irish character into habitual acceptance of the solid material virtues of self-help, thrift (he considered hire-purchase an economic enemy), civic discipline and the full and fruitful cultivation of Ireland's native resources. Critics of his policies may offer the view that he has become irrelevant with the accession of Ireland to the European Community. They may point to the alluring prospect of an Ireland sharing in European prosperity, as if no other formula were needed to achieve it beyond ink on paper. It is hardly likely that the gardeners of Alsace will cultivate the onion-plots of Castlegregory. Nor is it likely that Europe will have respect or place for any other kind of Ireland except the self-resourceful country Griffith worked his life out for. He never spared himself. An old Dublin trade unionist, who lived in the same house in Dublin's Summerhill as the Griffith family and remembered Arthur Griffith working into the small hours of night, told the present writer that "he had no use for anything else except work".

One of Griffith's ambitions was to diversify Ireland's economy and way of life by achieving an agreeable balance between agriculture and industry. Ireland's positive, if unspectacular, industrial growth before her accession to Europe came about largely through his teaching and influence. This growth may be seen as an intermediate step without which progress to the wider possibilities promised in the European Community might be a very speculative thing. But there is a real danger that his dynamic and creative philosophy may be obscured. It would have gladdened his heart could it have been known to him that Ireland, according to recent discoveries, has considerable resources of mineral wealth.

Yet, he was no mere materialist. The Ireland he envisaged was one that would achieve, given his hopes came true, 'a dominance in Thought, Culture and Development rather than the vulgar dominance of Material Empire'. The words quoted were written by him in prison, for Griffith, though not a militant man, was a stubborn one, like his contemporary Gandhi, greatest of twentieth-century leaders, who followed his lead and duly acknowledged his example. He could write well. Offers were made for his talents but Arthur Griffith was unpurchasable.

He put forward his Sinn Fein programme as the inclusive compound of all the Irish traditions, unionist and nationalist. Official Ireland has been curiously slow to do him honour. Philatelists will consult our commemorative issues in vain for a sign of his remembrance. He is controversial, it is said, and therefore it would not be suitable. But he may, after all, have been right, and whether his actions be in dispute or not, he was great. It is past time that the strange and narrow taboos surrounding certain of our great men were sent for good and all to limbo. They should be no part of the free and liberal Ireland sought by the man who, for one thing, championed Canon Hannay against his detractors.

The analysis of Griffith's policies and philosophy made in this important book by Dr. Richard Davis will come as an enlightenment to readers whose impressions of the man may have been formed out of the controversies that clouded the last months of his life. In its wide and generous perspective of a significant era it casts into relief the personality whose influence in shaping it was of major importance.

Is saothar tábhachtach, bunúsach é seo. Tá léamh riachtanach ann do gach duine, ó mhac léinn go fear stáit, ar mhaith leis stair nua-aoiseach na tíre seo a thuiscint i gceart.

SEAN O LUING
Dublin

Author's note

THE current wave of bloodshed and violence in Northern Ireland has drawn attention once more to the nature of Irish nationalism. Old myths and patriotic fallacies do little harm in a settled community. The glorification in the 1970s of former Irish violence can, however, lead to disastrous results. It is therefore incumbent on scholars to provide a less one-sided account of the Irish revolution. The passive resistance tradition in Irish history has hitherto received little attention. Virtually no analytic work in depth on the exceptionally important decade in which Arthur Griffith outlined his Sinn Fein policy has been published in English. The present narrative is an attempt to fill both these gaps. The Irish Republic has commemorated Gandhi with a postage stamp and Thomas Davis with a statue but has not yet shown much interest in the application of their ideas to the current problem of partition.

This book grew out of research originally completed for a master's degree at the University of Dublin in 1958, followed by ten years teaching Irish history in Australia and New Zealand. In 1970 I was granted sabbatical leave by the University of Tasmania and a research fellowship by the University of Manitoba which enabled me to visit Ireland to extend my researches and revise my existing material.

I should like to acknowledge my debt to Mr. W. T. Cosgrave, Mr. Denis McCullough, Mr. Bulmer Hobson, Mr. Sean McGarry, Mr. Patrick McCartan, Mr. William O'Brien, Mr. Cathal O'Shannon, Mr. C. J. Dolan, Mrs. W. R. O'Hegarty, Mr. John Sweetman, all now deceased, and Mr. Padraig O Caoimh, Professor Liam O Briain, Mr. George Shackleton, all of whom supplied, by interview or correspondence, valuable material. I am particularly grateful to Professor F. S. L. Lyons, who guided my early researches in this field, and Mr. Sean O Luing for his continued encouragement and practical assistance. Colleagues who provided valuable criticism and suggestions for the later drafts are Dr. John Kendle and Dr.

Francis Carroll of the University of Manitoba and Dr. Michael Roe, Dr. Asim Roy, Mrs. Mary Nicholls and Mrs. Diane Caulfield of the University of Tasmania. Finally, without the encouragement and forbearance of my wife this book could never have been completed.

In the following narrative 'nationalism' denoted by lower case refers to patriotism in general, while upper case 'Nationalism' means the Irish parliamentary party.

Introduction

At 11.30 p.m. on 5 December 1921 the British prime minister, David Lloyd George, sat with three of his senior colleagues, Austen Chamberlain, Lord Birkenhead and Winston Churchill, in the cabinet room of Number Ten Downing Street awaiting the response to his final ultimatum to the plenipotentiaries of the revolutionary Irish Republic. The alternatives were a treaty giving Ireland dominion status, or an immediate and terrible war to destroy the Irish Sinn Fein government and army. Tension mounted in the cabinet room as the tantalising minutes ticked past the stipulated deadline. At last the Irish delegation was announced. Arthur Griffith, the short, square and bespectacled founder of Sinn Fein, was followed by the tall, handsome Michael Collins, one of the great guerilla leaders of the 20th century, and the other delegates.

'Mr. Prime Minister, the delegation is willing to sign the agreements, but there are a few points of drafting which perhaps it would be convenient if I mentioned at once.'

When the minor corrections had been made, the atmosphere relaxed. Hands were warmly shaken by men previously divided by bloodshed and reprisal. Michael Collins fraternised with Britons who a few weeks earlier would have coolly ordered his execution. It was indeed a momentous occasion. For the first time since the Norman invaders appeared in 1169, Ireland's right to a government of her own was recognised by her more powerful neighbour. But little joy was felt by the Irishmen. Collins knew that by signing away the Irish Republic and accepting an attenuated allegiance to the British crown he had signed his own death warrant. His adversaries had also staked their political future. Apart from Winston Churchill, redeemed from oblivion by Hitler's panzers, the English politicians associated with the Treaty were to be relatively unsuccessful in future years.

The greatest responsibility lay with Arthur Griffith, leader of the

Irish delegation. On returning to his lodgings after signing the Treaty, he refused food and drink, and spent the rest of the night pacing the floor with his head in his hands. What should have been the triumphant achievement of a settlement with England based on the principles he had advocated for nearly twenty years was turning into bitter anti-climax. As he strode to and fro in the long grim hours of that momentous night Griffith had a timely opportunity to review the history of Irish nationalism and his own place in the tradition.

As a propagandist Griffith had delved deeply into Irish history. He contended that, in spite of frequent invasions and defeats, the Irish people were an historic nation, never psychologically conquered. Though religious divisions in the 16th century had increased the polarisation of Irish and English, Griffith believed that the liberal Protestants at the end of the 18th century, who forced England to recognise the partial independence of the Irish parliament and established the so-called '1782 constitution', had in effect united the subject Catholic majority and the Protestant ruling ascendancy. In 1800, however, Britain secured an act of union to conclude the Irish question by liquidating the Irish parliament and providing Irish representation at Westminster.

Modern Irish nationalism derives from the late 18th century. Two traditions, frequently merging on their peripheries, developed in opposition to the act of union. Physical-force republicanism is traced to the United Irishmen, led by the Protestant Wolfe Tone, who attempted to obtain French aid for the 1798 rebellion which was savagely crushed and used to justify the union. Robert Emmet in 1803, the Young Irelanders in 1848, the Fenians in 1867 and in Griffith's time the insurgents of 1916, all looked to Tone for inspiration in their unsuccessful rebellions. Though only the 1798 and 1916 rebellions caused the British government serious concern, the writings and speeches of each generation of Irish insurgents kept their names before the public mind. The Young Irelanders in particular produced some outstanding nationalist writers. The poems and articles of the Protestant Thomas Davis in the *Nation* newspaper, the *Jail Journal* of John Mitchel, another Protestant, and a set of articles by James Fintan Lalor in his *Felon* provided inspiration for subsequent Irishmen. The Fenian writings though copious were less significant, but the men of 1916 included Padraig Pearse, whose poems, plays and articles were nationalist propaganda of the highest order, and James Connolly, whose books give him a permanent place in the history of revolutionary Marxism.

The physical-force advocates were offset by a constitutional tradition of Irishmen who hoped to obtain a repeal of the union, or some lesser degree of Home Rule, by forming a parliamentary party from the 103 Irish MPs, strong enough to bargain with or blackmail the existing parties at Westminster. Physical force and constitutionalism usually followed each other in cycles of failure or disillusionment. Lines of demarcation were frequently fluid. Charles Gavan Duffy, editor of the Young Ireland *Nation* and once on the verge of transportation for treason, later led a constitutional movement at Westminster. He subsequently became premier of the colony of Victoria and accepted a knighthood. The Young Irelanders were themselves an offshoot of Daniel O'Connell's constitutional repeal movement.

O'Connell and Charles Stewart Parnell were the most successful constitutionalists of the 19th century. By levying subscriptions from his numerous supporters, calling mass meetings and insisting on a pledge-bound party, O'Connell in the first half of the 19th century anticipated many of the techniques of modern representative democracy. Though he won in 1829 the right of Catholics to sit at Westminster and subsequently used his parliamentary party to extract concessions from a Whig government, O'Connell patently failed in his attempt to force the Tories into conceding Home Rule by the bluff of huge intimidating demonstrations. O'Connell's determined opposition to violence was held against him by the revolutionaries. Parnell, who dominated the political scene in the 1880s, was more tactful than O'Connell in his dealings with the physical-force men and prevailed on many to give tacit support to his movement. When the divorce court destroyed his standing amongst moderates and clergy, Parnell in a vain attempt to re-establish his position in 1890-1 became dependent on the revolutionaries. Unlike O'Connell, he was elevated to the status of an honorary physical-force man.

Griffith was born of Catholic working-class parents in 1871. After education by the patriotically inclined Christian Brothers he obtained work as a compositor. He grew up in the orthodox physical-force tradition and eventually became a member of the Irish Republican Brotherhood or IRB, a secret society descended from the Fenians. But as Griffith approached manhood he became involved with other young Dublin working-men in Parnell's final struggle. This experience was to have profound consequences. Years later Griffith described a handshake with Parnell, on the way to the election meeting where he caught the virus which killed him.

After Parnell's death Ireland was plunged in despondency. The constitutionalists were split between Parnellites and anti-Parnellites, the house of lords rejected Gladstone's second Home Rule bill in 1893, and the physical-force advocates became disillusioned and lethargic. Quietly beneath the surface younger men were congregating in literary societies to study the Irish language and work out new schemes for the betterment of their country. Griffith played some part in this development, but later decided to emigrate to South Africa. He returned in time to edit a new nationalist periodical, the *United Irishman,* called after the paper John Mitchel had published in 1848.

The Sinn Fein movement grew out of several patriotic groups co-ordinated by the *United Irishman.* The physical-force IRB wanted an open propagandist movement to act as a front for their secret society, but Griffith now had other ideas. Believing that neither physical force nor parliamentarianism could succeed in an age of Tory supremacy and British military might, Griffith, out of a mish-mash of Irish and Central European history, developed his 'Hungarian policy'. Instead of violence he offered passive resistance; instead of parliamentarianism he offered an Irish abstentionist assembly in Dublin. In 1905 a movement along these general lines was inaugurated. But Griffith faced two great difficulties. Some physical-force men refused to give his *via media* a chance. A young Quaker from Belfast, Bulmer Hobson, and a London postal official and subsequent historian, P. S. O'Hegarty, found it impossible to work with Griffith. Though Griffith had the support of men like George Gavan Duffy, the solicitor son of Sir Charles, and Robert Lynd, the eminent essayist and literary critic, the movement wasted much of its energy on internal disputation.

Outside his movement Griffith was also unlucky. In 1905 the long period of Tory rule ended and the Liberals took office. At first they virtually ignored the Irish issue. Their leaders, unlike Gladstone, were at the best lukewarm Home Rulers and their large majority made them independent of the reunited Irish parliamentary party led by the lack-lustre John Redmond. In 1909 the situation changed radically. The Tory house of lords which had for many years sniped at Liberal legislation took the unprecedented step of rejecting David Lloyd George's 'people's budget' whose land tax appeared to threaten the estates of Tory landlords. Asquith's Liberal government decided to take up the challenge. To do so a general election was necessary. The contest of January 1910, however, eroded the huge Liberal majority and left the government dependent for its survival on forty Labour and eighty Irish MPs. The death of King Edward VII and a second general election in December 1910 saw the position virtually unchanged. The Liberal and Conservative parties were dead level with 272 members apiece, while the Irish and Labour parties held the balance of power. Never had Home Rule hopes soared so high. Redmond could not only insist on the permanent curtailment of the lords' power, certain to be used against Home Rule, but also compel the lukewarm Liberals to force through an adequate measure of Irish self-government. In Ireland all eyes were focused on Redmond, and the interest previously aroused by Sinn Fein quickly dissipated.

Luck soon ran out for the parliamentarians. The 1911 parliament act by limiting the lords' veto to two years ensured the passage of the 1912 Home Rule bill by 1914 at the latest. But the Conservatives having lost the parliamentary game refused to abide by constitutional rules. Like the extreme Irish nationalists, they appealed to force. Basing their strategy on the relatively compact body of Ulster Protestant unionists led by the brilliant advocate, Edward Carson, responsible Conservative leaders made violent speeches encouraging the signing of an Ulster covenant to resist Home Rule and the formation of an Ulster volunteer force. The Asquith government soon demonstrated its lack of stomach for a serious confrontation. In Dublin, however, the secret IRB accepted the challenge with alacrity and, using Professor Eoin MacNeill as a respectable figure-head, instigated the formation of a rival Irish volunteer force. Though Redmond later insisted on placing a number of his supporters on the volunteer governing board, his prestige in Ireland was considerably reduced by talk of partition at Westminster. Griffith's Sinn Fein, still technically in existence, attracted relatively little attention as Griffith and other members joined the volunteers.

The outbreak of the 1914–8 War again transformed the situation. Home Rule, nominally on the statute book, was suspended till the whole issue could be reopened and partition arranged at the end of hostilities. Redmond impulsively offered Britain the services of the Irish volunteers and the vast majority of members followed his lead. A small rump comprising five per cent of the whole refused all compromise with Britain and continued to drill under the direction of the IRB. Griffith whose newspapers were frequently suppressed by the government helped the IRB to disseminate anti-war propaganda.

At first the 'Sinn Fein' volunteers, as they were inaccurately called, were regarded contemptuously by most Irishmen. The War Office, however, showed a marked bias against Redmond's volunteers while giving Carson's men every encouragement to enlist *en bloc*. When Redmond refused a position in the war-time coalition government, his unionist opponents had no such scruples and nationalist Ireland saw erstwhile advocates of violence against Westminster working in harmony with Liberal ministers.

By early 1916 the IRB supreme council had made definite plans for an early insurrection. Sean MacDermott, Tom Clarke, an old Fenian, and Padraig Pearse, poet and schoolmaster, associated themselves with the tiny Citizen Army, designed to protect strikers after the 1913 lock-out of members of James Larkin's Transport and General Workers' Union. The Citizen Army was led by James Connolly during Larkin's absence in America. Official leaders of the Irish volunteers like Professor MacNeill and Bulmer Hobson

tried to stop the insurrection which they knew was certain to fail
without substantial German help. Pearse, more interested in a
redemptive sacrifice than success, with Connolly and the IRB leaders
nevertheless managed to hold Dublin for five days with the 1,300
volunteers mustered on Easter Monday. Griffith, who had assisted
MacNeill in his attempt to prevent the Rising, offered his services
when the hostilities began, but was rebuffed on the ground that he
was too useful a civil leader to risk death.

The British suppressed the Rising with the aid of artillery, round-
ing up the insurgents and all those who like Griffith had been
associated with advanced nationalism. Thirteen volunteers including
Pearse, Connolly, MacDermott and Clarke, were shot; the rest were
interned in England or Wales. At first the Irish who had many
relatives in the British army on the western front reviled the rebels,
but the martial law executions, drawn out over a ten-day period, and
the murder by an insane British officer of several bystanders, including the pacifist writer Francis Sheehy-Skeffington, soon created a
revulsion against the government. The mutually contradictory
expedients of David Lloyd George, who replaced Asquith as prime
minister in late 1916, failed to persuade the antagonistic Irish parties
to agree on a form of Home Rule. Most of the internees were soon
released, but many were subsequently re-arrested as participators
in an alleged German plot.

Supporters of the Rising now began to win by-elections against
the parliamentary party. In October 1917 Sinn Fein was recon-
stituted as a republican party. Griffith's original idea of an Anglo-
Irish dual monarchy, acceptable to moderate opinion, was now
definitely dropped. Griffith, moreover, conceded the presidency to
Eamon de Valera, a younger man who had played little part in the
pre-1914 debate but who now possessed the inestimable advantage
of being the senior surviving commandant of the 1916 Rising.

Griffith was now compelled to play a supporting role without
independent ideological initiative. He was elected in a by-election
for East Cavan in mid-1918. In the post-war general election of
December 1918 Sinn Fein won 73 Irish seats and annihilated the
parliamentary party. One of the main reasons for this startling
reversal of Sinn Fein fortunes was the British attempt to impose
conscription on Ireland earlier in the year. Though Sinn Fein, the
parliamentarians and the Catholic church were united in opposition,
the former group achieved the limelight. By withdrawing *en bloc*
from Westminster the parliamentarians themselves provided endorsement of Sinn Fein's traditional policy.

In early 1919 those Sinn Fein MPs who were not, like Griffith
and de Valera, in gaol met in Dublin and declared themselves Dail
Eireann, the parliament of Ireland. De Valera, who managed to

effect an escape from Lincoln prison, was elected president of the Dail, or prime minister. He appointed Griffith his home minister. While de Valera toured America in 1919 and 1920, raising funds, Griffith as acting-president was civilian leader of the Irish government for most of the Anglo-Irish struggle. Though the Sinn Fein civil government had many achievements to its credit like the establishment of arbitration courts and the raising of a loan, it was soon forced to operate underground. The military side of the movement then attracted most attention. In Dublin Michael Collins, also minister of finance, used his famous 'squad' to eliminate British detectives and secret agents, building up an elaborate system of espionage penetrating the very heart of Dublin Castle, the nerve centre of British rule in Ireland. In the country, leaders of IRA brigades and flying columns, often openly contemptuous of the mere politicians in Dublin, carried on their own guerilla war with reprisals against the police and members of the *ad hoc* counter-revolutionary formations known as the Black-and-Tans and the Auxiliaries. Though Dail Eireann ultimately accepted responsibility for the actions of the IRA, this was little more than a formality.

Griffith, who believed that the IRA should act defensively to protect the Irish government carrying out its functions, heartily disliked the increasing violence. On occasions he was able to veto some of the more sanguinary projects, but his initial knowledge of IRA actions was usually obtained from the newspapers. Unlike Mahatma Gandhi who had sufficient authority in the early 1920s to bridle Indian nationalist movements on the verge of violence, Griffith was compelled to maintain a public silence. The truce of July 1921 must have considerably relieved Griffith's inner tensions.

De Valera's initial negotiations with Lloyd George failed because of the republican issue. In a final attempt to achieve agreement, de Valera remained at home while Griffith led a team of negotiators to London. The Irish strategy was to ensure that the discussions broke down on Ulster's intransigence rather than Ireland's refusal to accept allegiance to the British crown. Griffith, whose preference for a dual monarchy was well known, was manoeuvred into accepting the promise of a boundary commission which might make the now separated six county area an unviable unit for the Protestants. When Lloyd George presented his final ultimatum on inclusion in the British Commonwealth, Griffith, neglecting to telephone de Valera, promised to sign and was followed by Collins, who feared that the IRA would not be able to renew the war. Other delegates eventually concurred. George Gavan Duffy, who had supported Griffith in his earlier controversies, was most reluctant to sign, as was Robert Barton, a Protestant landowner and ex-British officer. Even more hostile was Erskine Childers, the secretary of the delegation, who had served in the British navy with distinction in the war against Germany.

Griffith, therefore, had considerable food for thought as he anxiously paced the floor of his lodging in Hans Place on the cold morning of 6 December 1921. He had less than a year to live. As he no doubt foresaw, de Valera and his friends utterly refused to accept the Treaty which they regarded as a violation of the delegation's instructions.

After a stormy debate in Dail Eireann the Treaty was accepted by a small majority and de Valera and his supporters resigned, leaving Griffith as president. In his speech Griffith not only defended the Treaty as a stepping-stone to a fuller nationality, but insisted on the democratic principle that the Irish people had the right to decide their own form of government. He opposed the anti-Treaty party which denied that any majority had the power to disestablish the Republic. When Griffith told the Dail that he was acting in full accord with the principles of Thomas Davis, he made little impact on the Sinn Feiners of that period, more interested in revolutionary practice than political theories of the past. Like the new radicals of today many Irish nationalists believed in action before theory. A generation gap yawned between them and the 50-year-old Griffith.

In June 1922 a confused election enabled the Irish majority to endorse the Treaty. A number of IRA leaders, with the ambiguous support of de Valera, whose own alternative to the Treaty stopped short of a republic, decided to resist and civil war ensued. Griffith saw little of it. After taking the crucial decision to meet force with force, the president of Dail Eireann died suddenly of a stroke on 12 August 1922. Ten days later, Griffith's colleague, Michael Collins, was shot dead in an ambush. The fratricidal war against the opponents of the Treaty was brought to a successful conclusion by the Irish government led by William T. Cosgrave who had gained his administrative experience as a Sinn Fein member of the Dublin corporation in the early days of Griffith's movement. Cosgrave was ousted in 1932 by de Valera's new constitutional party, Fianna Fail, which had decided to regard the objectionable oath of allegiance to the British monarch, when required of Dail members, as a meaningless formality.

Though Fianna Fail, apart from two short intervals, has governed Ireland until 1973, little progress has been made in integrating the country. The boundary commission, upon which Griffith had relied, failed to reduce the territory of the six counties of Ulster which, with a two-to-one Protestant majority, enjoyed Home Rule under the aegis of Westminster. The excessive emphasis on allegiance to the British crown, so prominent in the Dail Treaty debates and civil war propaganda, distracted attention from the real issue of Protestant Ulster and probably hardened the attitude of the unionists. Ironically, it was not de Valera but the successors of Griffith who demonstrated the accuracy of the pro-Treaty stepping-stone argument by taking southern Ireland out of the British commonwealth in 1949. But by that time the action was both otiose and impolitic. India, with a history more venerable than that of Ireland, was demonstrating that a republic without loss of dignity could maintain its association with the British community; the problem of reconciling Ulster Protestants to a united Ireland was increased rather than lessened by the withdrawal of the Irish Republic.

In the following pages emphasis is placed on the story of Sinn Fein in the first 15 years of the 20th century. Griffith then possessed independent initiative and was able to work out, amidst the cross-fire of opponents committed to parliamentarianism or violent insurrection, a programme for independence by passive resistance which was noted by Gandhi while preparing his subsequent non-violent campaigns in India. In their internal disputes of the 1900–15 period Sinn Feiners raised several issues—force or peaceful non-co-operation; confrontation or compromise; ideological rigidity or tactical pragmatism—very relevant to current radical politics. Irish guerilla tactics in the years 1919–21 have provided precedents for many subsequent revolutionaries, but Irish contributions to the general theory of revolution have been less frequently acknowledged. Even in Ireland revolutionaries may find their contempt for political as opposed to revolutionary theory disadvantageous in negotiations with equally intransigent opponents.

The first section of this book narrates the development of the Sinn Fein movement up to the 1916 Rising. Attention is paid to relations with the parliamentarians on one flank and the advanced revolutionaries on the other, the latter hoping that Sinn Fein would become a propagandist front without independent political initiative. The final chapter in this section scrutinises the Sinn Fein party machine. The second section analyses the ideological debate within the Sinn Fein movement. To emphasise the contrast between the non-violence advocated by Gandhi in India, and originally by Griffith in Ireland, and exponents of physical force, an epilogue surveys the memoirs of three successful guerilla leaders of the Irish war of independence.

PART ONE
The Organisation

1 Literary prelude 1890-1900

IT is tempting to date the genesis of the Sinn Fein movement from the disillusionment which followed the death of Parnell in 1891. W. B. Yeats later claimed it was Parnell's death that persuaded him of the necessity for working in Ireland with young politically disillusioned men.[1] He celebrated the demise of the leader with a bad poem, 'Mourn—and then Onward', which received pride of place in the Parnell obituary number of *United Ireland*.[2] The falling star seen at Parnell's funeral also symbolised for the élitist poet the beginning of a new 'epoch of democratic bonhomie', which compared to the previous age 'seemed to grin through a horse collar'.[3]

In reality there had been a stirring of Irish youth several years before the death of Parnell. Yeats, who had not been interested in Parnell before his fall, seized the opportunity to fill the leadership vacuum with his poetry.[4] When the veteran Fenian John O'Leary (1830–1907) was in 1885 permitted to return to Ireland after imprisonment and a long exile abroad he soon gathered around himself a circle of poets, writers and artists which included the 20-year-old Yeats. O'Leary's nationalist history dated back to his association with Fintan Lalor in 1849, but more significant was his veneration for Thomas Davis whose works had, he declared, affected him in a manner analogous to religious conversion.[5] O'Leary had learnt from Davis that the end could not justify the means and there were things a man could not do even for his country. Self-perfection and tolerance were to O'Leary the vital constituents of nationalism.[6] Apart from his articles in the Fenian *Irish People*, 1863–5, he had himself published but one disappointing book. However, as a voracious reader O'Leary had entrée into the best Dublin literary circles, nationalist and unionist. His influence on Yeats's early career was considerable. Not only did O'Leary convert Yeats to nationalism but he provided the poet with Irish subjects and helped in the mundane though essential task of finding publishers for the youthful writer's works.[7] The O'Leary Fenians though extreme in theory were in practice tolerated as harmless by Dublin Castle and, as such, proved suitable associates for an ambitious nationalist poet.[8]

Another member of the O'Leary circle was Maud Gonne (1866–1953), a tall, beautiful girl 'with masses of auburn hair and strange golden eyes'.[9] A year younger than Yeats, Maud Gonne also came from a Protestant middle-class background. The death of her father, a colonel in the British army, and a small legacy gave her the opportunity to throw herself into Irish politics and agrarian reform. Yeats who first met Miss Gonne in 1889 was immediately bewitched, though he regarded her politics as wild. As he admitted, 'if she said the world was flat or the moon an old caubeen tossed up into the sky I would be proud to be of her party'. He anticipated that Maud would make many converts to her cause.[10] Maud Gonne certainly encouraged Yeats to participate in advanced politics and the IRB but her nationalist influence was not decisive in Yeats's development. Nevertheless, Miss Gonne's own platform presence and energy made her for a time one of the best known Irish separatists. Yeats had no hesitation in attributing Miss Gonne's nationalism to the O'Leary influence.

A slightly older friend of O'Leary and his sister was the poetess, Rose Kavanagh (1861–91), regarded by Yeats as a 'beautiful soul'.[11] Miss Kavanagh's much lamented death occurred several months before the demise of Parnell. But the poetess had played a not insignificant part in the nationalist revival through her juvenile column, 'Irish Fireside', in the *Weekly Freeman* and the resultant Fireside club. The object of this body, established in 1887, was not only to interest young boys and girls in Irish literature but also to encourage creative writing. Irish classes were organised with the assistance of the Gaelic Union, the less ambitious precursor of the Gaelic League,[12] founded by Douglas Hyde in 1893.

One of the earliest members of the Fireside club was William Rooney (1873–1901) who has been described as the Thomas Davis of the 1890s.[13] To his friend Arthur Griffith, Rooney was 'the greatest Irishman I have known or can ever expect to know'.[14] Unlike Davis, Rooney came from a Catholic working-class background. Though his parents were nationalists in the Davis-Mitchel tradition, Rooney was forced at 12 to end his education by the nationally-minded Christian Brothers and obtain work in a solicitor's office. Self-education, however, continued. In 1889 the 16-year-old Rooney read a precocious paper deploring the current neglect of good Irish writers in favour of second-rate books in English. In 1890 Rooney joined the Leinster Literary Society and began to contribute verse to *United Ireland*.

The internecine Parnellite split cut across this healthy and constructive development. Several of the new literary and debating societies were split between Parnellites and anti-Parnellites. Moreover, many of the separatists, headed by veteran John O'Leary, who literally hurled himself into the fray,[15] joined Parnell in spite of their previous antipathy to parliamentarianism. For his part, Parnell was happy to give the impression that he was also disillusioned with Westminster, but his speeches were still couched in ambiguous terms. Some separatists, including, if we can accept the memoirs written in her old age, Maud Gonne,[16] remained sceptical of the wisdom of allowing the conflict to distract attention from the new Irish-Ireland movement at home. The youthful Arthur Griffith devotedly followed the O'Leary line and unsuccessfully attempted to persuade a Parnellite MP, T. C. Harrington, to resign his Dublin seat in favour of Parnell.[17] Griffith, then a copyreader with a Dublin printer, was amongst the crowd of young Dubliners who farewelled Parnell at Broadstone station when, pale and weary, the Chief departed to address his last election meeting at Creggs.[18]

Rooney apparently differed on this occasion from his friend Griffith whom he had known since 1888. According to later writers, Rooney regarded Parnellism as a compromise which 'was killing the nation'[19] and struggled to keep his nationalist society from disintegrating, like many others, in the bitter strife created by 'the distracting fight which Mr. Parnell was making'.[20] Rooney was, however, compelled to write the final minutes of the Leinster Literary Society in December 1892. The vacuum was soon filled by the establishment of a more successful Celtic Literary Society. At a meeting held at Rooney's home in February 1893, when half a dozen members of the Leinster Literary Society appeared,[21] it was decided to form a club to study and support Irish language, literature, history and music. The political policy was 'independent opposition', the Parnellite slogan, which indicates Rooney's need to deal gently with the opinions of his followers. Such tact appears to have succeeded. According to one member, Rooney 'in a short time had the satisfaction of seeing nearly all the old members of the Leinster coming into the newly founded society'.[22] In the following year the political policy was changed to 'independent action', a sign perhaps that Parnellism was now superfluous.

The constitution and proceedings of the society have importance in that the Celtic was to a large extent the forerunner and model of other societies which later amalgamated to form an early strand of the Sinn Fein movement. Weekly meetings took the form of debates or the reading of papers, usually biographical studies of nationalists like the Young Irelander and American civil war general, T. F. Meagher, J. F. O'Donnell and the Fenian novelist, Charles Kickham. Once a month there was a reading of the society's manuscript journal the *Seanachie*. This journal, 'one of the greatest features of the society',[23] 'afforded an opportunity for expressions of ideas from "backwoodsmen" who were shy of the public debates, many of whom could write very well, but were indifferent speakers'. Rooney edited and 'contributed more to its columns in prose and verse, than any four others'.[24] Provision was made for Irish language classes, elocution lessons and musical reunions, to which ladies were invited, at the end of each session.[25] Women, even Maud Gonne, were not, however, eligible for membership.[26]

At a preliminary meeting, Rooney, as chairman, outlined the objects of the society, 'which were briefly, to spread as much knowledge of their own country amongst the working youth of Dublin as the utilitarianism of the time obliged them to know about others'.[27] John O'Leary gave his blessing in person to the new group. Though a man of some means, O'Leary regarded the artisan class as the best material for a nationalist movement.[28] While Rooney 'gloried in the title workingman'[29] it is by no means easy to generalise about the class composition of the club as a whole. Some members came from working-class families and rose to the bourgeoisie, while the social status of others, such as journalists and paid organisers, is extremely difficult to determine. It is, however, reasonable to accept the claim that the bulk of the membership belonged to the Dublin working class. The well-known writer and Irish Nationalist MP, Frank Hugh O'Donnell, appeared on the membership list.[30]

At the inaugural meeting of the new society, held at Costigan's Hotel, O'Connell Street, in October 1893, Rooney lectured on the poet, Sir Samuel Ferguson (1810–86), stressing the latter's interest in reviving the legends of the ancient Gaels.[31] Rooney concluded with Ferguson's lament for Thomas Davis. The poem's plea for an Ireland 'self-respecting, self-relying, self-advancing' summed up the future Sinn Fein ideology. Respect for Ferguson, a political unionist, anticipated another tendency of the subsequent movement.

Shortly after the foundation of the Celtic Literary Society there was controversy concerning the multiplication of Dublin societies, in *United Ireland*. The Leinster Literary and Debating Society, the Phoenix Literary Club, the Ninety Club, the Excelsior Social Literary Club, the Goldsmith Literary and Dramatic Club, the Henry Grattan Debating and Literary Club, the Sheridan Literary Society, the Edmund Burke Literary and Debating Society and the Eclectic Club all existed 'within a stone's throw of each other'. In 1891 and 1892 W. B. Yeats had founded literary societies in both London and Dublin. A correspondent arguing that 'no small society can survive the apathy with which the best are treated by our citizens and our newspapers', suggested that they 'amalgamate and form one good healthy, useful organisation'.[32]

Two main factors ensured the survival of the Celtic Literary Society in the Darwinian struggle. First, the Celtic Literary co-operated with another body, the Young Ireland League, with which O'Leary and W. B. Yeats were associated. The Young Ireland League had been formed prior to Parnell's death. 'By joint action they have succeeded in getting an Irish teacher appointed in the technical schools and that is practical work—work that any properly worked society ought to apply itself.' Some members of the Celtic objected to so close an association with the Young Ireland League, but the tact of Rooney, who was a member of both organisations, prevented another split.[33]

Such tact suggests a second reason for the Celtic's progress: the enthusiasm and leadership of William Rooney. Old members sub-sequently admitted that most of the responsibility for planning and its execution fell on Rooney's broad shoulders. As so often happens, 'most of his colleagues seemed content to admire his labours and feel secure in his efforts while they themselves remained at their ease'.[34] Possibly this is an exaggeration. When the society moved from the obscurity of Marlborough Street to its own rooms in Abbey Street, where 'we began to loom larger in the public eye', members worked hard to make the meeting rooms presentable, con-structing seats, bookcases and tables. Soon a respectable library was built up and pictures and statues obtained for decoration. The purchase of a piano was an important event in the life of the society.[35]

At this time Arthur Griffith played a distinctly secondary role. Rooney did not even nominate him for membership of the Celtic till October 1895.[36] At the end of 1896 Griffith emigrated to South Africa and did not return till 1898. He was suffering from bronchial trouble and needed a warmer climate for his health. There was also a slump in the Dublin printing trade. In later years Griffith was to demonstrate an almost superstitious reverence for Rooney.[37]

Rooney has often been compared to Thomas Davis. He himself shared the veneration for Davis shown by most advanced nation-alists of his time: 'The gospel of Davis is today as fresh and as applicable as when he lived and wrought.' To Rooney only the influence of Davis had saved Ireland from complete anglicisation. In his emphasis on the need for a broad educational movement to show the diversity of Ireland's untapped resources[38] Rooney was also in the Davis tradition. The diversity of opinion and frank discussions of the Celtic would have been congenial to Davis. 'Many a sore knock was given, and a hard hit delivered, at cherished opinions.'

An interesting example of the Celtic's open-mindedness can be found in a debate in December 1893 on the question 'could the Irish nation exist independent?'[39] Not only was the orthodox nationalist case for Ireland's abundant industrial and commercial potential well stated but a convincing attempt was made to present negative arguments. Irishmen, said the sceptics, were unable to unite and their success in other countries was no proof that they could do as well at home. Ireland, with a coastline inviting invasion, would never have the power to protect itself. Her natural resources were small and much of her area consisted of bogs and barren mountains. The prevailing tendency, moreover, was to form larger and not smaller national units.

Though these critical opinions were not dissimilar to the verdict of the German–American economist, Friedrich List, a future Sinn Fein hero, Rooney and Griffith insisted on the abundance of Irish resources. Griffith, making his maiden speech at the Celtic, provided an earnest of his future polemical style:

> If England believed that Ireland could not exist independent she would have tried the experiment long since of granting independence, and when Ireland, beggared and pauperised, would have crawled back to England for protection and assistance, England could treat her as she willed, and the Irish question would have been solved. That the experiment has not been tried is an argument in favour of the affirmative side of the debate.

The Celtic held several debates in this vein, discussing topics like the de-anglicisation of Ireland[40] and the benefits of English rule to the Irish. On the first subject Rooney took a moderate tone, and like Davis stressed the value of Anglo-Irish literature during the long interval before Gaelic could hope to prevail over most of the country. Opponents, however, insisted that it was now impossible to revive Irish and even that successful de-anglicisation would lead to the material ruin of Ireland. It was also asserted that all Ireland's progress 'in art, science, literature, or civilization, was the direct outcome of English rule'. A suggestion which bore some resemblance to later Sinn Fein propaganda was that the British empire provided an essential field for Irish talent.[41]

It makes little difference whether these views represented the speaker's real opinions or only their efforts to maintain debate as *advocati diaboli*. That an examination of the basic postulates of Irish nationalism was possible is in itself indicative of a new constructive spirit. The unionist T. W. Rolleston[42] and W. B. Yeats both praised the challenge by Irish youth to the tired conventional formulas of Irish patriotism. Yeats found more Irish in London than Dublin willing to abandon a 'hiss the villain' nationalism and a crude veneration for the letter rather than the spirit of Davis's writings.[43]

One of the earliest organs of the new nationalism was the *Shan*

Van Vocht, published in Belfast in the early 1890s by the poetesses, Alice Milligan (1866–1953) and 'Ethna Carbery' (Anna Johnston, later wife of the Donegal novelist Seamus MacManus). The *Shan* in 1899 merged itself in Griffith's *United Irishman.* Miss Johnston's father was an old-style IRB leader who nevertheless in the 1900s helped the younger generation to change the movement from a mutual admiration society of bar-room habitués to a serious revolutionary organisation.

While the members of the Celtic Literary Society carried out their constructive analysis of the basic premises of Irish nationality a number of developments vital to the subsequent Sinn Fein movement were taking place in Ireland. Though the parliamentarian leaders took some interest in Douglas Hyde's Gaelic League the more advanced nationalists began to dominate its councils. Yet not every enthusiast who started the study of Gaelic as a spare time pursuit was able to carry it as far as an intelligent appreciation of the masterpieces of Irish literature. The large sales of O'Growney's first book of Irish grammar were not repeated for the more advanced second and third volumes. As Hyde pointed out, if Irish had been as easy to learn as the notoriously difficult Dutch language Ireland would have soon become bilingual. The Gaelic League, however, was not simply an agency for language instruction but aimed at stimulating Irish industries, encouraging social activities like ceilidhthe (Irish dances) and learning Irish history from the works of the great unionist historian, W. E. H. Lecky.[44]

The difficulty of the Irish language had several important consequences. First, there was in the early 1900s considerable emphasis on the struggle, soon to be successful, for the inclusion of Irish in the intermediate examinations and for compulsory Irish in the new national university. Second, nationalists failing to make progress with their language studies became dependent on the inspired popularisations of Standish O'Grady and the adaptations of Irish saga and legend in the plays of the Irish dramatic revival.

In 1898 W. B. Yeats, Lady Gregory (1852–1932) and Edward Martyn (1859–1923) took the first steps in the establishment of what was to become the Abbey Theatre. Yeats was at this time such a strong nationalist that fellow poet, George Russell (AE), warned him against denying his own muse.[45] His early plays, 'The Countess Kathleen', 1899,* in which the heroine offered to sell her soul for the sake of her people, and 'Kathleen ni Houlihan', with Maud Gonne in the title role symbolising the sufferings and resurgence of Ireland, were immensely popular with the nationalists. Lady Gregory, who knew some Irish, also helped through her plays to create enthusiasm

---

*Popular mainly with advanced nationalists. Others were offended by the racial and religious implications of the play.

for Irish subjects, but was less actively political. She assisted Yeats in constructing 'Kathleen ni Houlihan', one of the best pieces of nationalist propaganda ever written. In her own way Lady Gregory may have been as good a nationalist as Maud Gonne.[46]

Edward Martyn was a wealthy Catholic landowner and playwright, whose Tullyra Castle was situated in Galway close to Lady Gregory's Coole Park, to which Douglas Hyde and the other great men of the national revival were invited. Though initially a unionist, Martyn was to become the first president of Sinn Fein. In 1900 Martyn, disgusted with the Boer War, resigned his offices as JP and deputy-lieutenant for his county.[47] His conversion to nationalism was not appreciated by his fellow members of the high Tory Kildare Street Club whose attempt to blackball the renegade broke down when Martyn's counsel, T. M. Healy, discovered a minute flaw in their procedure. Reinstated by court decision, Martyn continued to use the club. A somewhat eccentric bachelor, Martyn also played a part in the Gaelic League. His donation of £10,000 to establish a Palestrina choir in Dublin was, however, criticised by the impecunious advanced nationalists.[48] Martyn's political views were initially very moderate. He originally advocated a more obstructive policy by the Irish Nationalists at Westminster.[49]

A third consequence of the language movement was the intensified desire for some practical political activity to counteract linguistic disappointments. The defeat of the British Liberals in 1895 resulted in ten years' government by a Tory party determined 'to kill Home Rule with kindness'. One of the most significant measures of this ultimately unsuccessful attempt was the local government bill of 1898 which, by providing democratic organs of local government throughout Ireland, opened up new possibilities for the advanced nationalists. Associated with this development was John Sweetman, Sinn Fein's second president. Like Martyn, Sweetman was a Catholic landowner, but his estate in Meath was the fruit of his father's industrial success in Dublin.[50] While Martyn was a playwright, Sweetman was an inveterate correspondent in the daily press on political and economic subjects. Far from being a land-grabber, as his enemies alleged,[51] Sweetman, according to his own account, advocated agrarian reform before the Land League (1879–82) of Michael Davitt[52] and in the 1880s bought for subdivision into small farms 20,000 acres in Currie, Minnesota.[53] In 1892 Sweetman was elected to parliament as an anti-Parnellite. When he found that the parliamentary party had abandoned Parnell's policy of independent opposition by refusing to force a general election after the defeat of Gladstone's second Home Rule bill by the house of lords, he resigned. Sweetman, regarded as a renegade by his former associates, contested two seats as a Parnellite in 1895 but was defeated by small majorities.[54] He was, however, elected to the Meath county council and became vice-chairman.

Meanwhile, in the Wexford county council, Sir Thomas Esmonde, MP, scion of an ancient Catholic family deprived of its peerage by the 18th-century anti-Catholic penal laws, conceived the idea of a central council of delegates from the local authorities which could act as a *de facto* Irish parliament. Esmonde's circular was in tune with current Irish–Ireland thought and anticipated Sinn Fein in its suggestion 'that the many problems of Irish social life must be studied and solved by Irishmen themselves'. Following Wexford, in early 1899 the Meath council on Sweetman's motion passed a resolution, modelled on that of the patriotic Protestant Irish volunteers at Dungannon in 1782, asserting Ireland's right to her own parliament and denying the competence of any other body to legislate for Ireland. Anticipating Sinn Fein's subsequent passive resistance policy, the council declared that 'we will not yield willingly obedience to any but a native Legislature'. Each county council appointed three delegates and the general council of Irish county councils, largely financed by Sweetman, came into existence.[55] The unionist councils soon withdrew and the parliamentary party, reunited and more powerful after 1900, eventually secured the defeat of both Sweetman and Esmonde. This example of Irish self-reliance and initiative, however, was not connected with the separatist movement which was still floundering without a policy.

Maud Gonne and her friends were by no means politically inactive in the late 1890s, a period of agrarian unrest which created William O'Brien's United Irish League and eventually brought together the main factions of the parliamentary party. Yeats was forced to defend Miss Gonne's work on behalf of evicted peasants against John O'Leary who, in spite of his early association with Lalor, disbelieved in agrarian agitation. According to O'Leary, Miss Gonne was merely showing off her new bonnet.[56] More to O'Leary's taste was the series of protests and demonstrations which, in the period 1897 to 1903, built up momentum for the subsequent Sinn Fein movement.

British imperialism, reaching its zenith with Queen Victoria's jubilee celebrations in 1897, stimulated Irish nationalists to reply with the celebration of the centenary of the rebellion of the United Irishmen in 1798. Though separatists were to grumble that parliamentarians had captured the movement[57] some IRB circles became '98 clubs.[58] The celebrations which extended to small towns in far-off New Zealand also helped to achieve the unity of the parliamentary party. Maud Gonne, who in late 1897 visited America on behalf of the '98 movement, despite rumours that she was a British spy,[59] was supported by the anti-Parnellite Irish National

Federation of New York and even by Patrick Ford's *Irish World,* later a bitter opponent of Sinn Fein.[60] O'Leary was elected head of the '98 movement in Ireland while W. B. Yeats became president of the '98 centenary committee of Great Britain and France.

The most impressive of the numerous celebrations was John O'Leary's laying in August 1898 of the foundation stone of the Wolfe Tone monument (blown up in 1971) in St. Stephen's Green, Dublin. *Fainne an Lae,* the Gaelic League journal, 'praised the speech in Irish delivered by William Rooney as one of the many signs of the times'. In the London demonstration, Dr. Mark Ryan, the veteran Fenian, also spoke in Irish.[61] Arthur Griffith, though he had participated in a South African '98 celebration, did not return to Dublin till October 1898. With improved health and some experience as editor of a small South African journal, Griffith was ready to join Rooney in the establishment of the newspaper which inaugurated a new and constructive separatist policy.

Though it was easier in the late 19th century than today to establish a small weekly, the *United Irishman* was at first 'woefully under-financed' with only £30–£35 capital. However, the original proprietor, Denis Devereux, who had been an apprentice printer with Griffith, was eventually bought out. O'Leary was a strong supporter. The *Shan Van Vocht* suspended publication and its editors sent Griffith their subscription list.[62] Circulation was small, but Griffith and Rooney could count on the readership of separatists and IRB men. To advanced nationalists the advent of the *United Irishman* was epoch-making. As P. S. O'Hegarty said later, 'Personally, I can vividly remember how the advent of the *United Irishman* came to me with the headiness and bewilderingness of wine, with the sense of comradeship which made it certain that the views of Tone and Mitchel would eventually prevail over parliamentarianism which appeared "hopelessly and wickedly wrong".'[63] John MacBride, who after fighting the British in the Boer War, was executed for his part in the 1916 Rising, believed the *United Irishman* equal to a dozen organisers. Even those who disliked Griffith personally were constrained to admit his superb qualities as a propagandist. Some, however, subsequently played down Griffith's early contribution to the *United Irishman* and emphasised Rooney's leadership. But it is unwise to accept uncritically the suggestion that Griffith compared to Rooney was 'rather an indolent man'[64] and 'stolid and slow-moving'.[65] Though Rooney's best work may have been done in the first two years of the *United Irishman,* Griffith's own ideas can be detected from the first issue where, in spite of his orthodox separatist acceptance of the physical-force republican nationalism of '98, '48 and '67, the initial editorial quoted with approval Jonathan Swift and Henry Grattan who had advocated dual monarchy and a sovereign Irish legislature respectively. Even the limited Home Rule of the parliamentarians was not rejected out of hand, 'but we do assert that the whole duty of an Irishman is not comprised in utilising all the forces of his nature to procure its inception'.[66]

The task of the *United Irishman* was facilitated by the galaxy of literary talent available. W. B. Yeats and his father, J. B., George Moore, W. K. Magee ('John Eglinton') the essayist, AE, Oliver St. John Gogarty, the poetic physician and raconteur, and many others contributed to its columns. In wit and brilliance this group easily surpassed the talented young men who wrote for the *Nation* in the 1840s. As Thomas Davis had possessed close friends, D. O. Maddyn, for example, who were not nationalists, Griffith was acquainted with writers like James Joyce who had little interest in Irish nationalism or respect for the Gaelic revival. Griffith, who sometimes stayed in the Sandycove Martello tower (now the Joyce museum) overlooking the Forty-Foot, was once nearly drowned swimming in its icy water.[67] He was normally a strong swimmer and an energetic cyclist in spite of his small stature. Joyce's books contain a number of references to Griffith and his 'irreconcilable party'. Though 'Stephen D.' considered Rome a greater threat to Ireland than England, his creator, also a Parnellite, sometimes wrote sympathetically of Sinn Fein.[68] When Joyce found publishers in 1911 unwilling to accept a reference to Edward VII's adulteries in his *Dubliners,* Griffith published the writer's letter of protest.[69]

With Yeats, however, relations cooled when the poet championed J. M. Synge's peasant drama which appeared to Griffith and most nationalist leaders of the time a slur on the Irish people. In his patriotic period Yeats had himself hissed stage Irishmen in a London theatre. By 1903 Yeats had gained sufficient general publicity as a patriotic writer to reject Griffith's view 'that literature should be subordinate to nationalism' and insist 'that it must have its own ideal'.[70] In his *Autobiography* Yeats told disdainfully how Griffith, 'the slanderer of Lane and Synge', had in 1899 offered to bring down a crowd to cheer everything in 'The Countess Cathleen' that the Catholic church would dislike.[71] But in 1901 Yeats had humbly asked Griffith to review 'The Land of Heart's Desire', which would 'make people take me more seriously as a dramatist'.[72]

The Boer War rather than the talent of contributors probably assured the survival of the *United Irishman* in late 1899. Though Maud Gonne calculated that there were 50,000 Irishmen fighting for England,[73] most thoughtful Irishmen who were not unionists probably favoured the Boers. The British government made several attempts, including the Irish visit of the aged Queen Victoria in 1900, to persuade the Irish to look more co-operatively on the British cause. The situation initially favoured the separatists who

were encouraged not only to assist Major John MacBride and
Colonel Arthur Lynch, fighting at the head of Irish brigades in the
service of the Boer, but also to organise demonstrations at home.
Continued separatist advance, however, was checked by the parliamentary party, which after its reunification under John Redmond,
fought back grimly against any challenge to its authority.

Though John O'Leary was still an important figurehead and a
source of inspiration to the younger men, by 1900, apart from the
IRB leaders who were about to be ousted by their juniors, the chief
active separatists were Rooney, Griffith and Maud Gonne. Of the
three, Griffith was the least known and endowed with the least
outward magnetism. Canon Hannay (the novelist George A.
Birmingham) tells of Griffith's humourlessness, taciturnity and
frigidity of manner.[74] Revolutions, as Terence MacSwiney said later,
fail when their leaders have no sense of humour. Nevertheless,
Griffith's satirical verse indicated a lively sense of the absurd, and
Professor Liam Ó Briain, who knew Griffith better than Hannay,
insists that with the right people he could be delightful company.
Miss Gonne was then at the apex of her influence. At Easter 1900
she formed Inghinidhe na hEireann (Daughters of Erin), with Maire
Quinn as secretary, at the rooms of the Celtic Literary Society. The
organisation, something of a pioneer in the history of women's
liberation, was joined by the sisters of Rooney and Griffith. Like
the male societies Inghinidhe emphasised cultural activities and ran
free classes for children in Irish, history, music and dancing. In
opposition to the Boer War it started what its foundress described
as 'an intense campaign against enlistment in the British Army'.
Members of the society distributed to soldiers and their girl-friends
pamphlets denouncing, with extracts from army medical bulletins
describing venereal disease, the moral dangers to which British
servicemen were exposed. There were frequent fights when male
separatists defended their sisters and sweethearts who sometimes
dared to follow recruiting sergeants into public houses. 'Fighting
soldiers,' said Maud Gonne, 'became quite a popular evening
entertainment with young men, Arthur Griffith used to take part,
though Griffith, I think, hated it.'[75]

Miss Gonne had many other projects under way at the time. Most
hair-raising was the scheme for planting bombs on an English
troop-ship destined for South Africa.[76] Betrayal of the plan disillusioned Maud Gonne with the IRB. More peaceful and more
effective was the patriotic treat, attended by 30,000 children which
she organised in reply to the loyalist children's fête to honour Queen
Victoria. The *Irish World* considered the separatist treat, which
included a procession from Beresford Street to Clonturk Park, 'one
of the most remarkable Nationalist demonstrations ever held in

Dublin'.[77] A strong campaign was also mounted against loyal addresses to British monarchs. These challenges were the logical outcome of the Irish–Ireland movement of the previous decade.

Of the utmost significance for the future were Maud Gonne's visits to America in 1900 and 1901 when she campaigned on behalf of the Boers, contacted prominent Irish-American sympathisers and obtained a small though vitally important contribution of £100 for the *United Irishman*.[78] Her article in the paper denouncing Victoria's visit as 'The Famine Queen', led to the seizure of the issue by Dublin Castle. It was in her defence that Arthur Griffith after horse-whipping the editor of the *Irish Figaro*—which raised the old canard that Miss Gonne was a spy—and refusing to pay his fine, received his first short prison sentence.[79]

When, however, Maud Gonne with Major John MacBride (no longer useful to Boer guerilla tactics requiring familiarity with the terrain) addressed a New York meeting under Clan-na-Gael auspices, she was strengthening an association which ultimately reduced her influence on Irish affairs.[80] Against the advice of Arthur Griffith who realised that a union based mainly on nationalist conviction was unlikely to be happy, Maud Gonne and John MacBride were married in Paris two years later. In two years the couple separated; when she returned to Ireland after the breakdown of her marriage, Mrs. MacBride, once a popular idol, was hissed at the theatre. Her political influence was thereafter much reduced and she lived mainly outside Ireland till her husband's execution after the 1916 Rising.

But Griffith had suffered a greater blow in the death of William Rooney in May 1901, which as Yeats said, 'has plunged everybody into gloom. Griffith has had to go to hospital for a week, so much did it affect him.'[81] The magnitude of the disaster is shown by Griffith's belief that Rooney might have become the greatest leader in Irish history. It is profitless to speculate on how Rooney, who has left only a few essays and some poetry, not of the highest quality, might have handled the events of the next three decades. It is possible that the combination of Griffith and Rooney would have been stronger than Griffith alone. While Rooney had Thomas Davis's facility for winning the respect and co-operation of men of widely differing backgrounds and beliefs—even the egocentric novelist George Moore was prepared to follow his lead—Arthur Griffith, in reality shy, introverted and retiring, often appeared brittle and arrogant to associates from whom he was frequently estranged. Griffith had leadership thrust upon him when he would have preferred to act as *eminence grise* for a more popular chief. Had Rooney lived, the pressure of events in the first two decades of the 20th century would have made the reflective and open-minded nationalism which had been the hallmark of the Celtic Literary Society extremely difficult to maintain. Nevertheless, the mature Griffith was probably the greater man. Canon Hannay, writing after his disillusionment with Irish nationalism, in spite of his criticism of Griffith's personality reflected that 'he was a man of absolute honesty and no idea of self-glorification or self-advancement ever seemed to enter his head. He had a very clear intellect and was one of those rare men who never shrink from the logical conclusion of any line of thought, or seek to obscure meaning with hasty words.' A closer associate, *Sean-Ghall* (H. E. Kenny), praised Griffith's voluntary poverty in a venal age and showed that the latter's lack of magnetism could be exaggerated. 'I love him,' said Kenny to the historian Mrs. Alice Stopford Green, 'with as rich a love as my nature can yield.' Kenny who had been to school with that 'hero soul' William Rooney, likewise considered Griffith a 'great soul'. At a time when Irish nationalism appears synonymous with bullets and bombs it is important to realize that though he had nothing flamboyant in his make-up Griffith was no less a hero for being somewhat exceptional in the Irish tradition. [82]

2 Sinn Fein united

IF the diverse separatist clubs were to offer some serious challenge to the government, co-ordination was imperative. The establishment of the *United Irishman* was a vital first step. In early 1900 Griffith published an article suggesting a loose federation of advanced nationalist societies.[1] 'The utmost liberty of action' would be left to clubs adhering to the general object of securing a sovereign independent Ireland by cultural, economic or military means.

The article stimulated discussion and correspondence. At the end of September 1900 delegates from several literary, athletic and political societies (including the Irish Transvaal committee) met in the rooms of the Celtic Literary Society.[2] A new organisation, Cumann na nGaedheal, following closely Griffith's suggestions, was projected. Its aim was the total de-anglicisation of Ireland. Emphasis was placed on cultural activities but there was also interest in consumer protection for Irish industries and the development of an Irish foreign policy. Physical and intellectual training for the young was suggested. The public boards, moreover, were to be nationalised in some unspecified way. The basis was being laid for the Sinn Fein social policy of the future.[3]

The original programme was drawn up by Griffith and Maud Gonne. Yeats was interested and supplied Irish names for the bi-annual festivals.[4] Rooney presided at the first annual convention in November 1900 and was elected treasurer. O'Leary became president. Robert Johnston, the old Fenian, and Major MacBride were vice-presidents.[5]

Griffith hoped that member societies would not lose their individuality, but these soon began to function as branches of Cumann na nGaedheal rather than as separate clubs. The Cork Literary Society, for example, was specifically founded as a branch of the federation.[6] The activities of the Cumann na nGaedheal branches did not differ markedly from the non-political Gaelic League.

17

Though pious resolutions were passed in favour of arming Irishmen, little concrete political action was then possible. The organisation was basically a front for the secret IRB.

Though Cumann na nGaedheal made some progress in its first two years—spreading to the London Irish—it lacked a clear-cut political policy and *raison d'être*. The basic difficulty was that any attempt at open political action was likely to be regarded as a betrayal by the IRB members sworn to a republican physical-force struggle.

This possibility of future conflict was suggested in October 1902 when the Irish parliamentary party sent a delegation to the United States. The Cork Celtic Literary Society asked Maud Gonne, its president, to move a resolution of protest in Cumann na nGaedheal. As the protest criticised the parliamentarians for betraying the Irish republican tradition,[7] the vague Cumann na nGaedheal objective had first to be changed. Griffith, citing the absent president, John O'Leary, in support, insisted that 'sovereign independence' was a more suitable aim and won a vote on the issue against the Corkmen.

But Griffith did not spare the parliamentarians. In a lengthy speech he compared the passive resistance policy of the Hungarian Déak, who had boycotted the Austrian parliament until self-government had been conceded to Hungary, with the weak-kneed efforts of the Irish parliamentarians slavishly attending Westminster. Cumann na nGaedheal accordingly resolved that it would give no assistance to the Irish parliamentarians till they emulated Déak by withdrawing from Westminster. There was, however, no suggestion that revolutionary republicans should change their objectives.[8]

Griffith, responding to interest in the Hungarian analogy by a series of articles in the *United Irishman,* attempted to clarify the position by insisting that he was himself a supporter of the Hungarian republican physical-force leader, Kossuth. Kossuth, however, realising after the failure of the 1848–9 revolt that war against Austria would be impossible for some time, subsequently supported passive resistance. Ireland, said Griffith, was in exactly the same position and could only be saved from within the country 'by intellect and muscle', not abroad by 'cheek and tongue' at Westminster.[9] Though Griffith was suggesting that Irish revolutionaries give only partial support to a Déak-like policy he soon indicated a personal preference for non-violence by claiming that Hungary could declare sovereign independence from Austria without bloodshed after the death of the current emperor. 'Concentrated nationalism' not parliamentarianism or arms was Griffith's recipe for national independence.[10] When he signed the Treaty in 1921 Griffith anticipated a similar peaceful evolution towards full statehood.

Griffith's opponents have argued that his growing dissatisfaction with the IRB persuaded him to look for some other organisation as the vehicle for his new ideas. The national council appeared to provide a better basis for Griffith's views than Cumann na nGaedheal. Yet the origins of the national council appeared extremely militant.

In 1897 the Irish separatists led by Maud Gonne and the then relatively unknown socialist leader James Connolly organised a demonstration to offset the celebration of Queen Victoria's diamond jubilee. Miss Gonne had a flair for such protests. A coffin symbolising the British empire was hurled into the Liffey. At an open-air lantern slide display in Parnell Square demonstrating scenes of British oppression a police baton charge killed a woman onlooker. Professional revolutionaries have always understood the value of such incidents in estranging the masses from the government.

Three years later when the aged Queen Victoria visited Ireland the parliamentarians, and apparently even the IRB, were split on the issue of an official welcome. The Nationalist lord mayor of Dublin, Thomas Pile, earned the undying hatred of many separatists by reading a loyal address to the monarch from the Dublin corporation. Yeats's letters to the press denouncing the 'crime' of welcoming a foreign Queen[11] and Maud Gonne's nationalist children's party did not quite atone for the defectors.

In 1903 Edward VII visited Ireland. Maud Gonne MacBride, whose beauty had earlier caught the future monarch's roving eye, led a stalwart band, including Edward Martyn, who placed his Kildare Street club membership in jeopardy, and Arthur Griffith, into the Rotunda where a meeting of the United Irish League was in progress. Redmond and T. C. Harrington, the lord mayor, were on the platform. The deputation, acting on some information obtained by Griffith that a further loyal address by the Dublin corporation was in the offing, demanded that the lord mayor should tell the meeting if he intended to present an address to the king of England. The result was a riot which nearly ended in bloodshed.[12] As AE told Yeats, 'Mrs. MacBride rudely shocked last night in the most gorgeous row Dublin has had since Jubilee time. The Rotunda meeting was a free fight and two MPs are incapacitated.'[13] Griffith wrote a mordant article in the *United Irishman* suggesting that there was no difference in principle between an Irish home ruler who wanted Ireland to control its own gas and water, and an Irish unionist who wanted them controlled by Westminster. Both, according to Griffith, were West-Britons, loyal to a country not their own.[14]

It was next decided to issue a circular to persuade Irishmen of all parties to unite against the presentation of a loyal address, and to form a national council for the purpose. The national council's object was to gather together Irish representative men prepared to stamp out 'toadyism and flunkeyism'. Both home rulers and nationalists were welcome provided they believed in 'the absolute independence of the country'.[15] Though parliamentarians were ungraciously invited, a true nationalist was still apparently required to believe in more than the absolute independence of Ireland.

A large number of well-known people joined this organisation, which levied no subscription. Many of these were later prominent in the Sinn Fein movement.[16] Maud Gonne was one of the secretaries. After 'a short but intense campaign'[17] and a big public meeting in the Rotunda, the loyal address was defeated by three votes in the Dublin corporation. 'For the first time since the Norman invasion the capital has denied before the world the right of the king of England to rule this country.'[18] This was Griffith's first experience of working with people who were not republicans. As he was growing somewhat disillusioned with the political ineffectiveness of Cumann na nGaedheal, the prospect of a different type of organisation must have been attractive.

Inspired by its success the national council in August 1903 decided to extend its objects and adopted a new constitution in order to 'proceed vigorously with the work of nationalising the local representatives of the country'. Unlike Cumann na nGaedheal, membership was on an individual basis. All those 'opposed to the British government in Ireland', a relatively wide definition, were eligible. The council of the whole membership was to meet once a month while the annually elected executive convened each week. Membership was to be limited to the original group plus representatives of national societies adhering to the council's objectives and new members elected by the whole body.

The object was generally to assist all movements benefiting Ireland and particularly to ensure nationalist representation on elected bodies, especially the Dublin corporation. There was, moreover, a programme of progressive social reforms aiming at the abolition of slums, monopolies, and the police tax, plus the reduction of general taxation.[19] The emphasis of this programme was on local affairs. The national council was typical of many contemporary middle-class reformers who aspired to purify corrupt local politics in large cities. The council offered neither challenge to the parliamentary party nor demonstrated a desire to fight national elections.

Nationalist societies with overlapping membership were still proliferating in Dublin at this time. The limited separatist population was already supporting the IRB, the Gaelic League and Cumann na nGaedheal; now another organisation was added. As the rule was framed to admit non-separatists, it must be assumed that a certain number of these—nationalists by any other reckoning—had some influence on their more extreme colleagues.

Inexorably Griffith was led towards a less exclusive nationalism. Maud Gonne's matrimonial difficulties began in 1903 and the period of her dominance came to an end. Griffith without a serious rival became the most experienced man in the movement; John O'Leary was a veteran and the other men of Griffith's generation did not equal Griffith in ability. The stage was cleared for Griffith to put on a play of his own choosing.

Owing to the interest aroused in the Hungarian analogy, Griffith published between January and July 1904 a series of articles which gave a full, if highly coloured, account of the history of Hungary leading to the *Ausgleich* dual monarchy of 1867. Though still written from the standpoint of the republican Kossuth rather than the monarchist Déak, the final article drew a parallel between Déak's Austro-Hungarian dual monarchy and the Irish constitution of 1782. Suggestions were made for an Irish *de facto* government.[20] The argument, used by O'Connell in 1843, that the 1782 constitution was still the *de jure* constitution of Ireland—the Irish parliament not having power to surrender it—was a useful debating point against parliamentarians and unionists. Griffith had no intention at the time of initiating a new movement. He hoped that eventually some parliamentarians would be converted by his logic and withdraw from parliament. The separatists might then co-operate with them.

Some of Griffith's readers, however, thought immediately of an organisation to fight the parliamentarians and their United Irish League. John Sweetman, who had resigned from the anti-Parnellite party in 1895 and subsequently worked for the general council of county councils, was particularly interested in the new policy and may have had earlier unrecorded consultations with Griffith. In July 1904 he wrote to the editor of the *United Irishman* replying to the *Donegal Vindicator's* lament that there was no potential Déak in Ireland by pointing to Griffith himself as the obvious man to lead an abstentionist party.[21]

But this was to misunderstand Griffith's intention. 'The Irish Déak must be like his Hungarian prototype—a man who can say, honestly, that he desires no more than . . . the restoration of the constitution of 1782.' Griffith believed there were several potential Déaks in Ireland, probably hoping that Sweetman, a country gentleman and ex-MP, would himself take the rôle. The Hungarian articles were written for a limited purpose. 'As it is easier to convince the popular mind by example than by precept we chose to illustrate the policy Ireland should pursue, by telling the story of its success in a country which in its history . . . intimately resembles our own.'[22] There was nothing new in the Hungarian analogy which had been noted much earlier by the Irish parliamentarians and Patrick Ford's New York *Irish World*.[23]

Griffith may not have been entirely candid in 1904, for while declaring the purity of his nationalism in the *United Irishman,* he was negotiating with Thomas Martin of London, president of the Irish national society of Great Britain.[24]

The Irish national society was founded in London in 1902. Thomas Martin (1858–1926), an architect, had unsuccessfully attempted to establish a similar society in 1896. Like Griffith's supporters, Martin was opposed to parliamentarianism. A member of the Irish national society, R. D. O'Hart, claimed that it had initiated the Hungarian policy. The society, however, was generally less radical than the London Cumann na nGaedheal with whom it appears to have clashed. As the national society received a papal blessing soon after its foundation it appears to have been a Catholic rather than a non-sectarian organisation. The *United Irishman* attacked Martin's society for disparaging the Hungarian physical-force tradition and being an off-shoot of the United Irish League. Nevertheless, by 1903 it had several branches in London and individual members in other parts of England, Ireland and America.[25]

In 1904 Martin determined on a more dynamic policy of contesting elections against the parliamentary party and striving to establish a government in Ireland. Accordingly he invited a number of nationalists in Britain and Ireland to a conference in August. The brilliant barrister and Irish MP, T. M. Healy, was included but sent a polite refusal. The national council members were decidedly cool. Arthur Griffith insisted that the proposed date be changed and refused to speak for Sweetman whom he seldom met. Martin's enthusiasm appeared an embarrassment to the national council which was nevertheless compelled from fear of isolation to participate in the conference.

The meeting took place in Dublin on 4 August 1904. Griffith, Martyn, Tom Kelly and W. L. Cole met Martin and three other representatives of the Irish national society. Sweetman attended a later gathering. 'The Sinn Fein policy was discussed in all its bearings and a further meeting arranged for September 3.'[26] This was a most conservative group. It is almost certain that neither Sweetman nor the dramatist, Edward Martyn, was ever a member of the IRB, while W. L. Cole was one of Griffith's personal followers. As late as 1900 Martyn had only demanded more vigorous action by the Irish MPs at Westminster.

At the September meeting, it was decided to publish the Hungarian articles in book form. The advance was significant. Publication was due to the financial generosity of Sweetman, Martyn and apparently Martin.* Sweetman, to save his purse, wanted to print only the latter

---

*The circulation of the *United Irishman* and *The Resurrection of Hungary* both appear to have been about 30,000.

section of the pamphlet which dealt with the practical programme for Ireland and the '82 constitution, but Griffith, promising compression, believed that 'the parallel rather than the logic' would appeal to the people.[27] By playing down the 1782 constitution which had been rejected as an objective by many advanced nationalists Griffith hoped to tread a middle road between parliamentarianism and republicanism. The *United Irishman* letterheads at that time still declared policy to be based on the principles of Tone who had rebelled against the 1782 constitution. But unlike the conservative Martin, who wanted to fight parliamentarians, Griffith hoped to conciliate them. National council opposition to formal organisation was indicated in W. L. Cole's letter to Thomas Martin in late 1904. 'Will let you know in good time when the others here think best to launch Hungarian policy actively—'tho' I rather prefer personally letting it grow, as 'tis doing, without *any* organisation, of its own nature.'[28]

Further meetings were held in Dublin on 24 and 25 February and decided unanimously not to form a new organisation but to extend national council branches into the country.[29] A scheme drafted by Sweetman was submitted to the national council first annual convention in November. Meanwhile, the council prepared for the triennial elections of county and district councillors and poor law guardians. An address to the electors, only vaguely mentioning the Sinn Fein policy, was prepared.

On 28 November 1905 the long-awaited convention of the national council took place at the Rotunda.[30] Two hours after a private meeting lasting from 11 a.m. to 6 p.m., the public meeting began. In the morning Griffith proposed the objective demanding national development through individuals and movements working inside Ireland, and then made a lengthy speech adumbrating a practical Sinn Fein programme and system of economics, subsequently published and republished as the *Sinn Fein Policy*. There was no reference to the 1782 constitution but great emphasis was placed on the potentialities of the general council of county councils, about which he had no doubt been briefed by Sweetman, at this time chairman of the Meath county council and soon to become chairman of the general council. There appeared a fair chance that the general council might adopt Griffith's programme, especially as the parliamentary party had not previously taken much interest in local elections.

After Griffith's oration, the reorganisation of the national council was discussed. Opinion was divided on the subject of branches. Though the five chief members of the preliminary group, Griffith, Martyn, Sweetman, Cole and Martin, were present, they were not united. Martyn, as chairman, took little part in the discussion and

Griffith was probably exhausted after lecturing for three hours. Sweetman and Cole, however, arguing against the multiplication of societies, opposed the formation of branches in the country. They wished to maintain the organisation on an individual basis. This was also the policy of Griffith who desired a propagandist body rather than a political party. 'Griffith's idea,' said P. S. O'Hegarty later, 'and that of the Dublin men, and of Martyn and Sweetman, was to keep merely the central body in Dublin and educate by press and pamphlet rather than anything else; and they opposed the organisation at the first convention.'[31] Thomas Martin, however, supported by the provincial delegates, carried a motion to form branches in the country with combative intentions against other parties. Thus a new nationalist party was born. Ironically, Griffith was defeated by the combined vote of the left and right wings.

Most oratory was reserved for the public meeting at 8 p.m., sparsely attended but including a young barrister, P. H. Pearse. Martyn again presided, and John Sweetman moved that as no law was binding on the Irish people without their consent, the general council of the county councils was 'the nucleus of a national authority'. In the course of his speech he cited as examples of Sinn Fein in practice, a recent Russian strike and the boycott of British goods by native traders at Calcutta in protest against the partition of Bengal. Sweetman was seconded by Fr. W. Harpur of Wexford (regularly elected to the Sinn Fein executive during this period) who adapted the English socialist slogan 'curse your charity—we want work' to give it an Irish application: 'curse your concessions—we want our country'. He strongly appealed for tolerance and the ending of bigotry. 'Let them be good Catholics and good Protestants in their religion and good Irishmen in the brotherhood of the nation' (prolonged cheering). Fr. Harpur's ecumenical spirit was somewhat marred by some anti-semitic innuendo in an otherwise witty and able speech by Griffith's medical friend, Oliver St. John Gogarty. The IRB stalwart and trade unionist, P. T. Daly, anticipated future ideological difficulties when he asserted his belief 'in passive resistance until by active resistance they could end the foreign government of Ireland'. Moderates preferred an entirely non-violent struggle.

The movement which pre-empted the title 'Sinn Fein' (ourselves), a phrase in common currency at the time, had now been technically founded. The theoretically more militant Cumann na nGaedheal was still a separate organisation with overlapping membership. To complicate matters further a new advanced nationalist society called the Dungannon clubs had been established in Belfast.

The nationalist revival in Belfast was largely the work of two men, Bulmer Hobson and Denis McCullough, both destined to play a large part in separatist politics before the 1916 Rising. Hobson came from a Quaker business background. Though his father was only a Gladstonian home ruler, Hobson at the age of 12, while attending the Friends' School in Lisburn, began to subscribe to Alice Milligan's *Shan Van Vocht*. He left school in 1899 devoted to the ideals of Tone and his imagination fired by Standish O'Grady's popularisations of Irish sagas. These works, lent by Miss Milligan, 'opened up for me new ranges of hitherto unimagined beauty'. Employed in a Belfast printing house from 8.30 a.m. to 6.30 p.m., Hobson devoted most of his spare time to nationalist activity. At Anna Johnston's home he met Douglas Hyde, Maud Gonne and John O'Leary. Hobson started his own boys' club in 1900 and attempted in 1903 to establish a Protestant national society, which, though praised by the *United Irishman*,[32] had only a 'brief and unimportant life'. Hobson was also prominent in the Belfast Gaelic League. In 1901 he joined the local Cumann na nGaedheal branch, accepted as an open front for the secret IRB.[33] Hobson's background and advocacy of temperance made him appear somewhat remote and puritanical, fitting him better, it has been suggested, for work behind the scenes than for public leadership. Hobson was, however, an extremely effective platform orator.

Denis McCullough's background was entirely different. Born in Belfast in 1883, McCullough's father was a local Catholic publican and IRB stalwart in the movement's unregenerate days. When 'about the autumn of 1900',[34] his father swore him into the organisation at the side door of Donnelly's pub in the Falls Road, young McCullough was disgusted. As he said many years later, 'I was very unhappy with the effete type of men I found in the Organisation and as soon as I found my feet, determined to try and bring younger and more active men into the movement. My success in this work was limited. However, I cleared out most of the older men (including my father) most of whom I considered of no further use to us.' McCullough was assisted in his reorganisation by Robert Johnston, 'Ethna Carbery's' father. The reformed movement laid great stress on activism and absolute sobriety. One of the new members was Bulmer Hobson whom Denis McCullough had sworn in 1904. To McCullough Hobson always appeared something of a hero.

Both Hobson and McCullough were members of the Belfast Cumann na nGaedheal executive which had several active branches in Belfast. But they grew disillusioned with its lack of progress. According to McCullough, the branches 'were mostly composed of irresponsible young publicans and grocers' assistants, with little or no national tradition behind them, from their home environment. Their activities degenerated into Sunday night "Celidhs" and as most of them had easy access to liquor from time to time, so Hobson and myself decided to close down on the whole lot and start a new organisation, which would do some serious national work and which we could control in Belfast.'

The final comment shows that Dublin control was irksome from the beginning. At a preliminary meeting in Belfast on 8 March 1905 the Dungannon club was formed. Bulmer Hobson took the chair and nine others, including Denis McCullough and the poet Padraic Colum, were present. It was resolved that 'the attendance of Irishmen at the British parliament is inimical to the best interests of the Irish nation by admitting the right of any body other than the parliament of Ireland to make laws binding on this country'. In its objects, the restoration of the Irish constitution of 1782, the preservation of the Irish language and traditions, and the encouragement of Irish industries, the new organisation[35] followed closely the lines laid down by Griffith in Dublin. At a meeting held soon afterwards a resolution demanded 'that a deputation from the club wait on the several branches of Cumann na nGaedheal, to enrol members who will be willing to pay a levy weekly (fixed at 1d.)'.[36] There must have been some good material amongst the irresponsible young topers.

It is surprising to find that the Dungannon club formed from IRB men should have originally stood directly for the restoration of the 1782 constitution, a mere repeal of the union. No other Sinn Fein organisation made 1782 a direct objective. In his memoirs, written long after the event, Hobson stressed his disagreement with Griffith. The latter, Hobson maintained, carried the logic of the Hungarian policy too far. Griffith used the national council when Cumann na nGaedheal with its large membership showed little enthusiasm for the king, lords and commons of Grattan's day. Hobson claimed that the Dungannon clubs were republican, not for doctrinaire reasons but 'because we did not see how complete independence could take any other form in Ireland'.[37] The first published Dungannon club objectives in 1905 dropped the 1782 constitution.[38] When questioned in 1957, Denis McCullough played down any difference between Griffith and the IRB, 'I think I can say with confidence that no question of incompatibility between Griffith's "Hungarian Policy" and the frank Republicanism of the IRB, ever existed.' It is possible that not all the IRB men viewed the issue with the remorseless logic of Hobson.

With the aid of about 'thirty or forty young men at a white heat of enthusiasm' the Dungannon clubs made good progress in 1905 even in the 'Black North'. Though liable to heavy punishment not only from Orangemen but Catholic Hibernians, the Dungannon clubs organised street corner meetings, usually on the Catholic Falls Road. Before their first appearance 'we were frightened out of our lives', but the club courageously persisted and gave a magic lantern display. 'When one has learned,' said Hobson in a magnificent understatement, 'to handle a hostile mob in Belfast, other audiences seem pretty easy.' In several places, however, violence made immediate retreat imperative.[39]

Though his nationalist activity led to frequent dismissals from employment, Hobson was soon asked to speak all over Ireland and also in London and Glasgow. By October 1905 the fourth Dungannon club, London, had been formed by P. S. O'Hegarty who became secretary.[40] Eventually there were three or four clubs in Belfast and others at Derry, Armagh, Wexford, Carrickmore, Coalisland, Kildness, Ardboe and even Newcastle-on-Tyne. The movement was soon able to hire as organiser, at thirty shillings a week, one Sean MacDermott, a former pupil teacher who subsequently had been forced to take jobs as a bus conductor and bartender in England and Ireland. MacDermott was originally a member of the Ancient Order of Hibernians. In Dublin Patrick McCartan, a young medical student in touch with the US Fenian Clan-na-Gael while living in America 1900–5, formed a Dungannon club among the students of University College. This club may have predated Hobson's movement. The clubs were not centrally directed but part of 'a loose confederation' with 'no formal organisation' apart from the fact that they looked to the first Belfast club, of which Hobson was president and McCullough secretary, 'as the centre of the movement'.[41]

In 1905 Hobson published a *Dungannon Club Manifesto to the Whole People of Ireland* which though it made no mention of Hungary aimed at independence through passive resistance based on a *de facto* Irish government. Hobson afterwards argued that the total abandonment of the Hungarian policy 'did much to clear the air'. Parliamentarians like T. M. Kettle had launched detailed attacks on the Hungarian parallel which were difficult to defend at public meetings. But Griffith, said Hobson, 'wanted his teaching to be accepted as a whole'. Concentrating on his paper, Griffith appeared to have little understanding of the difficulties facing speakers confronted by inevitably hostile audiences.

But as the Dungannon club was still non-violent and discreetly silent on the vexed issue of republicanism versus dual monarchy there should have been room for co-operation between Hobson and Griffith. Hobson, admitting that the aims were similar nevertheless experienced 'a profound difference in their mental attitude and method of approach to various questions'. In challenging the Irish parliamentary party and its subsidiaries in Ulster, Hobson was forcing a conflict which made Griffith's policy of peaceful permeation impossible. Hobson may not have been entirely fair to Griffith when he accused him of aiming at a traditional political organisation as opposed to the Dungannon clubs' attempts to create a small vanguard of 'unbreakable psychological strength'. On firmer ground is Hobson's assertion that Griffith's national council remained pre-occupied with the Dublin corporation and municipal politics while Hobson stumped the country in a propagandist drive. Hobson may also be correct in his suggestion that Griffith resented the former's practical abandonment of 1782 and Hungary in his public speeches. Dungannon club men who had already hived off some branches did not in general attend the national council convention of November 1905 which decided somewhat reluctantly to follow suit.[42] In view of the existence of non-separatists in the national council the decision of both organisations to form branches in the country increased the likelihood of a clash.

Tension appeared in London where there were four important men, P. S. O'Hegarty, George Gavan Duffy, J. O'Sheehan, subsequently organiser of the Irish hospitals' sweepstakes, and Robert Lynd. All four became members of the London Dungannon club in October 1905 but none attended the national council convention. They were members of Cumann na nGaedheal,[43] but the national council's objectives appeared mainly of Dublin interest. The London convention of Cumann na nGaedheal in 1905 adopted a detached attitude to the Hungarian policy which it welcomed as 'a manly substitute for parliamentarianism' while insisting itself on 'full national independence'.[44]

Thomas Martin of the Irish national society who had demanded branches of the national council, was *persona non grata* to O'Hegarty and his colleagues. Having won his argument in Dublin, Martin naturally hoped to found branches and a subordinate executive in London. This was achieved in early 1906 and O'Hegarty and his allies became members. As there was no doctrinal division between the Dungannon clubs and the national council, these men were now members of two organisations with similar aims, one acknowledging the leadership of Hobson in Belfast, the other that of Griffith in Dublin. In the end it was London assisted by pressure from New York which brought Dublin and Belfast together.

The initial question of co-operating with Martin was thrashed out at a meeting of the London Dungannon club in April 1906. O'Sheehan and O'Hegarty objected to working with Irish national society members and wanted to break up the London executive of Griffith's national council. Duffy counselled tolerance till the national council convention but O'Hegarty was not convinced and decided to consult Lynd and Dr. Ryan,[45] the veteran Fenian, who had some influence on these younger men. His subsequent memoirs suggest that he favoured moderation on the ground that Sinn Fein, if not as advanced as Fenianism, was a step in the right direction.[46]

No real doctrinal issue had yet arisen but there was reluctance to co-operate with men who, from a separatist point of view, had a shady past. Thomas Martin resigned from the London executive of the national council in October 1906, on the grounds of age and family responsibilities. He was not asked to reconsider his decision.[47] Pressure may have been brought to bear upon him. Martin was, however, elected to the Sinn Fein national executive as a non-resident member in 1906[48] and 1907.[49] His position in the movement then appears to have depended on Griffith's support.

Apart from the inconvenience created by the existence of three organisations with overlapping membership and the Irish national society question, no open quarrel broke out until the second annual convention of the national council in September 1906. Bulmer Hobson was then preparing to publish a nationalist weekly in Belfast. His supporters suggested the *Republic* as a suitable title. The members of the London Dungannon club, however, considered *The Irishman* or *Young Ireland* more suitable. Hobson nevertheless persisted with the original suggestion though this was probably devoid of doctrinal implications. He told Gavan Duffy that he did not consider the 'Republic' an ideal title. The name was, however, striking and republicanism was a relatively popular idea, especially in the north where some Protestants feared a Catholic separatist monarchy.[50] Hobson was at the same time attempting an amalgamation with the national council. It may well be true, as O'Hegarty argued later, that many of his friends believed till the 1906 Sinn Fein convention, that the 1782 constitution and the Hungarian policy had been abandoned by Griffith. After September 1906, however, some national council members seemed determined to revive 1782 and 'crush out and antagonise the separatist spirit'.[51]

O'Hegarty played a prominent part in this second annual convention of the national council which met in Dublin in September 1906. Helping to obtain a more decentralised system, O'Hegarty, alongside Bulmer Hobson, was elected a non-resident member of the national executive. Nevertheless both Hobson and O'Hegarty felt grave misgivings. They were strong in the Belfast and London organisations but did not come often to Dublin where they were sometimes shocked and disquieted by the compromising attitude shown by Griffith and his supporters. They now began to feel that the 1782 constitution was being put forward as a serious alternative to separation.

Later in September Hobson expressed to Gavan Duffy his disgust with the Dublin situation and suggested an amalgamation between the Dungannon clubs and Cumann na nGaedheal. The national council seemed weak in Dublin and was 'not pulling well' with

Cumann na nGaedheal; 'altogether they seem a poor lot'. Though approached by Cumann na nGaedheal men Hobson was reluctant to cause a complete breach with the national council, but was in favour of a meeting to amalgamate the other two organisations.

O'Hegarty, secretary of both London national council and Dungannon club, soon received, as secretary of the Dungannon club, a letter from Hobson discussing the amalgamation of the three associations. Hobson demanded the dropping of the 1782 constitution and insisted on changes to give greater power to members of the national council executive living outside Dublin. The executive, for example, was to meet in the most convenient place and the expenses of executive members were to be paid. At a meeting of the London Dungannon club all except an extremist, Mrs. Dryhurst, agreed that amalgamation was desirable. But J. O'Sheehan dissented from Hobson's condition requiring the removal of the 1782 constitution.[52]

O'Hegarty soon had new quarrels with Griffith. It was essential to hold a big public meeting to create enthusiasm among the London-Irish and raise funds by a collection. As secretary of the national council O'Hegarty asked for speakers from Dublin, such as Cole or Griffith himself. No one was sent, but a hall in London had already been booked and a deposit paid. Hobson, who, fearing a public wrangle over 1782ism and separatism, had earlier been reluctant to share a platform with Griffith, agreed to preside over the meeting and it was held under the auspices of the Dungannon clubs.[53] Another source of annoyance was the high-handed action of the national council in Dublin when it affiliated a new London branch directly, by-passing the London executive in spite of the powers conceded to it at the second annual convention.[54]

As a result of these incidents, the question of unity was thrashed out at length. In London three organisations existed where one would have had a limited membership. O'Hegarty was instructed to ask the national council executive in Dublin if the Sinn Fein policy could be advocated on 'an avowedly separatist basis'. The Dublin executive replied that while individual members could support separatism the national council must continue to accept as members all Irishmen 'prepared to ignore and render nugatory England's legislation for his country'. The Londoners were not satisfied and inconclusively debated whether separatists in these circumstances would be justified in remaining on the executive.[55]

In Belfast, Bulmer Hobson, with £60 on hand, launched the *Republic* on 13 December 1906.[56] His policy statement used Tone and Lalor to repudiate the 1782 constitution. On the other hand, when Griffith's *Sinn Fein* succeeded the *United Irishman*, destroyed by a libel action in 1906, he dropped from the head of the leader column the quotation from Mitchel insisting on Ireland for the Irish rather than the nominees of certain peers. Mitchel's statement was an implicit repudiation of the 1782 constitution. The *Republic's* first editorial announced a more definitely republican doctrine, rejecting all compromise with England, than Hobson's remarks earlier in the year would have indicated. While some separatists wished to play down the gap between Griffith's policy and Fenianism, Hobson appeared to be deliberately widening it. The Belfast Dungannon club followed Hobson in rejecting by a large majority the 1782 compromise.[57]

Griffith was seriously disturbed by these events. His whole grip on the movement seemed to be weakened. He had adopted a new policy which might, if carefully manipulated, add less extreme men to the exclusive separatist ranks and achieve a numerically powerful movement. As O'Hegarty admitted in 1924, no one in the early 1900s really believed that all Irishmen, including businessmen, farmers and clerics, would in their lifetime be converted to Sinn Fein on a separatist basis. In private argument Griffith insisted, in opposition to O'Hegarty and his friends, that 'the mass of the people were not separatist, and would not actively support a rigidly separatist policy'.[58]

Even in early 1907 O'Hegarty could see the necessity of uniting the London organisations. He attempted to bring Griffith to London so that he could see the situation for himself, but Griffith, irritated perhaps by an invitation to Hobson to visit America, did not reply to O'Hegarty's letter.[59] The latter, convinced that 'the organisations in Ireland will never unite',[60] then toyed with schemes for arranging an amalgamation of the London clubs on his own responsibility. As relations between Griffith and Hobson were particularly strained at this time, O'Hegarty became something of a mediator. In early February 1907 Hobson visited America to put forward the Sinn Fein case. When he passed through Dublin, Hobson called on Griffith but 'was surprised at the coldness and hostility of his attitude'.[61] *Sinn Fein,* moreover, repudiated Hobson, a member of the national council executive: 'this visit is not authorised by the National Council, nor undertaken in its behalf'.[62] As P. S. O'Hegarty said: 'The note in last week's *Sinn Fein* about Bulmer was very bad. I hardly thought Griffith would do a thing which might possibly endanger the success of the mission.'[63]

Hobson believed that Griffith had himself hoped for an invitation to America and had written to John Devoy, editor of the *Gaelic American* and Clan-na-Gael leader. The success of Hobson's meeting at Finea in 1906, attended by 5,000 people and the local MP, Laurence Ginnell, who later sat in the First Dail (assembled after the December 1918 British general election), may have persuaded Devoy

to cable Hobson rather than Griffith. In 1908 Griffith was invited
to America but the visit did not eventuate. McCartan, assessing
for Devoy the relative merits of Hobson and Griffith as speakers,
remarked that though Hobson's delivery was more effective, Griffith's
matter was much better than Hobson's.[64]

In spite of the hostility of Ford's *Irish World*, always at loggerheads with the *Gaelic American*, Hobson's mission was a great
success though collections were not taken at his meetings. Hobson,
at 24, was an excellent orator; one American newspaper considered
him a 'wonder'. He was enabled to make contact with the Clan-na-
Gael leaders and transact IRB business. The veteran Fenian Tom
Clarke attended Hobson's New York meeting and may have been
moved to return to Ireland later that year to reorganise the IRB. D.
McCullough and J. M. McGarry ran the *Republic* during Hobson's
absence. Hobson claimed that 'his success in America exceeded all
expectations'.[65] The visit had two important consequences. First,
Hobson rather than Griffith was regarded by many Americans as
the Sinn Fein leader. Second, American supporters insisted on
unity as a prerequisite for financial aid.

There was nothing to keep apart the Dungannon clubs and
Cumann na nGaedheal. Neither had any interest in the 1782 constitution and Griffith, once powerful in Cumann na nGaedheal, had
now little influence in either body. His position was precarious,
for though he could usually count on the solid support of the Dublin
men there was a strong opposition in the national council itself.
O'Hegarty met him at a time when the amalgamation of the Dungannon clubs and Cumann na nGaedheal was in the air: 'He
wouldn't discuss anything, was quite hostile and sneering and never
even smiled. He is bitterer over this than I could have imagined
and I can't understand it.'[66]

It was a confusing situation. The IRB was undergoing the reorganisation which enabled younger men to take over in 1906 and
1907. Bulmer Hobson, Denis McCullough, P. S. O'Hegarty,[67] Sean
MacDermott, Patrick McCartan and Seamus Deakin all became
members of the supreme council at this time, while P. T. Daly was
one of the veteran members. Tom Clarke returned to Ireland in
1907, and after co-option to the supreme council, worked harmon-
iously with these young men; thus there came together some of
those active in planning the 1916 Rising. But at the time these
leaders, though looking eventually to force for achieving final
independence, considered passive resistance a useful preliminary
step. Griffith's 1782 constitution, however, appeared too compromising and pacific as an objective. Some of Griffith's supporters,
Martyn and Sweetman in particular, were not revolutionaries and
actively preferred 'the king, lords and commons of 1782' to a

republic. The issue was whether Griffith would persuade separatists to tolerate moderates in their midst or whether the separatists would force Griffith to renounce 1782.[68]

Early in April 1907 a meeting at Dundalk of delegates from the Dungannon clubs and Cumann na nGaedheal decided to amalgamate both organisations to form the Sinn Fein league. Its first object was 'the regaining of the sovereign independence of Ireland'.[69] Thus, while rejecting 1782, frank republicanism was not declared and room was left for compromise. At a further gathering on 21 April, P. T. Daly was elected president with McCullough and McGarry, honorary secretaries; Bulmer Hobson held only a place on the executive committee. The significance of this apparent demotion is that Hobson being *persona non grata* to Griffith might —if given higher office—have been less likely to achieve a settlement.[70] This desire to bring about a general agreement is visible in a statement by Daly soon after the amalgamation. He denied publicly that there was any split between the Sinn Fein league and the national council, for he was a member of both organisations and looked forward to complete amalgamation at the first opportunity. Daly cited the first resolution of the Sinn Fein league to this effect. The difficulty, he suggested, was that national council members differed in their objectives. Some 'do not wish to add "independence" to their constitution. Some believe the constitution includes this already. Others do not like to go quite so far.' Believing that 'to start weak is to end weak', the Sinn Fein league declared for sovereign independence. Daly promised an active policy, supported by American money, which would contest seats at general as well as local elections.[71] Griffith, plainly, was to be given the option of coming to terms or running his organisation without separatists or IRB men.

O'Hegarty announced the amalgamation to the London Dungannon club. There was no comment on the new rules and organisation.[72] But his three colleagues, Gavan Duffy, Lynd, and O'Sheehan tended to side with Griffith. O'Hegarty, pleading with Gavan Duffy to attend a meeting discussing amalgamation, poured out his frustration with Griffith. Griffith had shown himself 'more small-minded—mean almost' than ever by barely referring to the formation of the Sinn Fein league in his paper. Originally opposed to the establishment of an organisation, Griffith now demanded blind unreasoning obedience from his followers. O'Hegarty felt that Griffith wanted to drive out the physical-force men who might frighten away the priests and moderate businessmen whom he was hoping to conciliate. The other organisations were required to make a total submission to Griffith. O'Hegarty, who believed a split, but not total separation, almost inevitable, was convinced that Griffith would never be able, by utilising the 1782 constitution,[73] to beat the parliamentarians at their own game.

Unfortunately, little of Griffith's correspondence has survived. It seems unlikely that he was in fact trying to get rid of the separatists or physical-force men—and certainly not warranted by the facts —but it does seem probable that he wanted, as O'Hegarty suggested, 'the other organisations to dissolve and come into the National Council meekly and humbly'. O'Hegarty's conviction that the 1782 idea would never convert the parliamentarians is interesting. He also implies that Griffith was not safe in his own organisation and could be beaten. Though the practical management of the national council was in the hands of the resident executive, the annual convention might bring delegates from the country who could be persuaded to vote against Griffith. Had this happened Griffith would probably have thrown over the movement, which would have become a straight IRB front controlled through the supreme council,[74] and devoted his energies to propounding his policy in the columns of *Sinn Fein*.

It did not happen. Griffith's 1782 policy suddenly bore fruit. In June John O'Meara, MP for South Kilkenny, resigned his seat, later sitting in the First Dail; while two other MPs, C. J. Dolan and Sir Thomas Esmonde, whose county council work had anticipated certain Sinn Fein policies, announced their resignation from the parliamentary party. Though Esmonde, after some wavering, returned reluctantly to his former allegiance, Dolan accepted the challenge to re-contest his seat at North Leitrim as a Sinn Feiner. Dolan was a genuine 1782 man converted by Griffith's *Resurrection of Hungary*. He believed 'that under the circumstances existing in 1907, the restoration of the constitution of 1782 was a more practical objective than the establishment of an Irish Republic'. Dolan regarded 1782 as repeal of the act of union in contrast to the parliamentary party's demand for a legislature subordinate to Westminster.[75] Sir Thomas Esmonde, during his brief flirtation with Sinn Fein, showed a similar inclination in a letter read at both national council and Sinn Fein league demonstrations.[76]

Griffith, therefore, had been partially justified by results. It was now essential to drop all quarrels in the face of the common enemy. Though Griffith did not want to contest parliamentary elections, he was forced to fight at North Leitrim; though the Sinn Fein leaguers did not like 1782 men they were compelled to support Dolan. Griffith's organising ability was recognised by all. Denis McCullough wrote to P. S. O'Hegarty and asked him to assist in supplying 'C. J. Dolan with the sinews of war in the shape of "cold cash" ', remarking that the 'Party' were 'throwing all their strength and power into the battle recognising that their very existence hangs in the balance'. Hobson and MacDermott had already gone to Leitrim to begin the campaign.[77]

Immediately before the annual convention of the national council in August 1907, John Devoy, as editor of the *Gaelic American,* sent P. T. Daly, president of the Sinn Fein league, a cheque for £100, 'as an instalment on account of the North Leitrim Election Fund'.[78] As a result of Hobson's American tour and perhaps Devoy's own scepticism about the Hungarian policy, the Irish American sympathisers were recognising the Sinn Fein league as canonical Sinn Fein. Daly immediately sent the cheque to Griffith, who controlled the election fund, and thus further demonstrated the need for unity.

The long-awaited convention took place in the last week of August 1907. An agitated O'Hegarty, writing to Gavan Duffy to persuade him to cross over to Ireland for it, showed his concern: 'It is important that every man with a head on him be there. . . . Personally, I risk dismissal by going.'[79] Everyone was weary of the arid dispute. O'Hegarty exhibited considerable interest in the presence of members who differed from him in opinion.

When the delegates assembled, an exhausting two-hour discussion on amalgamation ensued. Daly, Hobson and O'Hegarty explained the views of the Sinn Fein league and intimated their willingness to 'join with the National Council in putting the Sinn Fein programme into active practice'. Griffith, Sweetman and others took part in the debate at which the new member, C. J. Dolan, outlined his views. Finally on the motion of P. T. Daly and John Sweetman it was decided amidst cheering to amalgamate the national council and the Sinn Fein league. The objective was now to obtain Irish independence, 'declaring that no voluntary agreement would be entered into with England until the British Government recognised the compact made between the parliaments of Ireland and Britain, and which stated that the only authority competent to make laws binding on the people of Ireland was the parliament of Ireland—a right which was acknowledged by Great Britain to be established and not questioned at any future time. It is further declared in the name of the Sinn Fein organisation that we are determined to make use of any powers we have, or may have at any time in the future, to work for Ireland's advancement and the creation of a prosperous, virile, and independent nation.'[80]

It is impossible to see how this position differed from that held by Griffith throughout the controversy. In a pamphlet by O'Sheehan, which O'Hegarty had previously criticised, it was also suggested that while all had different views about ultimate policy there was no reason why England should not first be kept to her compact of the 1780s.[81]

O'Hegarty maintained soon afterwards, and in 1952, that the new constitution was acceptable to the separatist, that 'the convention of 1907 did declare . . . against the constitution of '82 as a national basis', and that the constitutionalists had missed their opportunity to adopt 1782 openly. The clause dealing with the '82 constitution O'Hegarty explained away as 'merely a proviso that if England ever offers the '82 constitution we hold ourselves at liberty to consider it, but that the basic principle of the organisation is independence full and absolute'.[82] Hobson similarly insisted that 'we outvoted Griffith in his own organisation'.[83] The record hardly supports this claim. Republicans were compelled to swallow the renunciation act; Griffith's moderate ally Sweetman seconded the compromise suggestion. It was nevertheless true that those members of the IRB supreme council, who intended active resistance to drive out the British after passive resistance had demoralised them, were not bound by the strict wording of the national council constitution to accept the 1782 constitution as a stepping stone, but could apply force immediately. The fact that the IRB was a secret society made it difficult to state these 'hair splitting' views publicly.[84] If this interpretation is correct the arguments used by the physical-force men were casuistical in that moderates would hardly be attracted to the organisation if the most active adherents did not take its constitution seriously.

Sinn Fein was now technically united. Significantly, the decision to amalgamate was cabled to the critical Irish-American supporters.[85] It is perhaps a mistake to dwell too much on the arguments and mental attitudes of the different sections. The trouble can be partly explained by the geographical location of the adversaries and consequent personal differences. The IRB at that time had no hope of success in an insurrectionary policy—later events must not be allowed to obscure this fact—and all arguments on physical force versus passive resistance were then academic. Griffith's position at the centre of affairs, controlling the newspaper and dominating the resident executive of the national council, made the provincials and Londoners anxious to keep his influence within bounds. The compromise in 1907 may be regarded as a complete, if temporary, victory for him, and he was able to use his freedom of action in the next two years, often to the chagrin of the IRB men.

3 Redmond confronted
1900 - 14

THOUGH separatists and physical-force men had assisted Parnell in his last struggle, there was in the 1890s every reason for the reinforcement of their traditional hostility to parliamentarianism. The fiasco of Gladstone's second Home Rule bill and the vituperative strife between anti-Parnellites, Parnellites and Healyites were sufficient to disgust many long-term supporters of the parliamentary party. To separatists, not one of the rival factions possessed a redeeming feature. Anti-Parnellites and Healyites stood self-condemned as deserters of the Chief. Healy's venom in the battle against Parnell made him so unpopular that Griffith is said to have opposed for this reason his nomination as first governor-general of the Irish Free State.[1] Early Sinn Fein did not, however, neglect to utilise Healy's legal acumen in its not infrequent law suits. Redmond, though leader of the Parnellites, was, if anything, less popular with advanced nationalists who regarded him as a Judas wishing to betray his leader in 1891. It was maintained that Redmond by his refusal to replace the ailing Parnell as speaker at the rain-swept Creggs meeting had been the direct cause of the Chief's death.[2] Separatists in both Ireland and the USA continued to berate Redmond for a speech to the Cambridge union in 1895 when he wished to 'clear the way for the great imperial senate which in the future would govern the empire'. Redmond was also reported to have declared separation 'impossible and undesirable'.[3] Though Redmond complained of misrepresentation, these phrases were probably indicative of his real opinions.

This formal condemnation should not be regarded as a final breach between separatist and parliamentarian. Maud Gonne's work for evicted tenants and her visit to America in 1897 brought her into close touch with constitutional nationalists. The 1898 centenary movement was supported by both separatist and parliamentarian. Yeats was accused of using the movement to unify the Parnellites and anti-Parnellites.[4] The outbreak of the Boer War in 1899 provided further opportunities for co-operation. On the executive of the Transvaal committee, organised to provide an ambulance and medical supplies for the Boers and members of the Irish brigade, Maud Gonne, John O'Leary and Arthur Griffith worked with John Redmond's brother William and T. D. Sullivan, a Healyite MP. John Dillon, the anti-Parnellite leader, Michael Davitt and John Sweetman sent donations. Separatists certainly predominated in the committee, really a façade to cover the departure of Irishmen joining the Boers. Meetings were held in the Celtic Literary Society rooms.[5] At Westminster, Irish MPs spoke vehemently for the Boers and Michael Davitt ostentatiously withdrew forever, telling the furious English MPs that they were open to no other argument but force.[6]

Davitt's withdrawal might have led to another period of co-operation between separatist and parliamentarian as in the days of the Land League, now emulated by William O'Brien's new United Irish League which recaptured some of the old enthusiasm. Irish MPs were again cast into prison. Had the parliamentary party been reunited under a dynamic leader of Parnell's stature the separatists might have contentedly slipped into the background. It was not to be. Rather than rejoin the Fenians Davitt threw himself into the infighting which on 6 February 1900 resulted in the election of Redmond as chairman of the reunited party.

Moderate nationalists were pleased to see the healing of the fratricidal conflict. Even some separatists may have been gratified. William Rooney, less impressed than Griffith by Parnell, seemed to envisage some co-operation with the reunited parliamentary party. Though regarding parliamentarianism as 'a battered suit of mail', he suggested that it should be tolerated as one weapon in the nationalist armoury. Without stressing the doctrinaire need for abstentionism, Rooney suggested that the heavy expense of maintaining Irish MPs at Westminster might well be diverted to the maintenance of Irish trading representatives at foreign capitals.[7] Moderates like Martyn and Sweetman, who donated £10 to the reunited party,[8] were optimistic about the future of parliamentarianism.

Rooney's relatively tolerant article may have been a reply to Griffith's much more antagonistic statement, published in the previous week, which elicited a reply from Redmond himself. But even Griffith attacked Redmond on personal grounds, implying that co-operation under another leader would have been feasible. Physical-force men could not have denied the logic of Redmond's retort that in 1900 there was no sane alternative to constitutionalism.[9] Unfortunately for national unity, Redmond's election and

Davitt's resignation led inexorably to a bitter confrontation between separatist and parliamentarian.

Dillon and O'Brien had accepted Redmond's leadership in the hope of checkmating Healy whose influence in the country threatened the power of the United Irish League. The by-election caused by Davitt's resignation of the South Mayo seat was now a test case to determine the extent of League influence. A convention of the South Mayo UIL nominated its imprisoned organiser, John O'Donnell.[10]

The separatists meanwhile were contemplating a splendid gesture of defiance by securing the election of Major John MacBride, currently in arms against the British empire. The *United Irishman* publicised its intention on 10 January 1900—before the meeting which reunified the parliamentary party—and as late as 17 February professed disbelief in the possibility that any nationalist would oppose MacBride. The UIL argued that O'Donnell had been chosen by a convention of local priests and people before MacBride was mentioned.[11]

In normal circumstances a compromise would have been arranged. The Transvaal committee on O'Leary's motion endorsed MacBride's candidature and Mark Ryan's Irish national club in London expected O'Donnell to head the list of MacBride's supporters. Griffith himself approached O'Donnell to ask him to stand down, pointing out that he could have the seat after the inevitable declaration of MacBride's ineligibility. O'Donnell hesitated and wrote to O'Brien for instructions. Back came the cable: 'Fight MacBride to the end.'[12]

O'Brien was in a difficult position. In other circumstances he might have given his assent to MacBride's election. The gesture was not in tune with O'Brien's agrarian policy, besides being a needless affront to moderate unionist opinion. But Healy on hearing of O'Donnell's candidature had 'instantly cried out for any candidate to oppose him' and subsequently supported MacBride.[13] O'Brien now considered the future of the UIL at stake. Whether or not collusion existed between Healy and Griffith made little difference. Healy would in either case have benefited from the rejection of the candidate of the United Irish League. O'Brien had little choice but to fight the election. To Griffith, responsibility for the contest lay squarely with the parliamentarians.[14]

The result was never in doubt. O'Brien fought on his most favourable ground. Neither the IRB, which was behind MacBride, nor Healy was popular in Mayo. MacBride, a native of the district and a hero after his gallantry at the battle of Colenso, could not appear in person. In his speeches and those of his followers, O'Brien was careful to make Healy the object of his invective. He praised

MacBride, insisting that the latter was ignorant of the election, and mildly criticised his canvassers as innocent dupes. O'Brien also emphasised the great benefits obtained by the UIL and parliamentary unity which Boer victories could not achieve. 'One good fight for the grasslands of the west is worth a thousand Mauser bullets from behind a Transvaal kopje.'[15] 'It is for Mr. Healy you are asked to vote not Mr. MacBride.'[16] Use was also made of Davitt's letter wishing O'Brien success. The United Irishman regarded the letter as a breach of Davitt's promise not to intervene.[17]

MacBride's supporters included O'Leary, Mark Ryan, Griffith, Rooney and J. O'Leary Curtis. Maud Gonne was in America. Two old Fenians, J. F. Egan and John Daly, mayor of Limerick, who visited Mayo on MacBride's behalf, were attacked and stoned by a mob led by the parliamentarian, P. A. McHugh, who was to clash again with separatists. According to the Gaelic American, McHugh shouted to his 'drink-crazed blackguards', 'we must show the Irish in America that we were able to beat the Fenians'.[18] The incident passed into separatist folklore and made reconciliation with parliamentarianism more difficult to achieve.

Sufficient electors were convinced that by voting for O'Donnell they would not be insulting MacBride. Though only one-third of the constituency voted, MacBride polled a mere 427 votes against 2,401. The defeat was too crushing to be easily forgotten by the losers. The United Irishman naturally complained of misrepresentation[19] but the parliamentarians could afford magnanimity to Healy's innocent dupes.[20]

The hostility aroused could not easily be quieted. Though after the by-election O'Brien may have offered Griffith and Rooney seats in parliament, while Davitt later tried to tempt MacBride himself, the United Irishman totally opposed parliamentarianism at the general election later in 1900. In the following year Maud Gonne attacked the UIL in America. Though agreeing with its basic object, Miss Gonne claimed that she had done more to reinstate Irish peasants than any branch of the League. No co-operation from separatists could be expected, she said, when parliamentarians attempted to show their superiority to Fenianism by opposing men like MacBride and John Daly, the Fenian mayor of Limerick, while supporting loyal addressers in the Dublin and Cork municipal elections. Major John MacBride, who was touring America with his future wife, told his mother that he had been advised not to attack the parliamentarians, 'but I let them have it all the same'.[21]

Griffith learned much from the by-election. His subsequent criticisms were directed against Redmond and the League rather than Healy or Dillon. O'Brien received gentler handling when he later left the League he had himself founded. Abstention from

Westminster was the lynch-pin of the Hungarian policy which denied the validity of the union by boycotting the British parliament. Though it was now out of the question for IRB men and separatists to work behind the United Irish League as their fathers had worked behind Parnell and the Land League, the prospects for a direct assault on the League and party were not inviting. Hence the need for a compromise like the Hungarian policy. The South Mayo débâcle showed the hopelessness of fighting an election without funds. But Griffith's cautious policy of education and propaganda began to irk his more militant followers who demanded, if violent revolution was out of the question, at least the excitement of parliamentary contests. As president of the Sinn Fein league in 1907, P. T. Daly promised, no doubt with the support of Hobson and O'Hegarty, to contest seats at the next election.[22] Griffith's attempts to convert individual MPs appeared to Dungannon club members as suspect from the beginning. Sinn Fein consistently refused to put forward a candidate in any general election before 1918. The first meeting of the executive of the national council in January 1906, set the pattern by deciding unanimously to abstain from the elections and give the parliamentarians no excuse for not obtaining an Home Rule bill. In some Irish constituencies preparations had already been made for running Sinn Fein candidates but these were withdrawn as a result of the executive's decision.[23]

The general election of 1906 assisted Sinn Fein by returning a Liberal government with a majority sufficiently large to dispense with Irish assistance. The new Liberal leaders, moreover, had little enthusiasm for Irish Home Rule. While the Tories were in power Sinn Fein's criticism of the Liberal alliance sounded unreasonable; now Griffith's bitter attacks on Redmond's rejection of Parnell's opposition to alliance with a British party, without a Home Rule guarantee, seemed most justifiable. John Sweetman, a Sinn Fein vice-president, was able to republish his 1895 letter which had used this argument as justification for resignation from the anti-Parnellite party.

When the Liberal government attempted a token settlement of the Irish question in its woefully restricted Irish councils bill it almost succeeded in playing into Sinn Fein's hands. P. H. Pearse and Mrs. Alice Stopford Green, however, thought that the bill should be given a trial. Mrs. Green believed it would 'become one bit of standing-ground on which Irishmen shall be able in their own country to begin to fight out their own salvation'. Sir Antony MacDonnell, the under-secretary responsible, was 'the biggest Sinn Feiner of them all, only the Sinn Fein people are too ignorant and narrow to know it, and consequently they will not give any help'. From a writer whose work was an inspiration to the advanced nationalists, this opinion is surprising and another indication of the ideological fluidity of the period.[24]

Nevertheless, there was a powerful upsurge of dissatisfaction in the parliamentary party itself. At the 1907 United Irish League convention, which declared against this bill, several resolutions were suggested in an endeavour to force the parliamentary party into more aggressive action. Thomas O'Donnell, MP, proposed, and C. J. Dolan, the young and promising MP for North Leitrim, seconded a motion which showed clearly Griffith's opinions. It demanded withdrawal from Westminster 'to work in Ireland for the industrial, agrarian and linguistic betterment of Ireland, while demonstrating a defiant hostility to all English influence in our internal affairs'. This motion and another demanding top priority for Home Rule were lost while T. M. Kettle withdrew a proposal to boycott English goods.

After a meeting of the North Leitrim UIL executive had called on the parliamentary party to withdraw *en bloc* from Westminster as a protest against the Liberal 'betrayal of Ireland', Dolan resigned from the parliamentary party but refused to relinquish his seat. As he told the chief whip, Sir Thomas Esmonde, another dissatisfied MP, 'as long as I enjoy the confidence of my constituents, I shall not turn my back on them'. Dolan was thus able to reverse the argument against MacBride's candidature in 1900. On the former occasion the decision of the local League had been cited to justify resistance to the attempt of an outside body to foist a candidate on the constituency. But Dolan's conception of the party pledge admitted the Healyite idea of constituency autonomy. Though perfectly adapted to Griffith's policy for converting the parliamentarians piecemeal, it was opposed to Parnell's insistence, reinforced in 1900, on a united centralised parliamentary party. All modern parties normally demand the resignation of members unwilling to vote with the majority. In 1907, however, Devoy's *Gaelic American* ridiculed a pledge allowing MPs to defy their constituencies. There was nothing, it declared, to prevent the whole party going over to unionism. Dolan was slow to make his decision, but having done so, refused to change his mind.

In June 1907, because the *Freeman's Journal* was attempting 'to raise doubts in minds of honourable men', Dolan, though expressing confidence in the outcome, announced his intention of resigning. His hand was almost certainly forced by a Hibernian demonstration in Manorhamilton, followed by a public meeting attended by 6,000 people. Dolan, who put his case in terms that his opponent McHugh considered even more offensive than his preceding speech to the UIL directory, was defeated by a unanimous resolution in favour of Redmond's leadership. Several days earlier, McHugh had told

1. Arthur Griffith at his desk, 1922

2. The Volunteers of the city and county of Dublin
   in College Green

3. Interior of the Irish House of Commons, 1780

4. Henry Grattan

5. Theobald
Wolfe Tone

6. Robert
Emmet

7. Daniel O'Connell

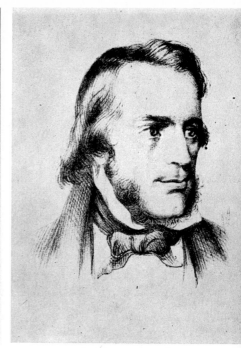

8. Thomas Davis

9. Isaac Butt

10. Sir Charles Gavan Duffy

11. John Mitchel

12. John O'Leary

13. James Fintan Lalor

14. John Blake Dillon

15. John Devoy

16. Michael Davitt

17. O'Donovan Rossa

18. James Stephens

19. Charles Stewart Parnell

20. Timothy M. Healy

21. William O'Brien

22. Douglas Hyde

Redmond that Dolan 'will be smitten hip and thigh. The constituency is solid for you.'[25]

Griffith after his experience at South Mayo was less sanguine than Dolan. 'Sinn Fein,' he wrote, 'did not seek the contest in North Leitrim but it accepts it.'[26] The parliamentarian, T. M. Kettle, nevertheless accused Sinn Fein of forcing the fight.[27] But Griffith realised that without large financial resources and the assistance of a daily paper a contest against the parliamentary party was doomed to failure. Like South Mayo, North Leitrim was a poor rural area whose inhabitants could not afford to antagonise the official United Irish League. As the *Gaelic American* pointed out, Sinn Fein would have had a much greater chance in Dublin, where four seats had been won in the 1907 municipal elections, than in Leitrim where 'the odds are heavily against them'.[28]

As sitting member Dolan had the initiative in deciding the date of the by-election. Immediate resignation, though capitalising on the general malaise in the parliamentary party, would have left Sinn Fein without campaign funds. Delay on the other hand gave Sinn Fein not only time to obtain money but to mount a propagandist campaign throughout the country. Griffith's experience in South Mayo, the potential split in Sinn Fein ranks in early 1907, and the realisation that a long campaign would have considerable long-term propagandist advantages, probably clinched the argument in favour of a waiting game. Judging by the parliamentarian reaction the decision to delay Dolan's resignation appears sound. McHugh commenting on Dolan's early propagandist work in the constituency, insisted that 'some steps should be taken to force him to resign at once'. Redmond, however, replied, 'I know of no way of forcing him to do so except by the action of public opinion. He certainly ought to be made resign at once if at all possible.'[29]

Devoy's *Gaelic American* was most co-operative. Pointing out that recent Redmondite tours of the USA and Australasia had raised funds to be utilised in the struggle not against Britain but the nationalists at home, Devoy opened a subscription list in July 1907. Though the final response was considered disappointing, by February 1908 $1,570 (£314) had been raised in America. The *Gaelic American* considered that Dolan had made a serious mistake in demanding only $500 to cover his bare election expenses.[30] Sinn Fein raised a total of £711 for the by-election. Of this sum nearly £250 was spent on the publication in Manorhamilton between August 1907 and March 1908 of a Sinn Fein newspaper, the *Leitrim Guardian*. The rest was devoted to travelling expenses and printing costs.[31] American money may also have affected strategy. When in early 1908 a convention of delegates from the newly formed

Sinn Fein branches attempted to dissuade Dolan from resigning his seat the latter pointed out that American money had been specifically subscribed for the campaign and could not be used for other purposes unless an agreement were reached with the parliamentary party.[32] That party, however, refused Dolan's suggestion that each side should donate £500 to local industry and, without recourse to British law, decide their differences by an unofficial plebiscite.[33]

The North Leitrim by-election was therefore no ordinary campaign but a bitter struggle lasting from June 1907 to February 1908. Defeat in view of the current disaffection might, as the *Gaelic American* suggested, have meant the end of the parliamentary party. If indeed other by-elections had been lost, the next general election might have seen a Sinn Fein victory anticipating, without the assistance of a rising in arms, the events of 1918. Overnight Sinn Fein, once contemptuously dismissed as the 'Green Hungarian band', became a power in the land and was also represented in the United States and distant Argentina.[34] Dolan was supported by James O'Mara (1873–1948) who after resigning his seat for South Kilkenny paid £10 towards Dolan's campaign fund. O'Mara did not immediately recontest his seat, but when he regained it with a two-to-one majority in 1918 he sat in Dail Eireann, not the British house of commons. Sir Thomas Esmonde also seemed to have come over completely to the Sinn Fein viewpoint; but after publishing a letter strongly criticising the parliamentary party he returned to it to avoid a split constituency. As the *Gaelic American* pointed out, Esmonde could not revoke his original letter, while the willingness of the party to receive him back into the fold demonstrated that it was losing its grip.[35] The parliamentarians, however, were careful to ensure that Esmonde was ousted from the chairmanship of the general council of Irish county councils.[36]

Parliamentary leaders at this time sometimes made favourable gestures in the direction of Sinn Fein. Redmond, claiming that he agreed with the whole Sinn Fein policy apart from abstentionism, argued that the dispute was simply a question of tactics. Grattan's withdrawal from the Irish parliament before 1798, he said, simply gave the government a free hand to repress.[37] The veteran parliamentarian Alfred Webb agreed with Redmond. But Joe Devlin, the chief home ruler in the north, was uncompromising. Sinn Fein, he said, meant 'the condemnation of every policy pursued by every recognised leader of the Irish people since the Act of Union'. Devlin also claimed Thomas Davis as a parliamentarian. John Dillon who had in 1877 or 1878 suggested in the privacy of his diary what was later to become the Sinn Fein policy of abstention, *de facto* government and passive resistance, was seriously worried in 1907. He concluded, however, that Sinn Fein would never become formidable 'because it has no one with any brains to lead it'.[38] A great deal of debate centred on Parnell. Both Sinn Feiners and parliamentarians[39] insisted *ad nauseam* that they were the true inheritors of Parnell's mantle, and their arguments will be analysed in a subsequent chapter.

Two intelligent young members of the ginger group Young Ireland branch of the UIL, Conor Cruise O'Brien and Francis Sheehy-Skeffington, displayed considerable ingenuity in their probing of Sinn Fein weaknesses at this time. O'Brien attempted to prise open the division between republicans and 1782 men.[40] Sheehy-Skeffington, who was on good personal terms with a number of Sinn Feiners, not infrequently attended their meetings. Though he admitted that Irish MPs would normally be more useful in Ireland than England, he rejected doctrinaire abstentionism.[41] The parliamentary oath he regarded as a mere formality which did not betray Ireland's rights. Like other parliamentarians, Sheehy-Skeffington teased Martyn and Sweetman for paying income tax to the British government. To this Sweetman replied not unreasonably that he was compelled to recognise the *de facto* government until a nation-wide campaign had been inaugurated.[42] In much the same way, Sinn Fein was criticised for accepting £50 from Robert Barton, the retired British army officer who later reluctantly signed the Anglo-Irish Treaty. The *Gaelic American* showed that the great 18th-century patriot, Lord Edward Fitzgerald, had also been a British officer.[43]

As in most conflicts of the period, religion was an important factor. Sinn Fein was attacked for anti-clericalism. Withdrawal of Irish MPs from Westminster, many constitutionalists insisted, would leave English Catholic education unprotected.[44] In Ireland Sinn Fein was accused of joining the current campaign against the system of clerical managers in the primary schools. A Leitrim priest ordered his congregation to boycott Hobson, sometimes accused of being an Orangeman,[45] because he was alleged to have attacked clerical school managers. Hobson denied that he had ever made a public statement on the issue.[46] Walter Cole also insisted that Sinn Fein had taken no position in the dispute. The *Gaelic American*, however, did not hesitate to attack clerical managers for helping to denationalise Irish education.[47] Moreover, W. P. Ryan's *Irish Peasant*, in which Hobson merged his *Republic*, was condemned by the primate, Cardinal Logue, for allowing a controversy on the managerial question. Dolan had, however, an apparent advantage in that his uncle was vicar-general in his constituency, but as McHugh privately told Redmond, the influence of the bishop of Kilmore was on the parliamentarian side and only two curates were likely to give even surreptitious support to Sinn Fein. Dolan's uncle played no part in the campaign.[48]

Dolan naturally attracted considerable abuse. He was accused of being a renegade Catholic, a place-hunter and the disloyal protégé of P. A. McHugh, member for Sligo and editor of the *Sligo Guardian,* who led the battle against him. In actual fact, Dolan had been educated at Maynooth where, on discovering a lack of vocation, he had been awarded a degree in philosophy. McHugh, according to Dolan, had opposed his nomination for North Leitrim but had offered to help him to an appointment in the Indian civil service. McHugh, himself a 'spoiled priest', was accused of owing his entire career to the good offices of Dolan's father.[49]

When Dolan finally resigned from parliament in February 1908 the stage was set for a particularly vicious final conflict. He had campaigned already for nearly eight months. With the aid of his paper and Sean MacDermott, the Sinn Fein organiser, Dolan had stimulated the formation of more Sinn Fein branches than in any other area outside Dublin. P. A. McHugh, manager of the campaign for F. E. Meehan, the new candidate, had been an active opponent of Parnell in 1891, while Sinn Fein had secured the attendance on their behalf of Anna Parnell, the Chief's sister, a considerable advantage in view of Sinn Fein's claim to the Parnellite succession. The parliamentary party could take no chances in view of Dolan's improved position.

Miss Parnell's oratory was something of an embarrassment. As a member of the militant Ladies' Land League of the early 1880s, dissolved by her brother, she denounced the male Land League leaders, including by implication Parnell, as 'a gang of scoundrels' and as 'cowards, imbeciles and impostors'. She had left politics after the destruction of her own League. Miss Parnell, who appears to have come to North Leitrim on her own initiative, opposed the parliamentarian 'humbugs', but had little interest in Dolan. 'Cast your votes not for his sake, not for the sake of Sinn Fein, but for my sake and for the recollection of old times.'[50]

Considerable propagandist capital, however, was to be drawn from the treatment Miss Parnell received during the campaign. The parliamentary party did not rely entirely on argument in their attempts to win over the voters. Since the days of John Mitchel and Smith O'Brien, who had been attacked by O'Connellite mobs, advanced nationalists had suffered violence from parliamentarian hands. Though Redmond had visited the constituency some time earlier, no major parliamentarian came to Leitrim for the final weeks of the campaign. The contest was left to P. A. McHugh, who had directed rough tactics in 1900 at South Mayo, and Dermot O'Brien, the United Irish League organiser. Members of the Ancient Order of Hibernians (board of Erin as opposed to American Alliance who tended to favour Sinn Fein) were imported from Belfast—including perhaps some of Hobson's old adversaries—to supplement those on the spot.[51] Joe Devlin wired to Meehan the party candidate: 'all expenses will be paid. Have the constituency thoroughly worked up. Wire House of Commons whatever assistance you require.'[52]

On 14 February the Glenkeen band, supporting Dolan, marched up to a meeting addressed by Meehan's supporters at Kiltyclogher and drowned the speeches with music. The band was chased away by Meehanites and the big drum destroyed. The unionist *Irish Times* feared 'a fierce outbreak of violence'. The Sinn Feiners, though the weaker party, did not attempt to conciliate their opponents. At Glenade, Dolan, unable to attract an audience, joined the crowd addressed by Dermot O'Brien and heckled him. The parliamentarians going to a meeting at Ballinaglera were stopped by a Sinn Fein cordon across the road.[53] However, the worst occurrence was at Drumkeerin. Dolan, Anna Parnell and George Gavan Duffy attempted to address a meeting there. Though the police tried to keep a hostile crowd away, the Sinn Feiners were pelted with mud and rotten eggs. Miss Parnell had a pail of water emptied over her head when she tried to address the crowd, while Gavan Duffy's formal but unsuitable tall hat was shattered by a stick. The police sergeant appealed to John O'Dowd, MP, to speak to the people as his local force was insufficient to keep the peace; and O'Dowd agreed on condition that Dolan did not attempt to hold a meeting. Eventually the Sinn Feiners were suffered to leave the town.[54] On 19 February a party consisting of Dolan, T. Kelly, and others were again assailed with mud and eggs at Kinlough by rowdies from Belfast. The police attempted to keep the two parties apart. The next day the motor car used by the Sinn Feiners was found with its tyres cut and damaged to the extent of £80. Their opponents sneered that it was an English car.[55] A meeting outside Dolan's shop in Manorhamilton was protected by police while Griffith and Dolan accused the Belfast men of causing the disorder.[56] Even in the polling booth on the day before the poll there was a scene; Dolan punched an intruder from Belfast who was ejected by the sub-sheriff before he could retaliate.[57]

Sinn Fein published a full exposé of the electioneering methods used by its opponents, which included payment for free drink and wages for roughs. Parliamentarians naturally denied these allegations. On both sides of the Atlantic stress was laid on the ill-treatment of Miss Parnell:

> When down to County Limerick
> They marched the other day,
> Who but the sister of Parnell
> Should cross them on their way.
> Those heroes, nothing daunted,
> When she came on the scene

Fired rotten 'spuds' and eggs at her
For the wearing of the green.
An' they're peltin' filth like heroes
For the wearing of the green.[58]

The parliamentarian retort that Miss Parnell had been lifted out of the car and carried to safety before the punch-up began is in itself significant.[59] William O'Brien, now totally estranged from the Redmondite party, believed that Sinn Fein had made too much of the disorder which naturally accompanies such elections throughout the world.[60] Ten years later, when Sinn Fein annihilated the parliamentarians at the polls it was the latter party which complained of violence and intimidation.

The result[61] of the North Leitrim election was a surprise to almost everyone. F. E. Meehan did win by what would normally be considered a huge majority, 1,946 (3,103 to 1,157), the total electorate being 6,324; but, to judge the true significance of this majority it is necessary to note the figures for the last contest in the constituency. At the 1900 election, P. A. McHugh defeated a unionist candidate by 4,025 votes to 383. It was estimated that there were 600 unionists in the constituency, an easy calculation in an area where the words unionist and Protestant were virtually synonymous. When a unionist candidate stood, most qualified unionists probably voted. Nevertheless, after the 1908 by-election P. McHugh, worried by Sinn Fein's large vote, insisted that 3,103 votes had been cast for Redmond, 657 for Dolan personally, 500 for unionism, but for factious Sinn Fein, none. According to the unionist *Irish Times,* however, Sinn Fein's attitude to England was 'so ridiculous and so disloyal' as to preclude absolutely any co-operation from loyalists.[62] The *Gaelic American* saw only a few known unionists at the polls and assumed that they would vote for the parliamentarians. Other assertions of an alliance between Sinn Fein and unionism were, however, made. In Tyrone in 1907 Sinn Feiners had been accused of marching in a body to vote for a unionist, Denis Henry, who was opposing the Liberal solicitor-general, Redmond Barry, a home ruler. It was later said that unionists had been advised to vote for Sinn Feiner W. L. Cole in the election for alderman in the Dublin Drumcondra ward.[63]

There can be little doubt that Sinn Fein had effectively split the nationalist vote. Considering the expense of the election this was a serious set-back for the parliamentary party. It is impossible to assess exactly the motives of those who voted for Dolan. A large number probably supported him on personal grounds; the propaganda which had been in progress before the arrival of the parliamentary battalions must have had considerable effect; a few voters may have been disgusted by the tactics of the opposition. Compared with the débâcle at South Mayo in 1900 the separatist cause had improved immeasurably. Both constituencies lay in congested areas where agrarianism was more likely to succeed than austere political separation. To counteract this disadvantage Dolan promised to foster industries in the area. In both constituencies, however, the separatists had certain initial advantages—MacBride's prestige was probably even greater than Dolan's—yet the results were very different. In 1908 the Sinn Fein organisation was undoubtedly better than the separatist organisation in 1900, and the movement had obtained far more publicity throughout the country. Yet Gavan Duffy, with his English accent, Tom Kelly, Griffith and the other Dubliners were regarded as virtual aliens and their efforts were neutralised by the Belfast Hibernians. William O'Brien's oratory may have been more effective than the rougher tactics of McHugh. It is significant that at the end of the South Mayo election O'Brien made a magnanimous and conciliatory speech while after North Leitrim McHugh remained vituperative, leaving all magnanimity to Dolan. McHugh's irritation may well have been increased by the fact that he and Redmond had tried, in the hope of sending down a candidate from headquarters, to dissuade Meehan, president of the Manorhamilton Hibernians, from seeking the nomination.[64]

While Dolan was almost pleased with the result, *Sinn Fein* was exultant, describing the by-election at which the parliamentarians had mobilised all their resources, as the declaration of Irish independence and an event of greater significance than O'Connell's election for Clare in 1828 which brought about Catholic emancipation.[65] The *Kerryman* agreed that it was 'a Pyrrhic victory for Parliamentarianism, and Sinn Feiners may look on it as a triumph for their cause'.[66] Though Patrick Ford's *Irish World,* dependent mainly on the unionist support theory, claimed that Sinn Fein had been 'crushed' in North Leitrim,[67] the Dublin *Freeman's Journal* showed some grudging admiration for the new nationalists. Most significant was the attitude of the unionist *Irish Times* which had not deigned to comment on MacBride's candidature in 1900.

The *Irish Times* was particularly impressed by Dolan's significant minority in what had been one of the parliamentary party's safest seats. Dolan had, moreover, been contending against all the resources, mobilised with frantic energy, which the constitutionalists could command. It praised the non-political elements in the Sinn Fein programme. Encouragement of Irish self-reliance was akin, said the *Irish Times*, to the principle of constructive unionism.[68]

Such opinion was a far cry from McHugh's contemptuous dismissal of the Sinn Feiners as 'a gang of political nonentities whose whole stock-in-trade is abuse of the Irish party' with an 'absurd and preposterous policy'. Sinn Feiners had, unlike the parliamentarians, generally supported the unionist Sir Horace Plunkett's movement for the agricultural revival of Ireland. The *Irish Times's* attitude may have encouraged Griffith (as a later chapter will demonstrate) to move further than some of his supporters desired in the direction of conciliating unionists. Before the foundation of Sinn Fein, supporters of the national council had been exhorted to vote for unionists rather than renegade nationalists who signed loyal addresses in the Dublin corporation elections. 'A foeman is to be fought—he may be respected. A renegade is to be loathed and crushed.'[69]

In the months following the North Leitrim by-election, Sinn Fein wore a confident appearance. At a meeting of national council branches in Manorhamilton attended by Griffith and Sean Mac-Dermott it was decided not only to continue the local Sinn Fein paper, but also to start, as the most suitable local industry, a boot factory. An appeal for capital was launched and Dolan was sent on a mission to America not only to raise funds but to learn the secrets of modern shoe manufacturing at St. Louis.[70] Soon afterwards a Sinn Fein meeting packed and overflowed the Dublin Rotunda rooms. Amongst those present were AE, Sean O'Casey, the great dramatist of the future, Countess Constance Markievicz, who was beginning her nationalist career, and the subsequent premier of the Irish Free State, W. T. Cosgrave. To embarrass the parliamentary party Griffith read a detailed list of Sinn Fein expenses at the by-election and challenged his opponents to reciprocate.[71]

By mid-1908 there were some indications that the tide might turn in Sinn Fein's direction. The old Parnellite, A. J. Kettle, resigned from the United Irish League, voicing the common dissatisfaction with the Home Rule guarantees given by Asquith and Winston Churchill.[72] At the triennial local body elections in June Sinn Fein gained 35 of the 69 poor law guardians in the northern and southern unions and won five local authority seats. In Manorhamilton a Sinn Feiner, John O'Donnell, defeated by 67 votes the new MP, Meehan. The Drumkeerin episode was revenged by the election of a Sinn Feiner for that area. Across the Atlantic, in August 1908, the Sinn Fein league of America was launched at Buffalo with a retired US army colonel, Robert Temple Emmet, grandson of the United Irishman Thomas Addis Emmet, as national president. The doughty fighter, Fr. P. C. Yorke of San Francisco, became vice-president and Joseph McGarrity of Philadelphia, treasurer.[73]

Clouds were, however, appearing over the horizon. Martyn, an invaluable source of money, had resigned the Sinn Fein presidency 'bitterly opposed' to the decision to fight the North Leitrim by-election.[74] His successor, Sweetman, was beaten after a determined campaign by the parliamentarians in the Meath county council election for Kells. This defeat plus the ousting of Esmonde from the chairmanship of the general council made it much less likely that the latter organisation could be used as the lynch-pin of Griffith's policy. By alerting the parliamentarians to the need to control local elections the North Leitrim by-election was undoubtedly a nail in the coffin of Griffith's peaceful penetration programme. On the industrial side of the movement Dolan's projected boot factory, shifted on paper from Leitrim to Dublin and then to Drogheda, eventually came to naught.[75] Dolan emigrated to the USA where he found a permanent position in the St. Louis legal department.

When Lloyd George introduced his 'people's budget' in 1909 he started a train of events which raised the popularity of the parliamentary party to a new height before dashing it on the rocks of total disaster. The budget when rejected by the house of lords led to the two elections of 1910 which reduced the Liberal majority and increased the influence of the Irish MPs. After the abolition of the lords' veto the passage of a Home Rule bill was certain had it not been for the unionists' unconstitutional resistance. Sinn Fein, which in this period could only criticise from the sidelines, was again the residuary legatee of a parliamentarian débâcle. As Griffith confided to AE shortly after the introduction of the Home Rule bill in 1912, 'If a good Bill accepted by Ulster had been introduced I and my party would have disappeared from Ireland. Nobody would have listened to us.'[76] In view of subsequent events Sinn Fein's arguments though discounted at the time became very important.

In 1909 Griffith mounted a strong attack on Lloyd George's budget, denouncing his land taxation as bearing too hard on Irish landowners and the spirit tax as discriminatory in that it hit Irish distilleries, not English breweries. Apart from the fact that the budget was a wedge to prise open the way to Home Rule, Griffith's defence of distilleries, considering early Sinn Fein insistence on temperance—Bulmer Hobson being so active in this respect—and the battle against the 'whiskey ring' in the Dublin corporation, appears misdirected and opportunistic. Sweetman, already under fire for his agrarian wealth, was not the best person to protest against a system of land taxation based on the views of Henry George who acknowledged Fintan Lalor as a forerunner.[77] Lalor's scheme, however, presupposed an Irish government. In spite of Griffith's complaints that the parliamentary party was not acting decisively to remedy these grievances, Sinn Feiners officially boycotted the general election in January and December 1910. At the October 1910 Sinn Fein conference Griffith insisted that they had no wish to increase the existing bitterness in Ireland, while Walter Cole frankly stated that a minority party had no right to obstruct the majority. Hecklers at the meeting demanded cheers for Redmond.[78]

In Connemara, however, Padraic O Maille attempted to win the Sinn Fein nomination for the district. The national council sent Sean MacDermott to meet the Co. Galway Sinn Fein committee to persuade O Maille to stand down. MacDermott, in view of his subsequent part in preparing for the Easter Rising, a surprising counsellor for inaction, had to persuade the local Sinn Feiners that their party was offering no other candidates, arguing that parliamentarianism, 'even if left unopposed will finally condemn itself in a few years'. He used the standard arguments against 'arousing violent political passions'. No repetition of North Leitrim was desired. O Maille withdrew with some reluctance, but remaining a loyal Sinn Feiner eventually won the seat in the general election of 1918. His doubt about the policy decision in 1910 shows the difficulty of linking condemnation in theory with connivance in practice. To O Maille the more opposition and harassment the parliamentarians received, the smaller their chance of 'injuring the cause of Irish nationality' by handing over Ireland 'body and soul to the English Liberals on the strength of a vague declaration from the leader of that party in reference to the self-government of Ireland'.[79] If, as Griffith and the *Gaelic American* argued, Redmond was botching the best opportunity for exploiting the balance of power since Parnell's time, Sinn Fein abstention at the polls was scarcely a dynamic policy.

The basic ambiguity of Sinn Fein's 1910 position was seen clearly by Frederick Ryan, an Irish socialist and humanitarian. Sinn Fein, he declared, was trying to be all things to all men and failing badly. Persistent abuse of the parliamentary party scarcely justified leaving it unopposed unless the abuse had been insincere. Sinn Fein inconsistencies, said Ryan, passed unnoticed only because the party itself was not taken very seriously by anyone. All knew that Sinn Fein was only rationalising its lack of funds which made electioneering impossible.[80] Professor Liam O Briain shares the view that financial inadequacy was responsible for the avoidance of contests.

But the executive's ruling was not always obeyed. In East Tyrone, however, McCullough's Sinn Feiners did have some success in early 1910. T. M. Kettle, in return for Sinn Fein support, whose strength he may have exaggerated, had to promise to prevent Hibernians boycotting Sinn Feiners and breaking up their meetings. In December, though the executive refused to support the candidature for the Dublin harbour division of James Brady, whose previous suggestions for compromise had nearly split the movement, the latter now professed to accept the Sinn Fein policy *in toto*. Failing to obtain its support, he renounced his association with Sinn Fein and, complaining of 'brutal intimidation' by the parliamentarians, was defeated by 3,244 votes to 631. Sinn Fein's assumption that the failure of 5,163 voters to poll was an endorsement of its policy did not carry much conviction.[81]

These facts and the decline, to be described in a subsequent chapter, of the Sinn Fein organisation after 1910, may encourage the opinion that Griffith's continued opposition to the parliamentary party was mere factionism which, by a mere quirk of fortune, subsequently achieved an undeserved popularity. In reality Griffith's policy in the 1910-4 period was quite subtle and worthy of serious consideration.

Griffith and most of the advanced nationalists like Hobson rejected, correctly as it turned out, the theory that Irish exploitation of the parliamentary balance of power was the certain harbinger of Home Rule. Parnell, Griffith argued, understood that it was not the house of lords but the English people who were the real opponents of Home Rule. Home Rule was inevitable, said Griffith in early 1912, not as the result of Irish parliamentary agitation at Westminster but of England's fear of Germany's navy and desire to use Ireland, 'her sword arm', as a recruiting ground for her armies. It therefore behoved Redmond to demand an adequate measure of Home Rule in return for friendship.[82] But Griffith was still sceptical of the Redmondite determination to restore Irish nationality rather than to secure a small measure of self-government inside the British imperial system. Griffith was particularly shocked by the attitude of a parliamentary delegation under Richard Hazleton (an MP who had taken part in the North Leitrim campaign) which toured New Zealand in 1911. These delegates disclaimed any intention of seeking Irish control over her army or customs and any power to deal with imperial affairs. 'Nothing meaner,' said *Sinn Fein*, 'in the name of Ireland has ever been spoken than the address of Mr. Hazleton to the astonished New Zealanders.'[83] New Zealand militant Labour, which during the Anglo-Irish war campaigned vigorously for Irish self-determination, was equally scathing in denouncing Hazleton's imperialism and penchant for closing meetings with 'Gor'save'.[84]

When in 1911 Redmond announced that in view of the lords' veto crisis no Home Rule bill could be introduced for a year, Sinn Fein, perhaps remembering his previous claim to support all aspects of their policy save abstentionism, challenged the parliamentarians to use their breathing space to help in the achievement of a long list of national council objectives.[85] Though Sinn Fein promised the parliamentary party a free field for two years—later extended—to implement its Home Rule promises, it did its best to create an Irish public opinion insistent on an adequate bill. In this respect *Sinn Fein* was more constructive than its more militant rival *Irish Freedom* which adopted a simplistic approach, arguing that if some Home Rule came it could be exploited by advanced nationalists; while if none were obtained physical-force men could capitalise on the ensuing disappointment. [86]

The earlier insistence on the 1782 constitution proved indispensable in the controversy over the Home Rule bill. Unlike the Republicans, official Sinn Fein had a realistic yardstick against which imperfections in the bill could be measured. The minimum conditions laid down at a meeting of the Sinn Fein central branch in October 1911, including exclusive taxation rights and the rejection of an English veto, came close to the dual monarchy concept which appealed strongly to the more radical parliamentarians. Germany, as Griffith significantly pointed out, had given substantial self-government to Alsace and Lorraine. The seizure of this territory from France in 1870 was one of the long-term causes of the 1914-8 war. [87]

The Home Rule bill of 1912 fully justified Sinn Fein suspicions. The memory of Poynings' Law, which had hamstrung the old Irish parliament before 1782, was invoked against the power of the British parliament to amend Irish laws. But it was the financial provisions which most irritated Sinn Fein. Right up to the Treaty of 1921 Griffith insisted that tariff autonomy lay at the root of Ireland's independence. The federal union for which Davis in 1845 wanted a fair trial differed from the 1912 bill in its control over customs and excise. [88] The new bill failed to give Ireland the power to collect her own taxes. Griffith surprisingly attacked the reduction of Irish MPs at Westminster on the ground that Parnell had insisted on the maintenance of the full quota under Home Rule. [89]

A Sinn Fein convention on 12 April passed seven resolutions against the bill, attacking the revival of Poynings' Law, the retention of British control over the land commission, the inability of the Irish to collect their own taxes, the power of Britain to tax Ireland without her consent, the procedure for questioning the validity of Irish acts, the joint exchequer board dominated by England and the nominated senate. On the following day a meeting of Sinn Fein sympathisers from all over the country criticised the bill. [90] Though Padraig Pearse attended the parliamentary party's demonstration in favour of Home Rule it was boycotted by the Sinn Fein organisation. [91]

At a public meeting at the Sinn Fein central branch on 1 May the bill was again fully debated. Though two ladies, Mrs. Wyse Power and Mrs. Smith, believed that the bill should be accepted, most speakers were extremely hostile. Sean Milroy argued that the demerits outweighed any advantages. Ireland was being asked to bow to the empire. W. L. Cole, denying that the bill represented any form of settlement, declared that Sinn Fein's critical attitude was now fully justified. Eamon Ceannt, then Sinn Fein organiser, agreed with Cole. The bill, he declared, was the product of England's failure to achieve a treaty with the USA to offset the growth of German naval power.[92]

In July Sinn Fein organised a meeting outside the old Irish parliament house, attended by 5,000 people, to protest in particular against the British collection of Irish taxes.[93] Eventually 15,000 signatures were obtained for a petition.[94] Particularly heartening from the Sinn Fein viewpoint was the fact that the general council of Irish councils, though under the control of the parliamentarians, was likewise insistent on Ireland's right to tariff autonomy.[95] In November 1912, however, Redmond announced that the Irish did not want control over their customs. According to *Sinn Fein,* evoking the memory of economically independent Grattan's parliament, 'the scene of November, 1783, is matched by the scene of November, 1912'.[96]

Had the parliamentary party been opposed simply by the economic arguments of Sinn Fein it might have weathered the storm. Colum shows that, in spite of the popularity of a new edition of Griffith's *Resurrection of Hungary* in the country at large 'there was not even a discussion about the withdrawal of the Nationalist members'.[97] The unionist revolt against Home Rule for a time distracted public attention from Sinn Fein. Griffith strongly criticised the parliamentary party for its failure to woo the northern Protestants with the same determination with which it had sought to attract British democracy. Like *Irish Freedom, Sinn Fein* had, since 1911, insisted that the threats of the Ulstermen were mere bluff. In the face of German power Home Rule was so necessary to England that even a Tory government would grant it.[98] Historical examples of Orange bluff, including the threats by Orangemen to give allegiance to their grand master, the duke of Cumberland, instead of Queen Victoria, were cited for the purpose. Hobson's *Irish Freedom* fully agreed.[99] When the Ulster covenant was signed, *Sinn Fein,* with tongue in cheek, promised, 'if and when the Ulster Unionists take up arms against the usurped authority of the Parliament of Great Britain to make laws to bind them, Unionist Ulster will receive the sympathy and support of Nationalist Ireland'. Furthermore, 'the country is labouring to new political births and the Ulster hysteria and the Ulster covenant are natural and necessary to its travail'.[100] Though it did not completely approve of Eoin MacNeill's attempt to cheer the Ulster volunteers in Cork,[101] *Sinn Fein* argued with some plausibility that the British Liberal government's 1914 retreat from Home Rule in the face of the unionists' plan for a provisional government, backed by these Ulster volunteers, was a copybook demonstration of the effectiveness of the Sinn Fein policy in practice.[102]

The negotiations in 1914 for a temporary partition of Ireland were bitterly attacked by Sinn Fein. At a protest meeting in March gathering representatives of all nationalist sections in the Sinn Fein rooms, a public meeting eventually attended by 500 was arranged for Easter week.[103] A committee of ten was appointed to bring a set of compromise proposals to the Ulster unionists.* Some of Griffith's previous allies criticised him at this juncture. Sweetman, who seems to have returned to his former party, thought that Griffith was needlessly embarrassing the parliamentarians in their extremity.[104] Alice Milligan, who had published Rooney's poems, but who rejected Griffith's later policy, considering partition an accomplished fact since the 16th-century plantations, suggested that temporary exclusion of the six northern counties would provide an opportunity for educating the unionists to a sense of Irish nationality. Griffith replied that the recognition of the Irish race at the Dungannon Volunteer convention ended the plantation era in Irish history. He asserted the unbending Sinn Fein position. 'The stern fact we have to look in the face is that Ireland cannot acquiesce in any partition of her territory without forfeiting *all* her rights as a nation.'[105]

Though standing firmly on the historical integrity of Ireland, Griffith was nevertheless prepared to safeguard the major Ulster interests. His reaction to the possibility of partition was more appropriate than Hobson's appeal to John Mitchel's adaptation of St. Luke 22:36, explained away by Erasmus: 'He that hath not a gun let him go sell his garment to buy one.' Recognising the economic pre-eminence of the area Griffith suggested that Ulster's representation in the Irish parliament be increased from 59 out of 164 to 74 out of 194, taking into consideration trade and rateable land values as well as population. The Ulster linen trade, 'nearly equal in importance to the staple industry of the other provinces' was to be exempted from Irish legislation, save with the consent of a majority of Ulster members. The chairman of the joint exchequer board could be an Ulsterman, and to meet the fear that Catholics would engross all civil service positions under an Irish parliament, these vacancies were to be filled by a permanent examination board appointed by the senate. The first session of the Irish parliament would be held in Belfast and future sessions would alternate between Belfast and Dublin. The most significant safeguard of all was that the Ulster volunteers under their own leaders were to be retained as part of the Irish volunteer force, committed to service within their own area except in the event of an invasion of Ireland.[106]

By any rational criterion these were fair terms. But herein lay

*The Belfast Trades Council was interested in Griffith's proposals for Ulster.

their weakness. Like the Marxists, Griffith attributed the whole problem to economics and neglected the religious, or tribal factor. His economic emphasis is demonstrated by the suggestion that Ireland's tariff autonomy by increasing the importance of the Protestant mercantile community would make discrimination against non-Catholics less likely.[107] But, as Canon J. O. Hannay, the novelist and church of Ireland rector from Belfast, and his son Robert demonstrated, Irish Protestants were deeply concerned about aspects of contemporary Catholic policy like the *Ne Temere* decree of 1908. This decree denied the validity of mixed marriages except when performed by the Catholic church and insisted that all children of such parents be brought up in the Catholic faith. As the decree abolished the former Irish custom by which the sons of a mixed marriage followed their father's and the daughters their mother's religion, Irish Protestants might well expect that Sinn Fein consistency required opposition to Rome as well as Westminster. But Griffith played down *Ne Temere,* pointing out quite logically that the decree did not affect the state law and was being misinterpreted by Orange bigots to work up hostility to Catholicism. In view of the Protestant record of anti-Catholic persecution the former had no right, said Griffith, to complain of *Ne Temere.*[108] Taken in conjunction with Sinn Fein's side-stepping of the mixed education issue, Griffith's approach, in a man who believed that Thomas Davis supplied the answer to all questions of Irish nationality,[109] may not have been completely adequate. That Griffith was alive to the problem is seen in his denunciation of the sectarianism of the Board of Erin Hibernians, and Cardinal Cullen, the great opponent of mixed education. He had also defended Hannay's *Seething Pot* which appeared to insult a Westport priest.[110]

On the outbreak of war in August 1914 Griffith's *Sinn Fein* for the last few weeks before suppression could do little more than assert that Ireland had no quarrel with Germany,[111] and, to ensure the passage of an adequate Home Rule bill, call on Carson and Redmond to set up a provisional government in Dublin. The Irish volunteer movement rather than the dwindling Sinn Fein organisation was the focus of advanced nationalist opinion in the years before the 1916 Rising.

The post-Rising landslide victory of Sinn Fein over the parliamentary party in the general election of 1918 raises an important, if unanswerable, question. Could Sinn Fein on the basis of Griffith's original programme have beaten the parliamentary party without the intervention of a sacrificial 1916 Rising? The possibility cannot be completely excluded. Even without the Rising, the credit of the parliamentarians would have run low by December 1918. The party's withdrawal to fight conscription in Ireland was a virtual capitulation to the Sinn Fein policy and left the initiative to the anti-parliamentarians. Sinn Fein had always opposed enlistment in the British army while the parliamentary party had been in two minds on the question. John Dillon's belief that the British government did all it could to ensure the victory of Sinn Fein[112] was but another way of saying that the parliamentarians had lost all value as allies of the British government. The limitations of the Home Rule bill and Redmond's embarrassment over the tariff issue would have been easier to exploit in 1918 than 1914. Moreover, as will be shown in a subsequent chapter, Sinn Fein would almost certainly have been able to draw on more substantial American funds than its opponents. Sinn Fein, it is true, had no real answer to the Ulster problem, though it is possible that a non-violent Sinn Fein *de facto* government might have been better equipped for negotiation with the hard-headed unionist leaders than the parliamentarians with their sectarian AOH associations. Griffith believed, after all, that the AOH 'had given the Orangemen the only explanation for their existence'.[113] Much would have depended on Griffith's control over his own supporters, and this subject now requires careful analysis.

4 Sinn Fein divided 1908-16

THE Sinn Fein compromise of 1907 had not resolved any of the essential differences between 1782 men and republicans. Nothing had been done to check the centralisation of the movement in Dublin and no provision had been made for giving greater power to non-resident members of the executive. *Sinn Fein* was still Griffith's organ and his freedom of action was in no way impaired by the convention.

Griffith had adopted the 1782 constitution because he hoped to use it as the basis of a wider and more powerful movement. In the early days of the *United Irishman,* Griffith had spoken out boldly against all compromise of the national separatist ideal and adopted a doctrinaire attitude to negotiation with non-separatists. He was only prepared to parley with unionists who accepted unequivocally Irish independence as the basis for discussion.[1] This meant in effect giving up unionism.

The Hungarian policy and the adoption of the 1782 constitution modified this exclusiveness. At first the organisation was mainly concerned with the admission to Sinn Fein ranks of members who though not technically separatists were more than home rulers. After the ambiguous amalgamation of the Sinn Fein league and national council, and the North Leitrim election the organisation acquired a new standing in the country and attracted the attention of other groups. Ironically it was Griffith's old enemy William O'Brien, now leader of a dissident rump of parliamentarians, who made the first approach.

O'Brien decided to call a conference of all parties. Already on good terms with Lord Dunraven and his liberal unionist group, he sent Captain John Shawe-Taylor who had helped to initiate the great land purchase act of 1903, which drew the fangs of Irish agrarianism by making the peasant the owner of his land, to sound out Sinn Fein in late 1907.[2] At this time the newly integrated

Sinn Fein was concerned with Dolan's candidature at North Leitrim. To offset the strength of the official parliamentary party, Griffith may have welcomed the intervention of other groups. Clearly Hobson, O'Hegarty and the other IRB men would have refused to consider a conference with O'Brien, but were not in a position to obstruct Griffith and his Dublin supporters.

According to O'Brien, the 'Sinn Feiners jumped at the idea' of an all-party conference and promised not to use it as a platform for 'their own peculiar doctrines'.[3] But Sinn Fein soon withdrew its support and the demonstration was still-born.[4] Griffith and some executive members may have favoured the proposal but feared the reaction of the Hobson–O'Hegarty junta.

Dolan's defeat at North Leitrim in February 1908 seems to have convinced Griffith that only by means of a daily paper could the Sinn Fein propaganda penetrate rural Ireland. A daily paper would pay its way only by appealing to a wider public than the Irish separatists. Griffith's new conciliatory approach was in sharp contrast with his earlier exclusive nationalism. Instead of rejecting all who refused to accept absolute Irish independence, Griffith now judged Irishmen by the consistency of their actions with their own political beliefs. All who loved Ireland in their own way would find solace in the daily *Sinn Fein*.[5] Greater efforts were made to conciliate the unionists than the parliamentarians.[6] Griffith was skating on very thin ice. Separatists like Hobson and O'Hegarty had already fairly demonstrated that they would tolerate no deviation from nationalist orthodoxy. What, moreover, could Griffith hope to achieve? If he played down doctrine to achieve a sufficiently wide circulation, would the paper have any propagandist value?[7]

Funds were difficult to obtain. Sweetman, one of Griffith's main sources of revenue, told Gavan Duffy: 'I did not subscribe to it [the *Sinn Fein* daily] at first, as I did not believe that sufficient funds could be obtained and I did not wish to encourage its starting.'[8] P. S. O'Hegarty informed Duffy that Griffith intended to make a start with £8,000 and felt that the leader should be supported 'even if he is not doing things quite justly'. O'Hegarty thought that Griffith was bluffing about his existing supporters and believed it would require a gift of several thousands from a millionaire to make up the first £8,000.[9] Even Griffith had doubts and told Sweetman: 'I think with you I won't get the £8,000 required, but for months past I have been receiving day by day letters from readers urging me to make the appeal.'[10] It was only after a severe struggle and constant requests that the *Sinn Fein* daily appeared from 24 August 1909 to 22 January 1910. Like the weekly it was independent of the national council, and Griffith thus had full scope for his policy of conciliating all parties.

Sinn Fein opinion on the paper was divided. The moderates considered it excellent, but the separatists, while admitting that it was a good newspaper, thought it entirely inadequate as an expression of nationalist opinion. O'Hegarty, who later told how Griffith by 'sheer obstinacy succeeded in winning over the Sinn Fein executive and forcing an appeal for funds',[11] was critical as usual. Everything was watered-down 'as low as he possibly can'. The whole emphasis was placed on the conciliation of unionists and an alliance with them was seriously proposed. O'Hegarty believed in conciliation 'but not at the expense of lowering our own practice or profession of nationalism'. Lynd, however, thought it a great paper,[12] and Sweetman sent £200 when he heard 'that the funds were nearly exhausted'. In a letter to Gavan Duffy, however, Sweetman demonstrated that O'Hegarty's fears were not ill-founded by revealing that the unionist Sir Horace Plunkett had donated £25 to the paper which Sweetman believed deserving of support by all parties.[13]

Griffith's gamble almost succeeded. When the daily was replaced by a weekly in early 1910, though only £4,000 of estimated minimum capital of £8,000 had been subscribed, revenue had reached 75% of expenditure.[14] Griffith's critics accused him of evasion on the position of the paper. He had, however, sent The O'Rahilly, who made a personal contribution of £100, to the United States. With him was 'Senor' William Bulfin, who had obtained $685 for the daily from Sinn Feiners in Argentina. Though Devoy was reasonably helpful funds sufficient to keep the daily alive were not raised. This seems largely due to the fact that Clan-na-Gael members were in close touch with Hobson and his friends who disliked many aspects of the new paper. The O'Rahilly and Bulfin were precluded by their instructions from making a public appeal.[15]

It was at this time that a new series of negotiations threatened to split Sinn Fein from top to bottom. In March 1909, William O'Brien made a second approach to Sinn Fein, again through the accommodating Captain Shawe-Taylor.[16] O'Brien's motive was obvious. In founding the All-for-Ireland League he hoped to unify all parties against the extreme unionists on one hand and the parliamentary party allied with the sectarian Ancient Order of Hibernians (Board of Erin) on the other. In his anti-sectarianism and his preference for unionists to parliamentarians he was in accord with Griffith. Like Griffith, moreover, O'Brien was critical of Lloyd George's budget and the land bill buying out Irish landlords. As O'Brien's strength lay in Cork and Griffith's in Dublin, an alliance appeared in the interests of both. The great obstacle to agreement was Sinn Fein's doctrinaire anti-parliamentarianism. Griffith, though 'in cordial agreement' with the proposal for joint action, would not consent to share a platform with the All-for-Ireland

League unless there was a resolution demanding withdrawal from Westminster. This O'Brien, believing it would alienate nine-tenths of his followers, refused to accept.[17]

With so much at stake, Griffith must have considered the possibility of an alliance deeply. Though he had never wished to fight parliamentary elections against the 'Party', no Sinn Feiner could then contemplate attendance at Westminster or alliance with a party which believed in it. Even the moderate Robert Lynd regarded abstentionism as the key-stone of Sinn Fein policy, for it asserted Ireland's confidence in its own ability to govern itself.[18] O'Brien and Griffith, therefore, had either to come to some agreement, violating the principles of neither—an almost impossible achievement—or see the decline of the All-for-Ireland League in Cork and Sinn Fein in Dublin.

In December 1909 William O'Brien's Dublin solicitor, James Brady, wrote to George Gavan Duffy suggesting that they both stand for Dublin constituencies with the backing of Sinn Fein and the O'Brien and Healyite parliamentary factions. Brady as a member of the Dublin corporation had been a 'loyal addresser' at the beginning of the century. In 1907, however, he began voting with Sinn Fein in the corporation and seems to have considered himself one of them. In 1908 Brady resigned from the Dublin corporation which he declared was a mere servant of the local government board and participated at the Sinn Fein annual convention.[19]

The most disturbing feature of Brady's letter, which Duffy showed to a shocked O'Hegarty, was the claim that reports in *Sinn Fein* and other papers indicated that Brady had 'practically succeeded in getting the Sinn Fein party here to admit parliamentary representation on certain conditions' such as its subjection to control by a council in Dublin. Duffy turned down Brady's proposal but promised to meet him in Dublin to explain his position.[20] Brady claimed that he was acting independently of O'Brien though his proposals were very similar to those of the latter.[21]

When the Brady proposals were finally discussed at a meeting of the Sinn Fein executive on 20 December 1909 they created a furore which soon split the movement.[22] Though the Hobson–O'Hegarty group was rigidly opposed to the smallest tinkering with the abstentionist credo, their Sinn Fein critics were, in the existing circumstances, not totally unjustified in their attempts to find some way out of an obvious impasse. Lloyd George's budget rejected by the lords had provoked a parliamentary crisis. The Liberal government now appeared likely to initiate a limitation of the power of the house of lords, perennially opposed to Home Rule. The election of January 1910 might be decisive. Any reduction of Liberal members would necessitate government support by a strong Irish party. The time was hardly ripe for doctrinaire Irish abstentionism. The only influence which Sinn Fein could hope to exert on the situation would be in conjunction with the more advanced parliamentarians following O'Brien and Healy rather than Redmond. Through them it was possible that a more far-reaching Home Rule bill might be obtained than if Redmond were given a free hand.

At the Sinn Fein executive meeting, Griffith tried to appear impartial, raising the question simply as a test of opinion. His advanced opponents, led by Hobson and Daly, were determined to needle Griffith into an admission that he personally favoured compromise. According to Countess Markievicz, who had just entered politics as a Hobson protégé, her faction was determined to 'kick him off the hedge'. Though there were but five of the 22 non-resident members present,[23] only eight members were prepared to support any form of compromise, while 11 voted stolidly against it. The moderates included Mrs. Wyse Power, M. D. Clare, T. S. Cuffe, Sean Milroy and Tom Kelly, but Sweetman and W. L. Cole on this occasion sided with H. Holahan, Miss Murphy and other allies of Hobson. There is, however, little correlation between attitudes on the Brady proposals and subsequent events like the 1916 Rising or the Treaty.

Though reports of the meeting are contradictory and confusing, the moderates appear to have attempted to secure a resolution allowing Sinn Fein to support an Irish council which would send MPs to Westminster as delegates when their votes were crucial, rather than representatives. This suggestion, sponsored by Milroy, would have surmounted several difficulties by enabling Irish MPs, normally resident in Ireland, to vote on matters like the abolition of the lords' veto or an Irish Home Rule bill. It had precedents in previous history when O'Connell's Repeal Association voted for the withdrawal of Irish MPs, except when Irish coercion bills and the like were under discussion. Smith O'Brien had been imprisoned by the house of commons for adhering to this resolution. Thomas Davis, though opposing the principle of parliamentarianism, once declared that it might be permissible to send Irish MPs to Westminster as delegates to vote for Home Rule.[24] In the 1910 context, however, the policy would have been impracticable as a pro-Home Rule government with a small majority required the constant support of Irish MPs to survive against an anti-Home Rule opposition.

Though Milroy's main suggestion was quickly disposed of, an attempt was made to introduce an amendment (which would have allowed Sinn Fein to send delegates to an all-party meeting), to an uncompromising resolution of Daly's. This was no more successful than the effort of Griffith to secure a rejection of Brady's immediate proposal rather than an absolute prohibition of all future negotiation with bodies rejecting the abstentionist principle. Though an attempt was made to make the final decision unanimous, a thoroughly irritated Griffith apparently declared that 'the matter would not end there', while on the other side Holahan resigned his membership of the executive because a compromise so inimical to the constitution had even been considered. When Brady eventually stood against an official parliamentarian for a Dublin constituency in December 1910, the Sinn Fein executive refused endorsement in spite of Brady's promise to abstain from Westminster. It is highly ironical that Daly, the tough opponent of compromise in December 1909, should have defied the executive by acting as Brady's election agent in December 1910.

The breach between the two groups was widened by the publication in the *Irish Nation and Peasant,* the residuary legatee of Hobson's *Republic,* of an embarrassingly frank and anti-Griffith account of the Sinn Fein executive meeting. The Sinn Fein general secretary, Aindrias O Broin, was directed to make a complete repudiation of the *Peasant,* and something of an internal witch-hunt began to find the executive member guilty of supplying information to the rival periodical. For a time suspicion fell on Countess Markievicz. O'Hegarty rushed into print in the *Peasant,* showing that the courageous leader of the Independent Orange Order, Lindsay Crawford,* later a Sinn Fein stalwart in Canada, had been promised national council votes in a Dublin constituency which William O'Brien had bought with a subscription to the *Sinn Fein* daily. O'Hegarty also revealed the contents of Brady's private letter to Gavan Duffy, much to the latter's chagrin. To O'Hegarty the 'amazing circumstances' of the Brady negotiations were at least partially attributable to the policy of the *Sinn Fein* daily which was attempting to show unionists 'how they may be unionists and good patriots at the same time'. The only remedy O'Hegarty could see was to make the paper independent of the Sinn Fein organisation.[25]

O'Hegarty's belief in the absolute validity of the abstentionist ideal did not, however, pass unchallenged. Earlier Fenians like John O'Leary and Mark Ryan had been somewhat sceptical of the policy of total withdrawal. O'Hegarty's London colleague, Gavan Duffy, denied that abstentionism was anything 'more than a canon of political conduct, which a minority of enthusiasts set up for the guidance of their countrymen'. Eamon Ceannt, shot as a signatory of the 1916 republican proclamation, believed in joining other groups as the Fenians had aided Parnell. Griffith would not have approved Ceannt's belief that 'John Redmond and Sinn Fein are the political descendants of Parnell and the Fenians', but his remark is indicative

*Crawford was expelled from the Independent Orange Institution in 1907 for advocating Home Rule.

of opinion at the time. Ceannt denied that Griffith was inconsistent in seeking compromise and cited the co-operation of Kossuth and Déak in Hungary.[26] Maud Gonne MacBride also believed in 1910 that Redmond had achieved the balance of power sought by Parnell, who, had he been alive, would have obtained Home Rule before the end of the year.[27] Liam de Roiste of Cork, who later sat in the First Dail, believed that the Irish MPs could be gradually converted to Sinn Fein ideas and persuaded to spend more time in Ireland.[28] This he thought more practicable than attempting to elect a Sinn Fein majority or compelling the parliamentarians to leave Westminster immediately.

The views of these representative nationalists indicate the danger of judging the opinions of 1909 in the light of subsequent events. The nationalism of Hobson and O'Hegarty was not necessarily sounder than that of Griffith or the advocates of compromise in 1909. In the existing circumstances there was nothing that either Sinn Fein or the IRB could achieve without modifying their exclusive principles. As a *Peasant* correspondent pointed out in September 1910 when the Brady controversy had been going on for nine months, it was laughable if not tragic to persist in debating nice points of compromise and principle when Sinn Fein itself was 'in the last stages of an inglorious existence'.[29]

The months between the O'Brien incident and the October convention of 1910 were used by Griffith and his supporters to restore order and centralise in Dublin the depleted organisation which had lost its daily paper earlier in the year. Griffith and Milroy were by no means perturbed by their rebuff in December 1909 and soon regained the initiative. In February Milroy proposed a motion 'deprecating the actions of members of the National Council assailing their fellow-members in regard to matters discussed at Executive meetings'.[30] In March, Milroy wrote to George Gavan Duffy to tell him of a new scheme for a national council of all parties which was being considered by the resident executive.[31] Executive members were required to sign as correct the official *Sinn Fein* version of the controversial December meeting. Only Countess Markievicz and Holahan refused. Hobson and McCullough accepted the statement but Patrick McCartan, now a member of the IRB supreme council, reported to Devoy that it would be used against them at the next convention. The report he believed was 'correct but incomplete'.

McCartan painted a dreary picture of the movement which was in a 'queer mess'. Seamus Deakin, another IRB supreme council member, McCullough and Countess Markievicz wanted to leave the movement to Griffith and his supporters, but Daly and the future Irish president, Sean T. O'Kelly, trimmed when they attended serious discussions.[32] The only hope appeared to lie in the resolutions which P. S. O'Hegarty was preparing for the next convention. If O'Hegarty failed it might be wise to start a new paper, controlled perhaps by the IRB. McCartan had discussed this issue with the veteran Fenian Tom Clarke whose tobacconist's shop was a favourite meeting-place for advanced nationalists.

O'Hegarty in London faced a difficult situation. The movement was declining rapidly. In January 1908 there had been five branches of the national council; in April 1909 there was only one.[33] The leaders meanwhile quarrelled among themselves. J. O'Sheehan resigned in May 1908 from the London executive, as a remonstrance against its decision, as a non-sectarian body, not to send a delegate to a protest meeting deploring the refusal of Westminster cathedral dignitaries to allow a service in Irish on St. Patrick's day.[34] Mrs. Dryhurst, once an extreme opponent of compromise, had 'developed into a Griffithite since her row with Madame Markievicz'.[35]

The relations between O'Hegarty and Gavan Duffy had been strained after the O'Brien affair. Duffy conceded that O'Hegarty was 'honest in his lunacy'[36] when he broke his pledge of secrecy by publishing the contents of Brady's letter. However, as the Sinn Fein annual congress approached O'Hegarty sent Gavan Duffy a list of his convention resolutions reducing Griffith's power.[37] Duffy, though 'utterly disgusted' by the executive's incompetence,[38] refused to support a campaign against Griffith, the only credible leader.[39]

The sixth annual convention of the national council, October 1910, met in a general atmosphere of unreality. The first general election of the year had captured the interest of the country, never particularly enamoured of Sinn Fein. The public meeting[40] was held in the mansion house by permission of the lord mayor on the humiliating condition that there must be no criticism of the parliamentary party. The weekly Sinn Fein no longer filled its front page with reports of branch activities and had shrunk to a smaller size: the annual convention received only a column on a back page.[41] This meagre treatment somewhat obscures the fate of O'Hegarty's resolutions. Two seem to have been accepted but no change in the basic composition of the national council was made. Instead 'resolutions re subscriptions to the executive and the composition of the executive were referred unanimously to the executive for consideration and report to the next congress'. It appears that several of O'Hegarty's allies either walked out in disgust or failed to attend.

The elections to the executive are significant; Sweetman, though absent, was elected president. Griffith and the executive tried hard to persuade Sweetman to retain his position. In spite of the plea that 'your resignation at the present crisis would be disastrous', they did not succeed in keeping him. Hobson, McCullough, Sean T. O'Kelly and Deakin were not elected to any position but O'Hegarty was placed, in his absence, on the non-resident executive. Tom Kelly and Griffith were appointed vice-presidents. Two men who had never previously held office, Patrick O'Keeffe and John O'Donnell, were elected honorary treasurers. Countess Markievicz and P. T. Daly remained as resident members of the executive and George Gavan Duffy a non-resident member. S. Milroy, the determined compromiser, topped the poll for the resident executive. Fr. Michael O'Flanagan and The O'Rahilly, a wealthy businessman whose claim to his exalted title was dubious, were elected for the first time.

The public meeting at the mansion house fully demonstrated the movement's decline. Letters of apology were read from Sweetman and Martyn, the latter remarking that he was 'in sympathy with almost all the Sinn Fein policy'. Griffith attacked Lloyd George's budget for imposing higher taxes on Ireland and suggested passive resistance by tenant-farmers required to make a declaration of land value for tax purposes. If Sinn Fein had possessed the confidence of the country, such resistance would have been afforded an admirable opportunity for opening the Sinn Fein campaign, but in 1910 general support was patently lacking.

Though several contemporaries believe that Griffith's final rupture with the IRB occurred in 1910 too much emphasis should not perhaps be placed on either the split in Sinn Fein or on the apparent decline of the movement between 1910 and 1914. The only frank account of the secession is given by Hobson who claims that interminable committee meetings in Dublin concerned mainly with Dublin corporation affairs and the impossibility of working with Griffith persuaded 'quite a number of us', including O'Hegarty and McCullough, 'to drop quietly from the Sinn Fein organisation'.[42]

Hobson became editor of *Irish Freedom* which as McCartan had suggested was controlled by the IRB. Its first issue of November 1910 took pains to associate itself with the republican tradition of Tone, Emmet and Mitchel. The new paper was less hostile to Larkin's Labour movement than *Sinn Fein*, but Griffith was treated with respect in *Irish Freedom's* columns as the movement's prickly but acknowledged *guru*. As Marcus Bourke argues, the nationalist resurgence which enabled the militant young group in the IRB to take over was largely the creation of Griffith himself.[43] Griffith sat on the general purposes committee of the Wolfe Tone and United Irishmen memorial association which was one of the organisations of the *Irish Freedom* group.[44] Irish Freedom clubs, moreover, paid small sums to keep *Sinn Fein* alive. P. S. O'Hegarty, a regular writer for *Irish Freedom,* maintained a foot in both camps by lecturing at Sinn Fein meetings. Countess Markievicz, though she remained technically in Sinn Fein, disliked Griffith and should logically have left alongside Hobson with whom she was organising Fianna Eireann, an Irish version of Baden Powell's boy scouts. She stayed on, however, because, as she said, Sinn Fein at that time was the only organization admitting women. Eamon Ceannt whose part in planning the Rising might seem to place him in the extreme camp was in 1910 a Griffithite. Sean MacDermott, however, retired from his position as Sinn Fein organiser and became manager of *Irish Freedom*. P. T. Daly, a Labour man and a leader of James Larkin's union, dropped out of the national council. He was subsequently excluded from the IRB supreme council for the embezzlement of £300 from Clan-na-Gael. The whole sorry story became public as the result of an unsuccessful libel action initiated by Daly in 1924. On the right-wing of the movement, W. E. Shackleton, the prosperous Protestant Lucan flour-miller, appears to have grown disillusioned with Sinn Fein at this time and subsequently supported the parliamentary party. Sweetman, though elected president in 1910, sent his apologies in the following year and Griffith at last became official leader of the movement. Martyn had withdrawn over the North Leitrim by-election. The O'Rahilly, on whose financial assistance Griffith was dependent in the years before 1916, fortunately possessed a vital resource in his motor car.

By 1911 Griffith had reverted to his 1903 position when the national council was set up to fight a loyal address to Edward VII. In 1903 Griffith had hoped to lead an educational campaign, based on a newspaper and a central committee in Dublin, providing the vanguard of a new revitalised national movement. Country branches and direct conflict with the parliamentary party were forced on him by more militant followers. Now that Hobson and his friends had withdrawn and Sinn Fein branches outside the capital were petering out, Griffith was able to revert partially to his former role, using the Sinn Fein central branch in Dublin as his pivot. The parallel between 1903 and 1911 is completed by the death of Edward VII which raised anew the loyal address question.

Now that there again existed a plethora of unco-ordinated national clubs, Sinn Fein was able to seize the initiative. By their voluntary withdrawal the Sinn Fein dissidents obviated the need for continual recrimination and time-wasting casuistry. A meeting in the Sinn Fein rooms, presided over by Griffith, set up a united national societies' committee to fight a loyal address.[45] An anti-coronation demonstration attended by 15,000 was held in Beresford Place behind the custom house. Griffith, McCartan, John MacBride, Countess Markievicz and Laurence Ginnell, the MP who had been almost converted by Hobson in 1907, played prominent parts. The mounted police charged and the foot police 'administered kicks and cuffs on all sides'.[46] At a further demonstration at Foster Place Countess Markievicz and her friend, the Abbey actress Helena Moloney, were arrested, the former, it was alleged, for kicking a policeman and throwing gravel in his face. Miss Moloney was congratulated by the Sinn Fein Ard Chraobh for refusing to pay her fine and accepting a gaol sentence.[47] On this occasion the Dublin corporation by a large majority resolved against the presentation of a loyal address. As already shown, the national insurance bill, the Home Rule bill, the prospect of partition, and eventually the Irish neutrality league, provided Sinn Fein with invaluable opportunities for taking the initiative on vital issues. The annual aonach, or industrial exhibition, held under Sinn Fein auspices between 1908 and 1914, helped to popularise the movement amongst Dublin businesses and emphasise its importance.

The small Sinn Fein organization after 1910 was also able to gain attention in other ways. For the campaign against enlistment the Sinn Fein anti-recruitment car was good advertising. The movement endeavoured to negotiate with foreign states. When in 1912 the direct shipping line between Queenstown (now Cobh) and the United States ceased to operate and thus made the export of Irish cattle difficult, Sinn Fein informed the German embassy that 'an ample supply of store and fat cattle' existed in Ireland.[48] The decision of the German Hamburg line to call at Queenstown was applauded.[49] The Sinn Fein writer Seamus MacManus, when granted an interview by President Taft of the USA, used the opportunity to refute the president's suggestion that the Irish parliamentary party after the 1910 elections was in a position to help Ireland.[50] The national council also wrote to President Taft in an attempt to persuade the American government to prevent further Irish emigration to the USA. The national council's arguments followed closely the traditional objections of American nativists against the Irish, that the low living standards of the Irish would displace American workers and that liquor dealers were the chief US immigration agents in Ireland. The saloon, said the national council, should not become a recruiting ground for American citizenship.[51] In Ireland, Sinn Fein spared no effort to discourage Irish emigration to the snowy Canadian prairies and sun-baked Australian outback.

In New York Sinn Fein had a partial ally in Devoy's *Gaelic American,* but as Hobson was the Irish correspondent its bias was somewhat against the national council. Sinn Fein did, however, congratulate the *Gaelic American* for its propaganda against the attempted Anglo-American treaty.[52] Like its counterpart in Ireland, the American Sinn Fein organisation, set up in a burst of enthusiasm after Hobson's 1907 visit, was declining after 1910. According to

Hobson, many years later, the American Sinn Fein league 'never grew to any size or importance'.[53] It did, however, organise opposition to Redmond's 1910 United States visit which the Gaelic American could then declare a failure.[54] Redmond was hated for favouring an Anglo-American alliance and opposing Irish industrialisation. The New York Sinn Fein branch seems to have been reasonably active and was still operational in 1913.[55] New York Sinn Fein, moreover, followed Griffith's line fairly closely. One of its leading members was the old Parnellite MP, Michael Conway, who provided numerous accounts of the Chief's betrayal by Redmond and other parliamentarians.

It was easy for Patrick Ford's Irish World to sneer at Sinn Fein which, like the three radical tailors of Tooley Street,[56] claimed to speak for Irish public opinion. But the national council was preparing the ground and establishing precedents for the men who, in the face of Britain's overwhelming power, would establish Dail Eireann in 1919. Sinn Fein in the 1910–4 period was not just one of the many nationalist societies—Wolfe Tone clubs, Inghinidhe na hEireann, Na Fianna Eireann—but the intellectual fertilizer providing nourishment for all. 'Ballingary' writing to Sinn Fein in mid-1911 suggested that Sinn Fein was still the best unifier of the 'excess of organisations' in Dublin, in spite of its 'grave blunder' of attacking parliamentarians head-on instead of by a flank movement. 'Ballingary', amongst other recommendations, argued that Sinn Fein should fight no more municipal or poor law elections but instead attempt to pledge all candidates.[57] He thus agreed with Hobson's criticism of the emphasis placed on the Dublin corporation but hardly did justice to Griffith's original intentions.

The departure of Hobson's group from the Sinn Fein organisation did not resolve controversy over violence versus passive resistance. While Griffith continued to emphasise passive resistance and the British Renunciation Act of 1783 as a basis for agreement, Sean Mac Giobuin (FitzGibbon), secretary of the Sinn Fein central branch, insisted, like Hobson, that passive resistance must lead eventually to stronger measures.[58] J. W. Biggar, auditor of the Trinity College Dublin Gaelic society, summed up the situation in 1913 when he said of Sinn Fein that 'the aims of the party seem to vary somewhat with the exponent'. Some believed in absolute freedom through physical force, while the 'more representative type' or 'true Sinn Feiner' was willing to settle for Grattan's parliament plus a democratic franchise.[59]

For Griffith, however, the formation of the Irish volunteers in late 1913 posed no intellectual problem. He had always believed with Mitchel that the right to bear arms was the hall-mark of citizenship, without neglecting to point out that Mitchel like the other Young Irelanders originally 'had a firm conviction that the

Irish Question could and would be solved without bloodshed'.[60]
But Griffith, while sneering at the 'illuminati' who in defiance of
Aristotle and the ancient Irish Solomon, Cormac Mac Airt, insisted
that war was 'impious and immoral', warned that arms would not
bring immediate independence. There was always the British fleet.
Griffith, in fact, valued the volunteers chiefly for their effect on
national morale. They could 'put a public opinion with backbone
into the country, to make men more conscious of their duty as
citizens, to associate the ideas of order and discipline with the idea
of liberty, to bring the nationhood of Ireland in touch with realities,
and to make it clear-seeing and fearless, an atmosphere in the
country in which the gasbag and flapdoodler will cease to be possible'.[61] Though the then circumstances of Ireland required the
nationalist to 'work through public opinion rather than through
force of arms', a public opinion lacking 'the confidence, the calm-
ness, the steadiness, the judgment, the resolution and the understanding' derived from training in arms would prove worthless in a
crisis.[62] One is reminded of the insistence of Gandhi (not by 1913
an Indian nationalist) and his subsequent demonstration that training in the techniques of non-violent resistance provided all the moral
benefits so often associated with martial pursuits. For those who
believed in the effectiveness of force, Gandhi advocated training in
arms.

Griffith played his individual part as a volunteer but was not in
the inner councils of the movement. O'Rahilly, regarded by his
biographer as the main force behind the volunteers, claims that
Griffith was deliberately kept in the background lest the movement
'might savour too much of Sinn Fein'.[63] At the volunteer meeting
in December 1913 Sinn Fein does not appear to have been officially
represented as an organisation, but Alderman Kelly and Sean T.
O'Kelly both participated.[64] On the volunteer provisional committee, established in May 1914, four members, The O'Rahilly,
Ceannt, FitzGibbon (Mac Giobuin) and Peter P. Macken were
designated Sinn Fein representatives.[65] Griffith, who had strongly
opposed the decision to bring in the Redmondites, was not included.[66] When Redmond's national volunteers broke away to
support Britain's war effort, the Irish volunteers were generally
referred to incorrectly—even in British secret service reports—as
the Sinn Fein volunteers. The Rising, though in no sense the action
of the Sinn Fein organisation, was similarly misrepresented.

It is difficult to disentangle the diverse attitudes of Sinn Fein
leaders in the months before the Rising. Hobson, once reckoned an
extremist, utterly refused to countenance rebellion without the
support of the mass of the people. Though volunteer quarter-
master, he was therefore excluded from the confidence of Mac-

Dermott and the group preparing for the Rising. Professor Eoin MacNeill, the volunteer chief of staff, had a parliamentarian, not a Sinn Fein background. Nevertheless, according to Colum, Griffith's views on the possibilities of revolution most closely approximated to those of MacNeill with whom John FitzGibbon, once secretary of the Sinn Fein central branch, was closely associated. FitzGibbon, like several others, had preached violence in the past but when the crunch came opposed insurrection.

MacNeill, like Griffith, believed that civil action supported by the people could obtain independence on the 1783 basis. Because the north was attached to the crown, Ireland should remain a monarchy. The volunteers were 'to function at police level'. Any sort of action against the British during the war should be defensive only, if, for example, an attempt were made to disarm the movement. These views certainly coincide with the opinions often expressed by Griffith. In 1915, MacNeill published a pamphlet on Daniel O'Connell and Sinn Fein in which he based his argument on the illegality of the union in constitutional law. Griffith and FitzGibbon, moreover, were both used by MacNeill in his attempt to prevent the mobilisation of volunteers before the Rising. Hobson, who had himself sworn Pearse into the IRB, was so hostile to the Rising that to silence him he was kidnapped beforehand. The O'Rahilly, also opposed, was killed in the fighting after deciding at the last moment to participate. Of all the leading Sinn Feiners, only Ceannt appears to have been in the councils of the instigators of the insurrection. Sean MacDermott had long dissociated himself from the official Sinn Fein.

The one curious feature of Griffith's position was that, unlike Hobson, in September 1914 he appears to have attended a meeting of Tom Clarke and the IRB leaders at Parnell Square where he was, according to Bourke, with O'Rahilly committed to a Rising before the end of the war.[67] Moreover, after the suppression of *Sinn Fein*, Griffith edited, by agreement with MacDermott and the IRB, his wartime papers, *Eire*, *Nationality* and *Scissors and Paste*. In the light of Griffith's views, publicly expressed earlier in 1914, it is difficult to believe that Griffith ever supported the idea of a sacrificial rebellion. As Colum has hinted, Griffith must have realised that a wartime rising in southern Ireland would make subsequent agreement with Ulster unionists well-nigh impossible. When the Irish volunteers were first formed Griffith had put forward the not completely chimerical suggestion that north and south might yet come together in some brotherhood of arms. In 1916 the heroism of the executed leaders of the 1916 Rising was matched a few months later in the battle of the Somme by the glorious assault of the Ulster division which was almost decimated. Though they differed in loyalties Irish nationalist and Ulster unionist should have learned to respect the courage of their opponents' convictions. If a stand were required before the end of the war to justify Ireland's participation in the peace conference, it seems likely that Griffith's propagandist ingenuity would have lighted upon some device short of the bloodshed he had always hated.*

Opinion is also divided on Griffith's actions during the Rising itself. Yet it seems to matter little whether he offered his services as a private soldier—the most likely possibility—or remained aloof. The difference between violent and non-violent policies is more subtle. During the 1914-8 war Gandhi, almost an exact contemporary of Griffith, acted as a recruitment officer for the British government. The real issue is whether Griffith's original policy might have led to a happier and more united Ireland than in fact emerged. The Italian Risorgimento, so impressive in the eyes of 19th-century liberals, seemed after the rise of Fascism to have been flawed from the start. For too long the failure of the Irish revolution has been attributed to excessive moderation rather than an unreasoning cult of violence. In the two preceding chapters Griffith has been shown as a man in the middle struggling, not always successfully, to maintain a precarious balance between left and right. To understand the full strength of the revolutionary alternative to violence offered by Sinn Fein requires a more detailed consideration of organisational machinery and ideology.

*Griffith was prepared to publicise his opposition to the Rising as late as September 1917. A survey in 1915 had shown him to be the most popular nationalist in Dublin, well ahead of Pearse.

5 The party machine

It has already been demonstrated at some length that Griffith and his immediate followers had no desire to establish Sinn Fein as a new political party in opposition to existing organisations. However, an alliance of both left and right wing sympathisers forced Griffith to accept the necessity for branches in the country, plus the full paraphernalia of elective offices required by a combative political party. Nevertheless, Sinn Fein activists proved no more successful in evading the 'iron law of oligarchy' than the rank and file members of contemporary socialist groupings. An organisation dominated by a leader who disbelieved in the necessity for its very existence obviously stood little immediate chance of success. But to assess with greater precision the exact nature and importance of the early Sinn Fein machine the sparsely attended inaugural meeting of November 1905 must be briefly revisited.

At this private meeting Griffith's priorities were clearly demonstrated in a speech, later published as *The Sinn Fein Policy,* which was to remain the economic gospel of the movement. His whole emphasis was on national unity as a prerequisite for the establishment of a *de facto* Irish government. The coalition idea is implicit behind the generalities of Griffith's proposed objective which sought 'national self-development through the recognition of the rights and duties of citizenship on the part of the individual and by the aid and support of all movements originating from within Ireland, instinct with national tradition, and not looking outside Ireland for the accomplishment of their aims'.[1] The plurality of movements to whom the appeal was made was the most significant feature of the formula.

It seems doubtful, however, if, after the generation of some enthusiasm in the country and amongst the Irish in England, Sinn Fein could have remained a mere propagandist body in Dublin. Aldermen Kelly and Cole no doubt found the Dublin-oriented national council sufficiently useful in their campaigns for election to the Dublin corporation, but the co-operation of delegates like Maurice Sweeney from Loughrea and Thomas Martin of London could hardly be obtained on so narrow a basis. Sweeney's insistence on branches to fight the United Irish League was fully endorsed by Martin who demanded 'an organization to meet the parliamentarians step by step, to advance as they retreat'. Cole's plea for propagandist individuals rather than formal branches, which he feared might compete with other societies like the Gaelic League, carried no weight with provincial delegates, insistent on an organisation strong enough to fight local elections. As Sweeney's friends pointed out, branches were necessary if seats on local authorities were to be won 'and the principles of the organisation advocated through the one medium where they would reach the ears of the country'. Blithely ignoring the possibility of a backlash effect, the provincials lacked Griffith's belief that more supporters might ultimately be gained through peaceful persuasion than aggressive electoral confrontation. It may have appeared to the provincials that Griffith was more tolerant of clashes in Dublin than in the country. This possible discrimination might have been justified by the claim that the parliamentary party intervened less directly in Dublin corporation affairs while the United Irish League tended to dominate rural elections.

Griffith and his Dublin friends might be outvoted on the organisational issue, but, as the failure of the Hobson–O'Hegarty group demonstrated, it was almost impossible to keep the Dubliners permanently subordinate to the movement in the country. The Griffithites could have been effectively controlled only by a really active and enthusiastic movement in the provinces. One of the main purposes of the subsequent analysis is to compare the relative vigour of Sinn Fein in Dublin and the country.

The 1905 conference sanctioned the establishment of branches of at least ten members in every electoral district. A scheme for a large unwieldy executive council, containing 25 members resident in Dublin city and county, four from Cork, four from Antrim, ten from Great Britain and two from each of the other Irish counties, was drawn up.

The new constitution consisted of eight articles. Article one admitted individual members subscribing a shilling a year, while two provided for branches of at least ten members, paying an affiliation fee of ten shillings. The consent of the executive was required for the formation of more than one branch in an electoral district. Clauses three and four demanded a pledge from all Sinn Fein candidates for representative positions to 'act and vote' on issues according to council decisions arrived at by a caucus containing all

Sinn Feiners belonging to local governing bodies. Clauses five and six dealt with individual membership. Central and branch committees had the right to veto any candidate proposed by two members. British servicemen and pensioners were totally excluded and those holding office requiring allegiance to the British crown were debarred till the position was relinquished. Clause seven established an annual summer congress as the governing body of the movement and the elector of the executive whose function was described in the final eighth article. Both the national and resident executives were required to meet at least once a month. The former controlled organisation, finance, press, propaganda and urgent issues.

The constitution was a compromise between the Dubliners and provincials in that it provided for both individual and branch membership. Branches were never an essential feature, and the organisation did not collapse after 1910 when most provincial branches became dormant. Unlike most modern parties, there does not appear to have been originally a provision for a system of branch delegation to the annual congress. This omission would increase the power of the Dubliners likely to obtain an individual majority at any annual congress. The huge executive containing representatives from each county did nothing to offset this initial advantage as it would have been impossible for any but the 25 members resident in Dublin to have attended regular meetings.

By January 1906 it was established that the full executive would meet only six times a year while the resident executive met monthly. The vital general purposes committee, consisting of the officers, met weekly. Though non-resident members were apparently well represented on the two other committees, few would have been able to attend monthly meetings. Dublin dominance was indicated in early 1906 when the first meeting of the national executive (10 January) resolved against opposing the parliamentary party in the 1906 general election, in spite of the claim that the Dublin municipal election had been 'a sweeping victory' for Sinn Fein policy.[2] Dublin corporation elections which particularly interested men like Cole and Kelly were still fought, but, as earlier chapters have shown, would-be Sinn Fein parliamentary candidates received short shrift.

The original constitution, moreover, gave predominance to elected local body representatives in the council who were to form the caucus which established the party line for all Sinn Feiners belonging to local authorities. Although not specifically ruled out, there is no explicit indication in the constitution that parliamentary elections were ever to be fought on the basis of abstention from Westminster. The pledge for Sinn Fein candidates was similar to that of the Irish parliamentary party, though it applied to Irish local bodies and not Westminster.

In the years before 1916 several Sinn Fein executive members sat on local bodies. James O'Flaherty was a district councillor for Loughrea; P. Hughes (Dundalk), Seamus MacManus (Donegal) and James Ward (Castlebar) sat with O'Flaherty on the non-resident executive. But Sinn Fein's greatest success was undoubtedly in the Dublin corporation. On the Sinn Fein resident executive of 1906 Councillors M. J. Lord and P. O'Carroll were honorary treasurers while Alderman W. L. Cole was an honorary secretary. Subsequently Alderman Tom Kelly and Councillors P. T. Daly, Sean T. O'Kelly, J. J. Reynolds and D. O'Healy became resident executive members. Mrs. Wyse Power, widow of a Fenian and owner of a Henry Street café frequented by advanced nationalists, was, with Miss M. Murphy, a poor law guardian and resident executive member. Hobson's criticisms of Sinn Fein's excessive interest in the Dublin corporation must be read in this context. His antipathy may have been accentuated by the fact that men like Tom Kelly and W. L. Cole were particularly moderate in their views. Desmond Fitzgerald, hearing Tom Kelly at a 1913 Sinn Fein meeting, considered him completely Dublin-orientated and oblivious of opinion in the south-west where large numbers were native speakers. Griffith, according to Fitzgerald, was able to transcend his Dublin background.[3] Griffith's Hungarian policy laid great stress on the local authorities. The Dublin corporation, of unsavoury reputation, which represented the area where support for Sinn Fein was greatest, seemed an obvious target for electioneering, especially as the parliamentary party and United Irish League were usually apathetic in the capital.

The national council had run candidates for the Dublin corporation before the official inauguration of Sinn Fein in 1905. The future Irish president, Sean T. O'Kelly, chosen as a candidate by lot from the Sinn Feiners of his ward, was in 1906 one of the three new members of the national council's successful team of six. As only two Sinn Feiners had been defeated and 1,100 votes polled for the party, Griffith claimed a victory. In 1907 *Sinn Fein* announced a majority of 1,992 in the Dublin divisions up for election. Three more Sinn Feiners and a sympathiser were elected.[4] Next year, though the *Irish World* insisted that they had been routed, Sinn Fein again won three seats.[5] The *Gaelic American* regarded these as 'stunning victories' in a straight fight in the working-class areas between Sinn Fein and the publicans.[6] A year later, in 1909, the United Irish League, now aware of the danger of allowing Sinn Fein free scope in the Dublin corporation, put up a more vigorous fight. Local clergy told the electors to oppose the Sinn Feiner, Sean T. O'Kelly, on the ground that every vote given against him 'was given for their religion and their God'. O'Kelly, a devout Catholic, was nevertheless re-elected. One of his Sinn Fein colleagues elected for the first time, W. T. Cosgrave (1880–1965), won in Usher's Quay ward the chance to gain administrative experience which stood him in good stead when he led the Irish government in the first ten years after the Treaty. Cosgrave believed that he had been nominated by Sinn Fein in the erroneous belief that he was a wealthy man. P. T. Daly, Sinn Feiner, Labour unionist and IRB supreme councillor, was disqualified on a technicality in 1909, but his place as councillor for the Rotunda ward was taken by Dr. Patrick McCartan. In this election Sinn Fein lost one seat and gained another.[7]

There were then about a dozen Sinn Feiners in a corporation of 60 councillors and 20 aldermen. It seems that, for a time, Sinn Fein members of the Dublin corporation adopted a form of the obstructionist tactics employed by Parnell at Westminster. On 14 June there was a particularly disorderly scene when the Sinn Feiners attempted to use a resolution attacking Lloyd George's budget to denounce Irish attendance at Westminster.[8] The hostile *Irish World* claimed that this action raised 'a storm of indignation that threatens to overthrow whatever hold the so-called "extreme" party ever possessed in Dublin', and made it hazardous to organise Sinn Fein meetings in Dublin.[9] In his memoirs, Sean T. O'Kelly described this violent opposition from parliamentarians at Sinn Fein public meetings in Dublin. Alderman Kelly was nearly blinded with lime; Sean McDermott was beaten black and blue with sticks; and O'Kelly himself was knocked down and kicked. This was the sort of provocation that 'Ballingary', who wished to end direct confrontation at the polls, had in mind. After 1911 the national council did take a less prominent part in Dublin corporation elections and followed this adviser in seeking pledges demanding opposition to loyal addresses and promising reforms in Dublin.

Sinn Fein's actions in the corporation were often dramatic if not immediately successful. Sean T. O'Kelly managed to ensure that Dublin corporation's inscription on its cleansing carts was in Irish. But Sinn Fein also worked hard to effect vital reforms. Attempts were made to force owners to keep tenements in repair. A list of corporation members holding tenement property was also mooted. Sinn Feiners tried to reduce unnecessary costs and to audit the moneys voted to the lord mayor. Interest was taken in the establishment of evening continuation schools.[10] The Sinn Feiners certainly played a large part in securing, in spite of the opposition of the Catholic hierarchy, a Dublin corporation resolution in favour of compulsory Irish in the National University. Griffith's articles played a very large part in this outcome. W. B. Yeats, however, was furious with the Sinn Feiners in the corporation when they rejected a £70,000-worth gift of pictures from Hugh Lane who had stipulated the building of a municipal gallery to house them. Sinn

Fein, said Yeats, in demanding an Irish architect, 'preferred their mouthful of east wind'.[11] Griffith, denying that Sinn Fein belittled Lane's gift, insisted that the movement had originally persuaded a reluctant corporation to accept it. He complained that Lane had stepped up his demands and now required a large gallery as a personal monument, far greater than any accorded to O'Connell or Parnell.[12]

Yeats considered Cosgrave 'our best supporter'.[13] The praise received by Cosgrave as minister of local government during the Anglo-Irish War, suggests the most important result of Sinn Fein's early work in the Dublin corporation. Though some of the original Sinn Fein aldermen and councillors dropped out of subsequent politics, it was the corporation which gave pre-1916 Sinn Fein the opportunity to act as a credible political party and exercise a modicum of power for the first time. In 1913 when the party machine appeared almost defunct, William Tierney could still be elected under Sinn Fein auspices to replace a resigning UIL member of the corporation.[14]

The partial success of Sinn Fein in the Dublin corporation did nothing to assist the progress of Sinn Fein in the provinces, England and overseas. Revolutionaries from Tone to Mao have seen the danger of concentrating on capital cities to the exclusion of the country. But Hobson, O'Hegarty and the Sinn Fein opponents of Dublin's predominance had two major problems before them. In the first place, like all advocates of party control over elected politicians, they faced an almost inevitable movement towards oligarchy. This was accelerated by the fact that only in Dublin did Sinn Fein really function as a political party. By the same token, proponents of party democracy could not hope to carry conviction unless supported by a healthy and vigorous movement outside Dublin. A weakness in their position is illustrated by the popularity of their opponents. At the annual election of 1909 for vice-president Griffith received 50 votes to Hobson's 29. While Tom Kelly headed the list of resident executive members, O'Hegarty, McCullough, Gavan Duffy and Robert Lynd were the last four elected to the 12-man non-resident executive, being beaten by three priests and moderates like C. J. Dolan and W. Sears, editor of the *Enniscorthy Echo*.

Between 1905 and 1910 O'Hegarty and Hobson fought hard for administrative decentralisation. Their disputes with Griffith have already been documented. Some further analysis of their proposed organisational reform must precede the investigation of branch strength before 1910. Consideration of the truncated but centralised Sinn Fein organisation of 1910–4 can then be completed by comparison with post-Rising Sinn Fein institutions.

O'Hegarty's and Hobson's attempts to modify the Sinn Fein structure appear ironical in the light of an uncritical eulogy by the popular writer Shaw Desmond. Desmond, taking the organisation at its face value, regarded it as 'one of the finest examples of disciplined democracy'. In spite of the 'iron hand' of the national council the organisation was democratic in the ancient Gaelic sense which recognised a spiritual aristocracy to which 'ungrudging obedience' is given.[15] To modern readers Desmond suggests Gaullism or 'guided democracy', but the evocation of memories of Cuchulain and the Gaelic past to justify the 'iron hand' of centralism which Michels and others have treated in less flattering terms was undoubtedly original. The actions of Hobson and O'Hegarty, even at this early stage, could nevertheless have been even more effectively rationalised as an attempt to oppose to proto-Fascist authoritarianism a genuine system of democratic control.

At the September 1906 convention,[16] O'Hegarty did achieve some success in re-establishing the national council, to which 21 branches were by then affiliated, on an efficient basis. He secured the acceptance of three proposals. The first set up the London executive, thus delegating the national council's powers. The second organised the national executive in a form not altered till 1917, though O'Hegarty himself subsequently attacked the system vehemently. The original unwieldy executive was scrapped and replaced by a new national executive of 31 consisting of a president, two vice-presidents, two honorary secretaries, two honorary treasurers, 12 members resident in Dublin and 12 resident elsewhere. The resident executive which comprised the officers and the 12 Dublin resident members was still, however, the real governing body. Acceptance of Seamus McManus's proposal for a paid organiser further strengthened the executive. The national executive, including non-resident members, though supposed to convene quarterly, does not appear to have met more than once or twice a year.

O'Hegarty's third 1906 resolution was framed to ensure representation on the national executive for a county with five or more branches. In 1908 the county committees were allowed, like the branches, to send two delegates to the annual congress.[17] This 1906 provision had little importance. As late as 1909 there were only six counties, including Dublin, with more than five branches. Some of these did not discharge their responsibilities.[18]

The ideological controversy over the 1782 constitution appears to have distracted attention from the organisational issue. The 1907 convention amalgamating the national council and Sinn Fein league did not introduce any structural change of note, thus reinforcing the view that Griffith's group was by no means defeated. The subsequent dispute reaching a climax in the O'Brien negotiations did, however, encourage O'Hegarty to seek new procedural devices to check such developments at source. He placed considerable misdirected hope in the 1910 convention.

Writing to the unsympathetic Gavan Duffy, O'Hegarty summarised his propositions:

No. 1. Put the finances on a proper basis.
" 2. Wiped out the resident executive and provided for monthly meetings of the central executive.
" 3. Provided for the meetings being held on Sunday so that we could all go.
" 4. Provided for such meetings being confined to carrying out instructions, not initiating policy.
" 5. Definitely forbade the Central Executive to touch minor questions.
" 6. Pinned the organisation down to its proper business—practical work and propaganda.
" 7. Cut organisation loose from the paper—which is absolutely essential.

But Gavan Duffy's reply provides a classic illustration of the difficulty involved in a half-hearted challenge to the authority of any political leader and must have expressed the private views of many members of the organisation. The movement, said Duffy, was in a dilemma. It could not exist without Griffith who would object to the reforms, but with Griffith might 'continue on its ineffectual lines' till the situation improved in the future. Duffy therefore rejected open war with Griffith till the emergence of a man fit to replace him.[19] As a previous chapter has shown, O'Hegarty's proposals proved inopportune in 1910. Though O'Hegarty himself remained for another year on the executive most of his allies quietly withdrew.

The dissidents naturally believed that there was a positive correlation between their loss of interest in Sinn Fein and the numerical decline of the organisation. According to Hobson, 'when we left there were about 135 branches in the country; in the following year there were six and a year later there was one'. Contemporary evidence, however, indicates that the situation had begun to deteriorate before the 1910 convention. As McCartan told Devoy earlier in that year, 'membership was falling rapidly'. Clubs which had once possessed up to 20, 30, 40, 50 or 60 members were being reduced to numbers like 6 and 13.[20]

Fortunately, some figures exist to throw additional light on the numerical strength and financial competence of Sinn Fein branches at this time. To the casual observer the movement exhibited a mushroom growth in the counties. In 1906 there were 21 branches,[21] 57 in 1907, with 12 in the process of formation,[22] 115 in 1908,[23] and

128 in 1909.[24] But the full report of the latter year revealed a deplorable situation.[25]

Only one of the nine American branches had paid its affiliation fee, while in Ireland 61 of a nominal 106 branches were financial. But 20 financial branches omitted to pay either membership levies of a shilling a head or money obtained from local collections. As the previous congress had insisted on the shilling subscription for all members, the report estimated 581, or six per branch, as the total effective Sinn Fein membership. Even the IRB, according to Hobson, had 1,500 members in 1912, of whom more than half lived in Dublin.[26] However, the influence of a secret society could hardly spread much beyond its members, while Sinn Fein's electoral successes in the Dublin corporation and North Leitrim elections indicated a much wider potential following.

To explain the unsatisfactory 1909 position, the Sinn Fein report cited the drain on members' finances due to the repeated appeals for capital to keep *Sinn Fein* in circulation. It suggested that subscriptions be in future collected by agents from Dublin instead of by branch secretaries. Branch revenue which had dropped since the previous year provided little more than one-sixth of Sinn Fein's total annual revenue of £700. Most money was obtained by donations stimulated by appeals in *Sinn Fein*. Thus centralisation had a financial justification.[27]

The table on the opposite page gives a break-down by county.

These figures speak for themselves. Only 23 counties appear in the list and 29 of their branches defaulted. The remaining nine counties shared 16 defaulting branches between them. Twenty secretaries forwarded affiliation fees to the national council but could not cajole subscriptions from their members. Such branches must have been partially active or the 10s. would not have been paid.

Returns from individual counties demonstrate that only Dublin contained any considerable number of members. According to the report, it doubled its financial contribution in spite of the ten municipal contests in the city. However, 215 is not a large financial membership, especially if the IRB claimed more than half their total of 1,500 in Dublin. Unfortunately no figures exist to show how many Sinn Feiners were IRB men and how many were moderates adhering to 1782 and non-violence.

In the rest of the country, Galway had six paid branches and 71 paid members, an average of over ten per branch. Though originally intended to form branches with a minimum of ten members, there were on average only six per branch. Clare had one very large branch of 60 members, bringing it into third place. Cork must have been a great disappointment for half of its six branches defaulted and only 39 members paid subscriptions. Probably the influence of

	County	Nominal Branches	Financial Branches (10s. affiliation fee)	Financial Members (1s. membership fee)	Branches Defaulting Completely
1	DUBLIN	16	14	215	2
2	GALWAY	7	6	71	1
3	CORK	6	3	39	3
4	WEXFORD	6	5	28	1
5	CLARE	3	1	60	2
6	LEITRIM	15	7	33	8
7	MAYO	1	1	12	–
8	LOUTH	8	6	55	2
9	KERRY	3	1	—	2
10	LEIX	1	1	35	–
11	LONGFORD	1	1	15	–
12	WATERFORD	1	1	—	–
13	LIMERICK	4	3	—	1
14	KILKENNY	1	1	—	–
15	ANTRIM	4	1	—	3
16	CAVAN	4	2	—	2
17	DONEGAL	2	2	—	–
18	DERRY	2	1	10	1
19	KILDARE	1	1	8	1
20	CARLOW	1	1	—	–
21	DOWN	1	1	—	–
22	MONAGHAN	1	1	—	–
23	WESTMEATH	1	1	—	–
	TOTAL	90	62	581	29

William O'Brien's rival protest party was responsible for this lack of interest in Sinn Fein. If so it must have influenced Griffith in his negotiations with that politician. Before the foundation of Sinn Fein, Griffith had asked William Bulfin to lecture in Cork. 'The city is very apathetic at present but there is a small band of young fellows who are all right and it will help them.' Unfortunately, one of these was Terence MacSwiney, the future lord mayor of Cork who in 1920 died on hunger strike in Brixton prison. MacSwiney refused to join Sinn Fein which seemed to him to be based on an unsatisfactory compromise.[28] According to his biographer, Mac-Swiney 'and a great number of other Nationalists rejected Arthur Griffith's strategic acceptance of the Crown'. In Leitrim, thanks to the energetic preliminary efforts of Dolan and Sean MacDermott, the election contest of 1903 had led to the precipitate foundation of 15 branches. In 1909, less than half these branches paid their affiliation, and only 23 members their subscriptions. In no case was the contrast between nominal and actual membership more striking.

Particularly disappointing was the failure of the American Sinn Fein league, established in August 1908 on the understanding that 'the chief need of the organisation now is money'. The American members were required to pay higher fees $1 (4s.) and branch affiliations of $10. The money was to have been sent through the central council to Dublin. It has already been suggested that the tension between Hobson and Griffith probably goes some way to explain the lack of enthusiasm in America. At the very first meeting of the American Sinn Fein league the fear was expressed that money sent to Ireland might be misused as in the past. To allay such suspicions the clear-cut constitution of the party and the reliability of Irish Sinn Feiners were cited.[29] The 1910 O'Brien negotiations must therefore have caused considerable concern to American Sinn Fein supporters.

Perhaps the most significant of the revelations in the preceding table is that the future Six Counties mustered only three affiliated branches and ten paid members. Clearly the optimism of the founders of the Dungannon clubs had been belied. Hobson's allies must have lost their sparkle after the amalgamation with Griffith, perhaps because Hobson himself was in Dublin for several years before 1909. The truth may be that the situation of the Catholic nationalists was too serious for many to be diverted from the parliamentary party and the AOH (Board of Erin) by what seemed to them a political red herring parading an unrealistic non-sectarianism. Sinn Fein was more likely to appeal to the younger sons of Orangemen, widening for a time the generation gap by reacting against their fathers' politics. Bulmer Hobson, himself a Protestant, told Gavan Duffy in 1906 that at a meeting in the centre of Belfast, though his audience of 400 was mainly Orange, 'they not only did not object but I had to appeal for a hearing for a man who wanted to ask questions'. On the other hand, as Hobson admitted in 1912, 'any Protestant who chose to think for himself on national questions has always been treated as an outcast by his Unionist or Orange co-religionists'. On the Catholic side, Sean MacDermott appears to have done some good organising work in Antrim and Derry in spite of what the *Gaelic American* called 'the Board of England'.[30]

The London executive of the national council was a subordinate body with subsidiary branches of its own. O'Hegarty had at one time toyed with the idea of achieving the amalgamation of the Sinn

Fein league and the national council by fusing the London branches of both organisations, but this came to nothing. The London branches were little stronger than the Irish country branches. In 1908, O'Hegarty told George Gavan Duffy that 'the local branches are all weak. It would be an advantage if they were all amalgamated with the central except Forest Gate. However, I suppose they wouldn't amalgamate.' Instead of amalgamating they dissolved completely. Next year he rebuked Duffy and Lynd for missing 'meeting after meeting'. Only 17 had attended the last gathering. 'Surely to God, four hours a month is not too much to expect from you if you have any belief at all in the movement. And if the leaders of the thing here, such as it is, drop it, how can we expect the crowd to take it up? I'd sooner bust the whole pretence of a branch up than go on this way.'[31]

But such exhortations were of no avail. By 1909 there was only one London branch, which disappeared in 1910.[32] So much for O'Hegarty's decentralisation policy.

Griffith's scepticism about country branches seems justified; after 1910 he was not too unhappy when reduced to one effective branch in Dublin. Many of the criticisms voiced at the first annual convention were borne out by the event; the organisation did not take firm root except in Dublin. If to Griffith at this time a practical achievement justified compromise in theory, this attitude, characteristic of a machine politician as opposed to an idealistic political philosopher, had been partially forced on him by the supporters who insisted on the establishment of a conventional party organisation under his leadership.

In spite of the decline at the grass roots, in 1910 a building in Harcourt Street was acquired as the headquarters of the organisation. The significance of this development was fully realised by *Sinn Fein* which exulted in the forthcoming centralisation of the movement[33] and by Patrick McCartan who denounced it to Devoy. Quoting Swift, 'when nothing's left that's worth defence, they build a magazine', McCartan claimed that 'the separate building was to be the first step towards doing away with the Clubs and having the organisation consist of individuals who will subscribe a shilling yearly, and the Executive, the Resident Executives and other humbugs will be gravely elected by the frequenters of the club where the children will be taught to break Ireland's chains with their song. It will be an easy matter to make deals with O'Brien or any other men then.'[34] McCartan was hardly just. The Sinn Fein rooms provided a valuable rallying place for advanced nationalists in the years before the Rising. McCartan failed to realise that Sinn Fein was at last taking the form originally desired by Griffith.

After the secessions of 1910 this centralising process continued apace, not so much from Griffith's design but from the exigencies of the situation. The likelihood of Home Rule detached many supporters,[35] especially as Sinn Fein could not interfere in parliamentary elections. O'Hegarty, later commenting on the dwindling of Sinn Fein to a central branch and perhaps 'two or three' in the provinces, showed that at least the skeleton of the organisation remained between 1910 and 1913. The newspaper continued, conventions were held and the central branch met regularly, 'but no political work other than indoor educational and propagandist work was done'.[36] Griffith, if Hobson is correct, had always disliked public meetings. The last congress before the Rising, a special convention at Easter 1913, appears to have elected no new officers. Griffith, indeed, stated that its function was merely to provide suggestions for resident executive action in the coming year. As *Sinn Fein* published a list neither of members present nor of branches represented, it can be inferred that the congress was small. Though a few branches still existed the organisation was being run on the old basis of individual members. An advertisement for new members, proudly citing adherents from Sydney, Australia, to Nova Scotia, Canada, popularised the idea that residence in Dublin was not a prerequisite for joining the organisation. In 1913 Sinn Fein could muster less than £40 in subscriptions. Nevertheless, as a previous chapter has indicated, Sinn Fein achieved something in the years of her apparent decline.

As every Irish schoolboy is aware, Sinn Fein was completely reorganised in 1917. But it is worth considering whether the alteration entirely removed all the controversial features of the old movement. The new object aimed at securing 'the international recognition of Ireland as an independent Irish Republic. Having achieved that status the Irish people may by referendum freely choose their own form of government.'[37] The movement thus looked outside Ireland to the future peace conference and jettisoned the 1782 constitution. The second sentence is believed to have been a concession to Griffith, though it hardly allowed the use of 1782 as a bargaining counter.

The new annual congress consisted of the standing executive plus one delegate from each constituency executive and two from each branch. Unlike its predecessor the emphasis was on parliamentary and not local body elections. The national executive comprised 15 members, of whom ten were resident near Dublin, plus one representative from each constituency. Not more than 20 members, a large enough number, were to be co-opted. It met quarterly like the old national council, while the resident members met weekly. Shaw Desmond, as lavish with his praise of the democratic nature of the new as of the old, was equally unrealistic. It is ironical that he should have compared Sinn Fein with the decentralised soviets of the early Russian revolution.[38]

Sinn Fein was not, however, to be 'a compass to the world' in anticipating the modern radical idea of participatory democracy. The new constitution was even more centralised than the old: 20 co-opted members increased the power of the bosses and the permanent non-resident members only numbered five against ten.[39] As in 1910 the resident members meeting weekly were able to dominate the organisation. Though text-book democracy was obviously impossible when leaders were subject to arrest by the British and on the run, it was the general support of the people rather than their actual participation in Sinn Fein deliberations that enabled the movement to speak for Ireland. P. S. O'Hegarty, who had fought the excessive centralisation of the earlier organisation, was equally opposed to the latter:

I had an illuminating insight into democracy in practice one day in 6 Harcourt Street. Harry Boland, who was then secretary of Sinn Fein, was sitting at a desk as I entered, and going over a list of names. He would read out a name, 'John Brown, We can't have him'. Then 'John Black. I wonder is he safe? I'll ask X.' Then 'John Green. He's all right.' Then he came to another list and he looked at it, and said to me: 'Gavan Duffy. Do you think, P.S., that Gavan Duffy is a good republican? Do you think we ought to let him go up?' 'Well, Harry,' said I, 'I don't know whether he is a good republican, and I don't know whether I am what you would call a good republican. I prefer to call myself a separatist. But I know that Gavan Duffy was working in the separatist movement twelve years ago when it was neither popular nor respectable.' 'All right,' said he, 'I'll pass him.' What he was doing, apparently, was going over the lists of proposals sent up from the constituencies and himself deciding who would be allowed to be nominated and who would not. For the first Sinn Fein election there was a case for that. It was uncertain how many seats Sinn Fein would win, and it was vital that all the deputies elected should be dependable and safe from the point of view of giving least trouble to the political machine. But for the second Sinn Fein election it was a different proposition.

Though O'Hegarty was writing after the Treaty when feeling ran high, his experience makes short work of Shaw Desmond's euphoria. In a recent study, moreover, Michael Laffan has demonstrated that the proliferation of Sinn Fein clubs in the 1917 to 1920 period (1,240 to 1,822) resulted in a rapid decline when the 'Troubles' got under way. Activity was restricted to the military side of the movement thereby neglecting constructive civil planning.[40] During the War of Independence local IRA leaders were almost entirely independent of the Dail government. Griffith's attempts when acting president of the Dail to prevent the perpetration of certain outrages are examples of beneficent if not very successful centralisation.

Sinn Fein in its earlier days was an organisation of intellectuals. It made few concessions to the masses. It neither fought general elections nor prepared for a rebellion. Apart from Dublin corporation elections there was little for ordinary members but meetings discussing Irish history and literature, and occasional protest demonstrations. Resolutions, appeals for conferences, and negotiations were all arranged by Griffith and his immediate followers. As most of the rank and file were also members of the Gaelic League and the IRB, Sinn Fein might even appear superfluous to the average member. Outside Dublin it was frequently misunderstood. A contributor to the *Irish Nation and Peasant* lamented that Sinn Fein held big meetings in Dublin but not the country where it was regarded as 'a foolish physical-force movement, bossed by a set of carping critics who only criticise other people's work, while doing nothing themselves'.[41]

The basic difficulty was that Griffith, whom O'Hegarty subsequently accepted as 'the man who was Sinn Fein',[42] did not give sufficient thought to developing grass roots in the country. He did not want to divide the nation by starting a new political party, but to unify it by peaceful permeation in opposition to England. While nine-tenths of his supporters demanded successful electoral campaigns, Griffith meditated on conciliation. Consensus politics, however, have palpable weaknesses. Unless the active, and sometimes fanatical, party workers are kept happy by a vigorous policy, disaster may ultimately eventuate. Outside Dublin the Sinn Fein branches achieved little and, in Griffith's eyes, may well have appeared a handicap. Yet had the initial interests of the years before 1910 been maintained, the excessive emphasis on militarism characteristic of the 'Troubles' might have been avoided. Branches are a necessary part of a healthy political movement. As a political machine early Sinn Fein was at its least impressive. It is better seen as the university wherein the revolutionary vanguard learnt its nationalism.

PART TWO
Ideological Controversies

6 Revolutionary perspectives

THE Irish Revolution has supplied numerous precedents to subsequent nationalist and radical movements. Irish violent resistance
has been closely studied by terrorists like the Jewish Irgun.[1] Ho
Chi Minh was particularly interested in the 1916 Rising,[2] and the
modern IRA has obviously repaid the compliment by deriving many
of their tactics from Vietnam. On the other side, Griffith's original
programme of passive resistance was used by Gandhi in planning
his non-co-operation movements in India.[3] In the 1920s the advis-
ability of following Sinn Fein tactics in the Indian struggle was the
subject of a controversy between Gandhi and Jawaharlal Nehru,
who had attended Sinn Fein meetings in 1907 and 1910.[4] Griffith's
description of Déak's movement in Hungary has been included in
a recent anthology of writings on the theory and practice of non-
violent resistance.[5]

The perennial debate on the practical and moral advantages of
non-violent resistance over physical force has considerable relevance
to the past decade when numerous radical protest movements
switched from peaceful non-co-operation to violent retaliation
against apparently incorrigible opponents. As Nehru said against
Gandhi, in words virtually echoing those of Griffith's critics, to call
off a national independence movement because it was breaking into
violence gave established authorities power to destroy any campaign
by a judicious use of their own military resources.[6] Today it is less
easy to assume that non-resistance will assuage violence; indeed it is
arguable that an unaggressive posture may in some cases encourage
the sadistic feelings of an opponent. The assassination of Martin
Luther King provides justification for the Black Panthers and the
discomfiture of Northern Ireland civil rights marchers at Burn-
tollet clears the way for the provisional IRA.

Griffith, however, was never an exponent of the full-blooded
doctrine of non-violent resistance with its emphasis on human

brotherhood, self-sacrifice and love for opponents so clearly stated in the writings of his contemporary Tolstoi.[7] Though Gandhi claimed that Tolstoi had converted him from a belief in violence,[8] even the Mahatma was unable to follow the Russian's total rejection of patriotism as the chief source of world violence. Gandhi's patriotism was more liberal than Griffith's 'integral nationalism' which appears to have been drawn straight from the German school of romantics, with a dash of Mazzini. When he emphasised the nation and rejected the liberal individualism of the 18th-century Enlightenment, when he appealed to Irish history and Gaelic culture to justify Ireland's independence, and above all when he insisted on a protectionist policy based on Friedrich List to underpin his sovereign state, Griffith was very much in the late 19th-century European nationalist tradition. It is significant that Hans Kohn selected a passage applauding List's national economy for Germany as Griffith's most representative contribution to nationalist theory.[9]

Ironically, as will be shown, it was Griffith's early Sinn Fein opponents, advocating violence, who based their philosophy on the natural rights philosophy. They denounced Griffith's élitism and emphasis on Hungary. Hungary might indeed be regarded as a classic example of the worst evils of 19th-century nationalism. The Magyar landed aristocracy was determined to dominate an area where they were a racial minority. After their victory in 1867 the Magyars, maintaining, by vigorous gerrymandering, their supremacy over the Slavs and Romanians in their half of the Austro-Hungarian dual monarchy, proceeded to extirpate the cultural and linguistic diversities of their subject races. By a subtle process of blackmail the Magyars were also able to exert an inordinate influence on the foreign policy of the Austro-Hungarian empire. Thus the Magyars, a people which Mazzini classified alongside the Irish as lacking a moral claim to national status, acquired an influence in central Europe out of all proportion to their numbers.[10] That Griffith should take them as his model helps to explain some of the more grandiose objectives of his power philosophy.

Though Griffith's eulogy of Déak's passive resistance in Hungary patently ignores some of the less pleasant realities of the central European situation, early Sinn Fein did make a few ambiguous steps in the direction of non-violent ideology. Sinn Fein does not appear to have taken much notice of Gandhi's early *satyagraha* campaigns in South Africa.[11] Before 1919 Griffith would not have regarded Gandhi, who abandoned the term 'passive resistance' because it was compatible with subsequent violence,[12] as a full nationalist. But Griffith was keenly aware of contemporary Indian nationalism and exchanged information with several Indian patriotic journals. The Indian *Swadeshi* movement, which *inter alia* rejected British manufactures, Griffith considered the equivalent of Sinn Fein and this interest was reciprocated by Indian writers who complimented their Irish contemporaries.* Young Jawaharlal Nehru after visiting Dublin in a Cambridge vacation in 1907 reported to his father that Sinn Fein was similar to the advanced section of the Indian Congress party which under Tilak was breaking with the easy-going moderates.[13] Griffith was particularly impressed by the views of the eminent Bengal leader, Bipin Chandra Pal, who anticipated Gandhi by insisting that Indians must not hate the British but maintain towards them an attitude of 'benevolent indifference'.[14] Lala Lajpat Rai, leader of the Punjab nationalists, was approached on behalf of London Sinn Feiners and considered as a potential lecturer.[15] Though O'Hegarty at this time jibed at Sinn Fein talk about loving its enemies 'as positively maudlin', he later insisted that in spite of its vigorous attacks on England and the Irish parliamentary party, early Sinn Fein 'had no hatred for either'.[16] Griffith had certainly done much to conciliate the unionists.

The nearest Sinn Fein approach to doctrinaire non-violence came from the pen of Robert Lynd (1879–1949), an Ulster-born essayist and *New Statesman* critic sometimes compared with G. K. Chesterton and Charles Lamb, whose contributions to *Sinn Fein* and the movement's Irish year book were signed in Irish. Lynd, who was probably conversant with Tolstoi, insisted that a non-violent struggle would not only preserve the unity of the country but would provide a greater problem for the British, who could easily suppress a violent rebellion by superior physical strength but who were bound to flounder when confronted by an Irish character stronger than her guns.[17] This was precisely the argument of Gandhi's *Hind Swaraj* which also appeared in 1909. Diametrically opposed was O'Hegarty's insistence, anticipating Nehru, that Britain could always 'disorganise any purely passive resistance movement and drive it into premature and unprepared insurrection'.[18] Lynd's first suggestion, that violence was likely to further alienate the Irish unionist population, has received insufficient attention in recent Irish history.

In the last analysis the difference between the objectives of non-violent resistance and modern guerilla warfare may not be diametrically opposed. Both aim at winning over the masses, without whose tacit co-operation alien government is impossible. Psychological victory over the minds of men, not military success in formal warfare, is the aim of most wars of liberation. Violence operates more rapidly on public opinion, requires less discipline and is able to utilise secrecy, but pacifists insist that it arouses hatreds and fears which are impossible to eradicate when ostensible

*Griffith's pamphlets were apparently translated into a number of Indian languages and widely distributed.

victory is won. Nevertheless the distinction between violence and non-violence is not always easy to draw. A boycott, for example, may be physically non-violent but coercive in effect; a soldier, on the other hand, says the *Bhagavad Gita,* may be psychologically non-violent if he fights as a duty without hating his adversary. Though Gandhi attempted to interpret this passage metaphorically as referring to the individual's war against his evil passions,[19] many of the Mahatma's own statements were decidedly ambiguous on the subject of absolute pacifism. 'Taking life,' Gandhi once said, 'may be a duty.' Courageous violence was always preferable to cowardly acquiescence in iniquity, except where the subject was qualified by training in the ethic of non-violent resistance. When Gandhi refused to follow Sinn Fein tactics in the early 1920s he was as much concerned that the Indians lacked the self-discipline to emulate the Sinn Fein abstention from elective assemblies dominated by the British as repelled by the Irish movement's current association with violence. 'I would,' declared the Mahatma, 'risk violence a thousand times than the emasculation of a race.'[20] His subsequent meeting with Irish guerilla leader, Dan Breen, illustrates this attitude.

As Tolstoi showed, divisive nationalism was the greatest enemy of the non-violent ethic. In their emphasis on Irish language and the ancient Irish sagas, late 19th-century Gaelic leaguers shared most of the characteristic attitudes of contemporary European linguistic patriots. There was a belief, even amongst those who like W. T. Cosgrave admitted that they knew no Irish, that Gaelic was a purer language with a greater literature than English.[21] Advocates of the de-anglicisation of Ireland would have sympathised with the pacifist J. G. Herder's injunction to Germans to 'spew out the ugly slime of the Seine'. Others agreed with the Lutheran, Friedrich Schleiermacher (1768–1834), that 'only one language is firmly implanted in an individual' and insisted that that language should not be English.[22] Thomas Davis, the father of self-conscious Irish 19th-century nationalism, was subsequently criticised because he did not envisage Irish as the main spoken language of the whole Irish people.[23] Griffith, forceful and expressive in English but relatively weak in his command of Gaelic, was too honest to take an extremist approach on the language question. He pointed out that though a national language was desirable it was not a prerequisite for nationality and cited Switzerland and the USA as examples.[24] Many other Irish nationalists were content to pay lip-service to the view, traceable to Fichte, that a nation's soul can only be discovered by the recovery of its ancient pure language, regardless of the latter's lack of literature or restriction to remote isolated villages. Gandhi also stressed linguistic nationalism.

As has been shown above the difficulties of the Irish language made rank-and-file nationalists dependent on translations of the old sagas by Anglo-Irish writers like Yeats and the 'Fenian' unionist, Standish O'Grady. These epics, of which the *Tain Bo Cuailnge* treating the most heroic feats of the legendary hero Cuchulain is the most famous, tended to glorify violence. Standish O'Grady's vivid prose rendering of the sagas may have weaned the young Quaker Bulmer Hobson from his ancestral pacifism. Though the Irish poet and agriculturalist George Russell (AE) sought a theosophical interpretation of the epics and criticised O'Grady's complacent acceptance of wholesale slaughter and carnage,[25] no Irish pundit succeeded in doing for the *Tain* what Gandhi had done for the equally bloody *Mahabharata* which includes the *Gita*. Gandhi interpreted Arjuna's war in the *Gita* as spiritual conflict, just as Erasmus had spiritualised the sword demanded by Christ in Luke 22:36. Not much ingenuity would be required to provide a non-violent moral to the *Tain's* story of selfish ambition, blood lust and intrigue. Something could be made of a dying hero's complaint when unfairly defeated that 'by way of deceit no good can come'.[26] Allegorical interpretation cuts both ways. While Cuchulain is taken as the symbol of the heroic insurgents of 1916, Ulster unionists can argue with some plausibility that Cuchulain, far from standing for the unity of Ireland, achieved his greatest fame defending Ulster against the rest of Ireland.[27] The liberal and humanitarian would probably agree with Goethe's view that mankind needs clarity and serenity, usually absent from primitive folk poetry which one reads 'and for a while is interested, but only to cast it aside'.

If the Gaelic revival and the late 19th-century emphasis on Irish history encouraged in general a more aggressive and violent nationalism this was not true in every case. Men like Douglas Hyde, founder of the Gaelic League, were content to refute Mazzini's dismissal of Irish claims by developing Irish cultural identity without overt political content. Griffith's nationalist historicism was liberal in that it emphasised the place of a non-Gaelic and Protestant patriotic tradition. The history of Ireland in the 19th century abounded with precedents for passive resistance movements, many of which have hitherto received, as a consequence of the apparent success of violence in the 1916–21 period, insufficient attention. Too often Irish historical figures have their real views bowdlerised to fit into an 'orthodox' Irish nationalist tradition. In reality few Irish leaders of note have restricted themselves to any single means but have utilised constitutionalism, passive resistance or physical force as the situation demanded.

Many of the basic items in the quiet resistance tactic can be found in the writings of that misanthropic Irish 18th-century Protestant dean, Jonathan Swift. Swift, who greatly influenced Griffith,

not only advocated a dual monarchy in which Ireland's only connection with England was a common crown, but also made several
non-co-operation suggestions. His injunction to burn everything
English but her coal was frequently quoted by Sinn Fein and literally
practised by Gandhi in India.

Theobald Wolfe Tone, often regarded as the founder of the
Irish republican tradition, was another Irish Protestant who began
where the dean had left off. Only when forced into exile in 1794
did Tone advocate total republicanism in a bid for the assistance
of revolutionary France. His *Memoirs* refer to the need for a
complete break with England, but as this passage closely follows
an acknowledgement of Swift it is possible that Tone would have
then accepted a dual monarchy. Such a compromise implies a
non-violent struggle. Tone, when he suggested that if the government arrested the leader of the Catholic committee all the members
should follow him to gaol, and when he worked for the Catholic
assembly whose pressure helped to secure the repeal of most anti-
Catholic laws in 1793,[28] shows some interest in the possibilities of
passive resistance.

Thomas Davis in the first half of the 19th century came closer than
Tone to non-violent theory and was later cited by Robert Lynd as
one of its advocates. Though Davis insisted, like Gandhi, on the
right to bear arms, he pleaded for the use of peaceful means as long
as they had any prospect of success. He seems to have envisaged
some active form of non-co-operation. 'Never yet did argument
unloose a conqueror's grasp. Knowledge, virtue and vigour backed
by millions—these are the means of liberation which must triumph
without the sword.'[29] Again like Gandhi, Davis emphasised the need
for national self-improvement and the conciliation of opponents.
Orange and Green united were to carry the day. Thus the distance
between Davis and Gandhi, who was prepared to countenance the
defensive physical force of those not fully converted to non-violence,
is less than absolute. Some of Davis's writings suggest the ideal
of blood sacrifice which reached its apogee with Pearse in 1916.
Gandhi's fasts to the death, however, also belong to this tradition.
Had the Mahatma's hunger strikes been fatal widespread disorder
would almost certainly have occurred in India. This 'Hara-Kiri'
theory of national awakening leads frequently to general violence.
It is also unpleasantly close to the European cult of bloodshed which
has played so prominent a part in Irish history from the days of
John Mitchel (whom Griffith nevertheless claimed as a supporter,
where possible, of peaceful revolution), Pearse and the provisional
IRA. *'Dulce bellum inexpertis'*, says Erasmus, but even Gandhi
considered war in some ways heroic. Tolstoi, a Crimean war veteran,
was less naive.

Davis, as Griffith showed in the Treaty debates, like Swift believed that Ireland could share a monarch with England while preserving her essential independence. He died too soon to break completely with his old leader O'Connell or to participate in the fiasco of the 1848 rebellion. O'Connell has never been able to live down the fact that he was the only major Irish leader to reject bloodshed unequivocally as a means to national independence. But even O'Connell on occasion prepared to utilise ambiguous threats of force. O'Connell provided valuable theoretical precedents for Sinn Fein by his claim that the act of union, as a breach of Britain's renunciation act of 1783, was illegal, by his plan for a council of three hundred to act as an Irish *de facto* government, and by his not very determined attempts to boycott the Westminster parliament. Davis's writings endorsed these suggestions, and after his death Gavan Duffy's *Nation* in 1847 produced another plan for an Irish assembly which would obtain independence 'without firing a shot'.[30] At about the same time Fintan Lalor adumbrated a comprehensive passive resistance programme which was, however, expected to end in violence. Lalor hoped to rouse the masses by a rent strike in the manner that Gandhi challenged the Indian salt laws in 1930. Lalor's proposals were partially applied by Davitt's Land League in the late 1870s and early 1880s. Irish Nationalism of this period influenced Tilak[31] who preceded Gandhi as the most forceful Indian leader.

After 1848 there was a more obvious polarisation between tepid constitutionalism on one side and Fenian conspiratorial violence on the other. The imprisoned Fenian O'Donovan Rossa was elected for Tipperary in 1869 and the outlawed John Mitchel for the same constituency in 1875. Though Mitchel stood explicitly as an abstentionist, it was the election of Parnell for Meath in the latter year that laid the basis for a new policy and reopened a theoretical debate.

By eventually achieving a disciplined Irish party comprising a vast majority of Irish MPs, Parnell made total withdrawal a feasible policy. His personality and deliberate ambiguity of utterance raised a number of issues of importance to the early Sinn Fein movement. Parnell provides a bridge between orthodox constitutionalism, dependent on votes at Westminster, and the Sinn Fein ultra-constitutionalist insistence on the continued validity of the old Irish parliament. The following chapter will examine these issues and demonstrate the influence of Parnell's example on Griffith's racism and quasi-imperialism. To obtain a full understanding of Griffith's position *vis-à-vis* Sinn Fein critics his dual monarchy is next analysed. As the Hungarian nationalists were strong believers in racial inequality, Griffith's general attitude falls into place. Finally, Griffith's economics are discovered to fit into the same general pattern of 'integral nationalism' which places the competitive national groups before the individual in the natural order of the universe. Only Griffith's genuine desire for a non-violent consummation saved him from sliding into totalitarian authoritarianism.

7 Parnell and Sinn Fein

In the preceding chapters the continued efforts of Sinn Fein to appropriate the mantle of Parnell have received considerable attention. Since the parliamentarians naturally used Parnell as a justification for attendance at Westminster, a lively controversy, reaching its peak at the time of the North Leitrim by-election, ensued. So protracted was the dispute that a Dublin publisher brought out a book entitled *Words of the Dead Chief.* For a man who less than 20 years earlier had been opposed by the vast majority of the Irish political leaders, the swing of opinion towards Parnell was remarkable. As the *Gaelic American,* edited by John Devoy (according to *Sinn Fein* second only to the 'Chief' in ensuring the success of the Parnellite party), remarked in 1908, both Sinn Feiner and parliamentarian now accepted Parnell's greatness, 'though from the fact different arguments are deduced'.[1] To avoid the confused thought which Devoy found characteristic of the discussion on Parnell, lying as it does close to the heart of the Sinn Fein policy, the issue is analysed under three heads: (1) the theory of withdrawal from Westminster, (2) the 'union of hearts', and (3) Parnell's ultimate objectives.

(1) THE THEORY OF WITHDRAWAL FROM WESTMINSTER

Abstentionism, as the debate on the Brady proposition showed, was regarded by many as the crux of the Sinn Fein programme. In 1919 it was effected with eventual success. But Parnell who spent his whole political life as a member of the house of commons is nevertheless regarded as a Sinn Fein hero. Why this striking incongruity?

To understand the issue some background is necessary. In 1869 the Fenian O'Donovan Rossa was elected for Tipperary.[2] Friedrich Engels, seeing a significance which was not realised till the foundation of Sinn Fein, considered it an event forcing 'the Fenians out of empty conspiracy and the fabrication of small *coups* into a path of action which, if legal in appearance, is still far more revolutionary than what they have been doing since the failure of their insurrection'.[3]

This isolated occurrence, motivated by the desire to secure Rossa's release from prison, seemed an important innovation in Irish revolutionary policy. There was, however, no immediate sequel. C. J. Kickham failed to recapture the seat when Rossa was excluded. Though John Mitchel won the seat again some years later, the conditions were not ripe for a movement of general withdrawal, as the decision of his friend, John Martin, to attend Westminster indicated. Martin originally wished to protest but not fully participate in proceedings. Sean MacDermott in later years considered it a mere accident that John Martin had gone to Westminster and thus started the parliamentary movement. Nevertheless, the election of one such candidate as Rossa was an extremely effective demonstration. As Griffith pointed out, it forced down the price of Consols and turned the attention of the European press on Ireland.[4]

It was, however, John Martin's action that prepared the ground for the Irish Home Rule movement and Parnell's appearance at Westminster in 1875. The Sinn Fein argument that Parnell supported the withdrawal policy was based on the latter's activities in the early Land League, 1877–9, the conflict with Gladstone's Liberal government, 1881–2, and Parnell's final struggle after the divorce, 1890–1.

To Griffith the Land League was a '*de facto* government in Ireland' which 'paralysed British rule'.[5] Moreover, 'the policy which Mitchel tried to carry out in 1848 was in essence the policy with which Parnell emancipated the Irish farmers 30 years later'.[6] Mitchel's 1848 programme was based on the ideas of Lalor. It is noteworthy that Griffith by omitting Davitt's vital role gives a distorted impression of Parnell's significance. However, the non-violent boycott tactic of the Land League was an important precedent for Sinn Fein. The Land League's opponent, Captain Boycott, has given his name to passive resistance movements throughout the world. Griffith once revealingly altered the phrasing of a speech, delivered at Greenock in September 1877, in which Parnell, citing O'Connell's achievement of Catholic emancipation, justified his contention that action outside the house of commons was more effective than parliamentarianism. Griffith's personal preference for non-violence was shown when 'fear of an impending insurrection' became 'outside action'.[7]

Historians are still divided on the significance of Parnell's action in 1881–2. Griffith had no such doubts. He claimed that in 1881 'Parnell proposed to his followers to abandon the British House of Commons altogether and following the Hungarian precedent, return to Ireland and carry on the Home Rule government *de jure*. His parliamentary followers refused to follow him—they held they would gain Home Rule quicker by action in Westminster—and they are there still, and Parnell is dead.'[8] Though Michael Davitt in his *Fall of Feudalism*[9] and James O'Mara, who resigned his seat in 1907,[10] accepted the view that Parnell was in favour of secession, Davitt's biographer Sheehy Skeffington, writing in 1908, disagreed. Skeffington had been debating the withdrawal policy with Sinn Fein and criticised the new movement directly. Nevertheless, he attributes to Davitt in 1881 a secessionist policy very similar to that of Sinn Fein. The Irish MPs were to demand the repeal of the union, and if denied, were to return to Ireland to establish 'an informal legislative assembly'.[11]

Modern scholars agree only on the importance of the year 1881. Thus Griffith's interpretation was not *prima facie* absurd. Parnell may have reflected on withdrawal in 1885 or 1886, when, instead of the score of reliable followers in 1881, he had a disciplined party of 85. Even Gladstone 'was haunted by the fear' that Parnell might establish a *de facto* Irish parliament in Dublin. As the fear was voiced in May 1885,[12] before the election which gave Parnell his 85 colleagues, it obviously played a part in persuading Gladstone to introduce his first Home Rule bill. Gladstone subsequently stated in an interview that had he been an Irishman he would have denied the moral basis of the act of union. A Parnell speech referring to Austro–Hungary in 1885 was duly noted by Gladstone.[13] The Irish Home Rule party had sent condolences to Hungary on Déak's death shortly after Parnell became a member.

When Parnell made his appeal to 'the hill-side men' after the 1890 split, he became more explicit in his suggestion that he had never been a committed constitutionalist. C. J. Dolan, for example, was able in 1908 to quote against Redmond Parnell's declaration: 'if our constitutional movement were to fail I would not continue one hour at Westminster'.[14] Michael Conway, the ex-MP and New York Sinn Fein president, advertised the fact that he had been present when Parnell made this statement.[15] In the Parnell funeral issue of *United Ireland,* a sub-leader by 'a physical-force man' gave as a personal impression, derived from conversations with Parnell in the weeks before his death, 'that the great Chief himself was latterly losing heart in the so-called constitutional side of his work'.[16] P. S. O'Hegarty and C. J. Dolan, on opposite wings of the Sinn Fein movement, insisted that Parnell regarded parliamentarianism as merely a temporary expedient.[17] The facts do not, however, justify this contention, so useful as propaganda. Parnell's extreme speeches, 'if you examine them closely, usually contained traces of his habitual ambiguity'. Parnell hoped, right to the end, for victory in a general election.[18] Yet had Parnell won a majority of seats at this time, it would have proved the strength of the physical-force element in the country and thus increased the pressure for a withdrawal policy which, especially after the lords' rejection of Gladstone's second Home Rule bill, might have proved good tactics. Sinn Fein's contention that Parnell used parliamentarianism as a temporary means is supported by the suggestion that numerous nationalist politicians have oscillated between constitutional and revolutionary action.[19] But the argument could cut both ways. While Griffith and his friends attempted to demonstrate that Parnell was at heart an abstentionist they may well have convinced themselves that dogmatic abstentionism was not intelligent politics. The apotheosis of Parnell may explain the Brady negotiations.

(2) THE UNION OF HEARTS

A similar controversy centres on the 'union of hearts' issue. The idea that English and Irish democracy should work together for mutual advantage was strongly opposed by advanced Irish nationalists. Sinn Fein continually denounced the apparent tendency of the post-Parnellite parliamentary party to form a close alliance with the English Liberals. Opposition to union of hearts was of course the corollary of Sinn Fein's total rejection of action outside Ireland and demand for the establishment of a *de facto* Irish authority. The clash between Sinn Fein and Redmondites has already been discussed. Parnell was utilised for propagandist purposes. Sinn Fein maintained that Parnell rejected the idea of a union of hearts; the Redmondites and subsequent historians insisted that the Chief was responsible for the whole development. The issue can be seen from three angles: (1) acceptance by the Irish parliamentary party of British constitutional conventions; (2) amiable co-operation between the Liberal party and Irish MPs; (3) attitudes towards continued inclusion in the British empire. The third question, inextricably entwined with ultimate objectives, is considered with the latter controversy.

Irish separatists based much of their veneration for Parnell on the belief that he was totally opposed to Westminster. The awkward oath of allegiance was usually ignored, though a Sinn Fein meeting roared with laughter when Francis Sheehy-Skeffington suggested, anticipating the subsequent argument of de Valera in 1927, that the oath could be regarded as a mere formality.[20] The Sinn Fein argument that attendance at Westminster constituted recognition of the illegal act of union was always difficult to square with Parnell's activities. But, by a curious paradox, it was Parnell's action in the commons which raised him to the status of a Sinn Fein folk hero. As P. S. O'Hegarty argued, this success had a most unfortunate result, not achieved by O'Connell, Gavan Duffy or Butt, of riveting Irish eyes on Westminster.[21] Standing eye-ball to eye-ball with the rulers of the world's greatest power, Parnell cast defiance in their faces.[22] He made the 1880s the 'Age of Parnell'. Colonial politicians were forced to lobby the Chief to secure the passage of legislation vital for their development.[23] No other Irish leader since the 18th-century battle of Fontenoy, where Irish exiles helped to defeat the English, had achieved such pre-eminence. Wolfe Tone may have caused Pitt some private uneasiness; Robert Emmet's speech from the dock may have infuriated a third-rate Irish judge; some English intellectuals may have been mildly irritated by Mitchel's *Jail Journal;* but O'Connell whose political power most closely approximated Parnell's had suffered humiliation when forced by the government to cancel a mass meeting at Clontarf in 1843. Fifty years before Gandhi strode half-naked to negotiate on equal terms with the representative of the king-emperor, Parnell had humbled the representatives of the same authority in their own chamber. According to Griffith, who believed that from Shane O'Neill to Parnell the only Irishmen really feared by the English were Swift and Davis, 'Parnell outmatched all her statesmen, outgeneralled all her diplomats'.[24]

Much of the material for this image of Parnell was derived from the relatively brief period of obstruction in the late 1870s. L. Paul-Dubois, perceptive French visitor, argued that separatists regarded Parnell's obstruction as a form of physical force.[25] This obstruction certainly appealed alike to men such as Sean MacDermott,[26] who ultimately planned a rather more violent protest, and to moderates who had sat at Westminster like Stephen O'Mara, Sweetman and Dolan. Sweetman believed Parnell's policy was 'to make Party government impossible in England until Home Rule was given to Ireland'.[27] Dolan agreed that Parnell went to Westminster 'not to legislate, but with the avowed object of making legislation impossible'.[28] Dolan also quoted Parnell's ally Biggar: 'No Irish Bills but stop English Bills. No legislation, that is the policy.' In San Francisco Fr. Yorke insisted that Parnell's policy was distinctly Sinn Fein. The Irish MPs, he said, acted as a foreign body in the commons. Parnell told both Tories and Liberals that he did not care what they thought of him. Such reasoning supported Milroy's proposal to send delegates but not representatives to Westminster. Even Sir Charles Dilke had declared of Parnell, 'dealing with him was like dealing with a foreign power'.[29] In short, Parnell's obstruction could be regarded by separatists as a form of war by other means, exempt from the normal strictures against parliamentarianism. In New York in 1908, the late Parnellite MP, Michael Conway, lashed the Redmondite 'slavish reliance on Parliamentary methods' as 'so contrary to the teachings of Parnell'.[30] The appeal of the myth is seen in Maud Gonne MacBride's memoirs where she claims to have watched obstruction by Biggar at Westminster some years after the latter had in fact died.[31]

A recent historian has shown that Parnell attempted to justify his obstruction by arguing that an arrogant majority in the house of commons was flouting constitutional principles protecting the minority. Parnell's object was not to win Home Rule by obstruction but to dissociate himself from the discredited Irish parliamentarians and win popular approval in Ireland.[32] In this latter objective, Parnell's success was considerable. As late as 1907, Sinn Fein justified its policy on the ground that obstruction was no longer possible.[33]

Apart from intransigence at Westminster, opponents of the 'union of hearts' argued that Parnell had always opposed any form of close alliance, political or social, with an English party. Griffith campaigned for Parnell after the split when the Chief's main argument against his opponents was that they had submitted to English Liberal dictation without exacting their price in return. Parnell in 1891 claimed, 'I did not want a close alliance. I did not make a close alliance. I kept away from the Liberals as much as I could . . . I did not want the Irish MPs to rush into English clubs, or into English society.'[34] Sinn Fein consequently emphasised Parnell's independence of both parties and determination to oppose all English governments save those actively forwarding Home Rule.[35] Griffith quoted Parnell's insistence that the alternative to Home Rule was crown colony rule in Ireland, against the United Irish League, whose alternative 'to the British parliament passing Home Rule is to support the British Government in its warfare with the British Conservatives and aid it in its contests with the British Labour party'.[36] Though it is undoubtedly true that Parnell's liaison with Mrs. O'Shea, and perhaps a congenital love of secrecy, maintained a considerable distance between him and the Liberals, his policy gave his subordinates no choice but to work closely with their English allies.

The modern argument that Parnell's failure to attempt the conciliation of English opinion helped to bring about his downfall,[37] is close to the position taken by Sinn Fein. Sinn Fein, said Griffith, laud Parnell because he declared, 'I do not believe in conciliating the English. Conciliate them to the Day of Judgement and you will not get the breadth of a nail from them'.[38]

Sinn Fein's opposition to any union of hearts with England implied a justification for Parnell's retention of the leadership after the O'Shea divorce scandal. To Griffith the private morals of a politician, who also happened to be a Protestant, should have as little effect on the electorate as a murder by Michelangelo on an appreciation of his art.[39] Parnell appeared as a Gaelic hero knifed by the small-time politicians who resented his manly and independent policy. According to P. S. O'Hegarty, Parnell did not wish to see the parliamentary experiment continued for more than five or six years as he felt it an impossible task to keep his party independent longer.[40] *The Seething Pot,* by Canon Hannay, then a sympathiser with certain aspects of Sinn Fein, was defended by Griffith and Fr. M. K. O'Connolly, a member of the Sinn Fein executive, against the fury of Westport Catholics. It portrays in John O'Neill a Parnell toppled by clerical authorities without the aid of marital scandal. The book implies the orthodox Sinn Fein argument that the divorce was a mere pretext for destroying Parnell. It may be that Parnell's desire to retain the leadership was a shade less irrational than modern historians suggest. The issue is not, however, Parnell's real views but Sinn Fein's conception of them. It must now be seen whether Parnell's career can throw light on Sinn Fein attitudes to imperialism.

(3) ULTIMATE OBJECTIVES

To Griffith the real Parnell appeared in the celebrated speech at Cincinnati in February 1880 declaring his dissatisfaction 'until we have destroyed the last link which keeps Ireland bound to England'. Cincinnati is offset by the remark to Barry O'Brien, 'I have never gone for separation. I never said I would. The physical-force men understand my position very well.'[41] Apart from the fact that the Cincinnati speech was delivered to an ardent Irish–American audience, the breaking of the last link does not in reality exclude a dual monarchy. Griffith, moreover, couples this speech with the still more famous oration at Cork in January 1883[42] where Parnell refused 'to fix the boundary of the march of a nation'. As these words were placed on Parnell's monument they are universally remembered. Less well-known, however, are the two preceding sentences which epitomised Sinn Fein policy: 'We cannot ask for less than the restitution of Grattan's Parliament, with its important privileges and wide, far-reaching Constitution. We cannot, under the British constitution, ask for more than the restitution of Grattan's Parliament.' Parnell also made numerous speeches agreeing to accept limited Home Rule as a final settlement. In 1910, however, F. H. O'Donnell, at various times obstructionist MP, historian and member of the Celtic Literary Society, complained that the inscription on Parnell's statue had been bowdlerised. The feeble Home Rule bill for which Redmond was then working bore no relation to Grattan's parliament which Parnell had demanded as an absolute minimum. As for the limited Home Rule bill of 1886, O'Donnell quoted John Morley in support of the view that, had it not been for the secession of Chamberlain's followers, the Irish would have fought the bill in committee.[43]

Sinn Fein does not appear to have made much use of Parnell's Cork speech. Griffith's reference occurred in the early days of the *United Irishman*. Subsequent mention of Parnell tended to refer to tactics rather than ultimate objectives. In his 1907 address to the men of Leitrim, for example, Griffith claimed that Parnell had favoured withdrawal from Westminster in 1882, but said nothing about Grattan's parliament.[44] It is possible that Parnell's suggestion that even Grattan's parliament might be regarded only as an initial step, came rather too close to the cleavage between separatists and 1782 men in the Sinn Fein movement.

There is much evidence to show that Parnell agreed to Gladstonian Home Rule as a final settlement, desiring, as is shown by his acceptance of £10,000 from Cecil Rhodes, a compromise between Irish Nationalism and British imperialism.[45] The Rhodes gift was an awkward fact for Sinn Fein to explain away. John Sweetman tried to do so on two occasions. On the first he took refuge when needled by the *Freeman's Journal* in mere assertion: 'Mr. Parnell would never have voted for a resolution which set up a Local Parliament subject to the supreme authority of the Imperial Parliament.'[46] Later he was constrained to admit that Parnell, though not so culpable as Redmond, had limited his objectives in this instance.[47] Sweetman could have made out a better case. The correspondence between Rhodes and Parnell shows the latter willing to accept £10,000, but by no means enthusiastic about imperial federation. A number of colonial statesmen, however, hoped that an Irish Home Rule bill, retaining MPs at Westminster, would serve as a precedent for colonial representation in the British parliament. Associated with this scheme, Ireland would have been quickly identified with the almost completely self-governing colonies who desired Westminster representation to increase rather than limit their existing power.[48] In such a campaign Parnell's 'imperialism' may again have been a tactical manoeuvre rather than an expression of deep inner conviction.

But what of Griffith's own position? The Hungarian policy, which Hobson complains was taken too far, led to some unexpected results. When Parnell in 1885 cited the Austro-Hungarian settlement, Gladstone interpreted his reference as indicating a desire for imperial federation.[49] In spite of the abuse of Redmond's party, Griffith appears to have been moving in this direction by 1911. His pamphlet, *Pitt's Policy,* could be interpreted as a plea for a form of Anglo-Irish imperialism:

An Empire equally governed by Dublin and London was possible of expansion beyond all that the Empire had been. But it would cease to be England's Empire. It would be the Anglo-Hibernian Empire. In the rule of Empire England must bear no brother near her throne. Irishmen might be servants of Empire, but they must not be co-rulers. The Dual Monarchy must, therefore, be substituted by a single Monarchy.

In 1913 Griffith commended Australian Orangemen for referring to the Empire of Great Britain and Ireland. 'I thought the expression was a good one, and I often wondered why it was not more extensively used.'[50] This opinion is a far cry from Pearse's belief that 'the nation is of God; the empire is of man—if it be not of the devil'. The distance between Griffith in this mood and Standish O'Grady, whose unionism was based on the belief that, as the Irish were the natural superiors of the English, the former would dominate their joint empire, is small. Griffith's attitude on this issue, moreover, has logical corollaries in other aspects of his thought. He was obviously impressed by the manner, described in the previous chapter, in which the Magyars repressed their subject nationalities and at the same time dominated the external relations of the Austro-Hungarian dual monarchy.

The difference between acceptable and intolerable imperialism was hinted at in Griffith's contention that Parnell's Cork and Cincinnati speeches demonstrated that the Chief, unlike John Redmond, would not 'stoop to base the Irish demand on an admission of the validity of the co-called English conquest'. Parnell, as John Devoy argued,[51] is not easy to fit into the Gaelic tradition. He may have once invited a priest to say grace in Irish, but even Gladstone was shocked by Parnell's ignorance of Irish history. Parnell was certainly a patron of the GAA—an achievement which today would preserve his family for many generations from any imputations of shoneenism, the desire of Irishmen to be second-rate John Bulls—but he was also a passionate enthusiast for the foreign game of cricket. Unlike Redmond, however, Parnell believed in the industrialisation of Ireland. Griffith, no less than certain modern historians,[52] would have regarded this as an essential ingredient of advanced nationalism.[53]

Redmond, then, was at fault for attempting to keep Ireland a subordinate part of British imperialism. Griffith might have tolerated an imperialism, recognising Ireland as a co-equal mother country. The significance of this aspiration lies not in the likelihood of its realisation in the 20th century but in its revelation of Griffith's mental processes. The rejection of the liberal-humanitarian ideal of racial equality may have resulted partly from Griffith's sojourn in South Africa, partly from his reading of John Mitchel, and partly from an over-reaction, similar to that of Mitchel, against the popular 19th-century English and American nativist belief in the Irishman as a white nigger.[54]

In his famous introduction to Mitchel's *Jail Journal* Griffith refused to apologise for those views of Mitchel which modern radicals would not hesitate to brand as Fascism. Mitchel, said Griffith, correctly asserted that 'the right of the Irish to political independence never was, is not, and never can be dependent on the admission of equal rights in all other peoples'. On another occasion, however, Griffith qualified his statement by saying, 'he who wishes to serve humanity at large can only do so effectively when he serves it through the nation'. Though this was pure Mazzini, central European history indicates the difficulty of implementing such an objective. Such views are not easy to square with non-violence if we accept Tolstoi's insistence that pacifism was an integral part of the American W. L. Garrison's opposition to slavery. The other Irish pacifist, Daniel O'Connell, lost much American support by his opposition to slavery.

P. S. O'Hegarty fully supported Griffith's introduction to Mitchel in his *Irish Freedom* review.[55] But Griffith was narrowing his sympathies and providing easy targets for opponents. For example, Griffith's acceptance of the Boers as the authentic South African nation and dismissal of the Uitlanders as the British garrison, ignored the vast subject majority of native Africans. He was similarly blind in his failure to see that the Hungarians were an aristocratic caste whose oppression of the Serbs and Croats in the years before the 1914–8 War was notorious throughout Europe. On the other hand, Griffith, like other Irish nationalists, accepted the Indians as fellow freedom fighters, as befitted the inheritors of an ancient civilisation with many philological links with Irish Gaelic culture.

There are two factors mitigating Griffith's racism. In Ireland Griffith insisted that the volunteer convention at Dungannon and the resultant 1782 constitution ended the old polarisation between Celt, never in fact conquered, and Saxon, thus establishing a united Irish nation. Griffith agreed emphatically with his future enemy, Erskine Childers, who argued in his *Framework of Home Rule,* 1911, that 'Ireland is no colony. She has no claim based on colonial rights. . . . Her leaders in 1782 repudiated any right or claim on colonial grounds.'[56] Moreover, Griffith praised the suggestion by a Catholic parliamentarian who preferred an Irish Protestant parliament to a mixed assembly at Westminster.[57] These views are more liberal than those of modern ultra-patriots who wish to reject as alien to Ireland any tradition not totally Gaelic.

In the second place, the views of Griffith and Mitchel must be seen in the context of the racist views which were popular at all levels in 19th-century England. The great Victorian savants, Macaulay, Froude and Carlyle, expressed theories on Ireland so crude as to find modern parallels only in the literature of extreme racist paranoia. It was natural that men like Mitchel, whose intellectual debt to Carlyle was enormous, should turn the sages' weapons against themselves. Macaulay, to take one example, habitually referring to the Irish Celts as 'aboriginals', delighted to distinguish between them and the Anglo-Irish ascendancy. Mitchel insisted that the object of the *History of England* was not only to flatter the racial pride of the English but to prevent others from sympathising with 'so abject a race as those starved-out Celts'.[58]

Griffith and Mitchel over-compensated with an aristocratic conception of Irish liberty akin to that of the Greek, Roman and American slaveholders. This spirit was spread and accentuated by the Gaelic revival which demonstrated that Ireland possessed an aristocratic tradition as exclusive and as warlike as any in the world. Instead of Carlyle's rat to be squelched by the British elephant, the Irishman thought of himself as Cuchulain alone in the gap of danger defying fearful odds. But it was Parnell perhaps more than any other figure in Irish history who embodied the Irish aristocratic ideal. However modern historians shuffle their contemporary documents, Parnell the mythical hero was at least as important as Parnell the historical figure. As David Greene and Sean Ó Tuama recently demonstrated,[59] the Parnell legend has every ingredient—victory against odds, passionate sexual involvement, downfall through treachery, widespread belief in the hero's eventual return—of an Irish saga of the golden age. Thus Parnell's personal style was his greatest contribution to the separatist tradition.

Parnell's influence on Sinn Fein development was therefore considerable. Paradoxically, he not only supplied an image of heroic intransigence, but when quoted by ex-parliamentarians like Sweetman and Dolan, seems to have exerted a strong pull on Griffith in the direction of compromise or political realism. Parnell's career may have helped to persuade Griffith that the 1782 constitution was worth emphasising in the face of much separatist hostility. It is noteworthy that men like Devoy and O'Hegarty, arguing that Parnell's views by 1907 were passé, were notably less impressed by the Chief's posthumous mythological status. Moreover, by his examination of Parnell's attitude to abstention from Westminster, Griffith may have been encouraged to take that more flexible attitude to parliamentarianism which caused such a *furore* at the time of the Brady negotiations.

There was one irreconcilable contradiction in Sinn Fein's appeal to the memory of Parnell. Though the Chief's career may have been in full accord with the traditional Irish veneration for dictatorial leaders it was precisely this aspect of the national character that Sinn Fein had set out to replace by individual self-reliance. The San Francisco *Leader* put the problem in a nutshell in its criticism of Parnell for declaring martial law on the Irish mind, checking the rise of independent public opinion in Ireland till the emergence of Sinn Fein.[60] Men as far apart in political ideology as P. S. O'Hegarty and Sir Horace Plunkett concurred in this judgement.[61] This ambivalence which was to plague Irish politics in the future was not, however, peculiar to Irish nationalism.

8 Republicanism and dual monarchy

In recent times Irish republicanism has consisted of a nebulous set of opinions whose common denominator is the belief that physical force is the answer to all Irish problems. Reasoned political philosophies are not infrequently rejected with contempt in favour of the 'gospel of continuity' which seeks to base present policies on apparently successful applications of force in the past. A less one-sided history is now mandatory.

Though Tone had adopted republicanism to satisfy the French, the rebellion of 1798 and the act of union obscured the newly raised republican issue. In the early 19th century, patriots were too concerned with the problem of regaining the Irish parliament to emphasise the imperfections against which the United Irishmen had rebelled. Thomas Davis was no doctrinaire republican, but believed that 'repeal would give us a senate, a militia, an administration, all of our own'.[1] John Mitchel, however, seems to have been one of the first eminent nationalists to revive the republican ideal. At a meeting of the Irish confederation shortly before his arrest in 1848 he criticised T. F. Meagher for his willingness to accept the 'humbug' of the 1782 constitution and hoped it would not be seen again. A republic, he argued, was the only satisfactory settlement.[2]

In the quiet seclusion of his prison hulk, Mitchel came to the same conclusion. He cared 'not a rush' about republicanism in the abstract but believed that monarchical institutions—though once appropriate—were quite worn out for the western nations 'until we shall have advanced to them again, via barbarianism, in the cyclical progress of the species'. In England the monarchy only continued to exist as a prop of the evil *laissez-faire* system.[3]

For most of the 19th century the republican idea remained enveloped in the same Celtic mist which still shrouds it in the 1970s. Even the Fenians were divided in opinion. The letters IRB were taken by some to stand for the Irish Revolutionary Brotherhood and others for the Irish Republican Brotherhood. According to John O'Leary, Thomas Clarke Luby, like O'Leary himself, favoured the first interpretation and James Stephens the second.[4] Although the oath, which O'Leary never took, would appear to leave the matter in no doubt,[5] the Australian historian, Sir Keith Hancock, who knew a member whose political theory was Catholic monarchism, correctly states that the IRB 'was not particularly interested in republican theory nor particularly committed to it'.[6] In 1922, during the Irish Civil War, the anti-Treaty side accused the IRB, dominated by Michael Collins, of destroying the republic.

It was P. H. Pearse who changed republicanism from a vague formula to a powerful and compelling if still nebulous doctrine: 'Like a divine religion, national freedom bears the marks of unity, of sanctity, of catholicity, of apostolic succession.'[7]* He developed the theory that the demand for national independence, binding on every generation, was immutable. But when Pearse cited Tone's desire to 'break the connection with England' as the ultimate justification for republicanism he was factually on dubious ground. Pearse cited Davis, Mitchel, Lalor and Tone as the four fathers of Irish nationalism, adding Parnell as an afterthought. The dogmatic republicanism of Tone, Davis and Parnell is open to question. Pearse, therefore, fell back on the type of argument used by Griffith with regard to Parnell, that republicanism was implicit in Davis's career. The 1916 Rising, however, 'gave a halo to the abstract theory of republicanism',[8] and made it impossible to continue the advocacy of Griffith's alternative.

There were, in fact, two alternative theories to republicanism held by advanced Irish nationalists:[9] Catholic monarchism and dual monarchism. The first doctrine may have been held by a small number of nationalists but it suffered from the fact that if a Catholic king was established—a complete impossibility at the time—both Protestants and democratic Catholics would be alienated and national unity made even more difficult to achieve.

The formulation of a second doctrine, that of dual monarchy, is usually attributed to Swift who stated in *Drapier's Letters* that though Ireland and England shared the same king there was no ground for English intervention in Irish affairs: 'We have indeed obliged ourselves to have the same king with them, and consequently they are obliged to have the same king with us.'[10] In a word, it suggested that the king of England as a private individual and not the English king-in-council or king-in-parliament should reign in Ireland. It was the position which the American colonists had attempted to maintain before the revolution, and the result finally

*Pearse, however, was apparently prepared to accept a German king during the Rising.

achieved by the British dominions after the passage of the statute of Westminster. Today Canada, Australia and New Zealand possess far greater effective independence from Britain, with whom they happen to share a monarch, than the Republic of Ireland. Theoretically, a dual monarchy means separation from England if the common monarch is constitutionally bound to accept the advice of an Irish executive responsible to an Irish parliament. In such a case the modern Irishman, unlike his 1782 counterpart, would owe allegiance to a king of Ireland and be in no way governed by England. John O'Leary fully understood that it was not form of government 'but simply freedom from foreign control' that mattered. Like Swift, O'Leary was prepared to swear allegiance to an Irish monarch 'even though the Queen or King should happen to be Queen or King of England'.[11]

O'Leary's position had been criticised in the 1840s by his old associate, Fintan Lalor. Lalor denied that equality between England and Ireland could exist under a dual monarchy. The idea was repugnant to common sense and experience. 'Two wheels in the same machine, of equal power, independent, unconnected and not under the control of the same prime mover, would be a better arrangement.' Lalor correctly prophesied the collapse of the Swedish–Norwegian dual monarchy. He was, however, prepared to consider the possibility that Ireland, after becoming independent, might wish to enter a federal union with England.[12] It is paradoxical that advanced nationalists professing a belief in Machiavellian power politics should have naively thought that the mere symbolism of a republic would have prevented England from exercising a dominating influence over Ireland.

John Devoy, answering critics who claimed that O'Leary was not a true Fenian, demonstrated that the latter had felt the difference between a well-organised republic and a liberal constitutional monarchy too slight to make it worth changing from one to the other. O'Leary, moreover, had worked loyally for the republic which 99% of active nationalists desired.[13] Should Griffith have done likewise or was there positive justification for his continued demand for dual-monarchy?

Like earlier Irish nationalists Griffith became fascinated by the Austro–Hungarian dual monarchy. Hungary, unlike Ireland, had an historic monarchy, and Hungarian nationalists claimed that the emperor of Austria possessed authority over them as king of Hungary only. In 1848 Kossuth led a republican revolution which failed because of the intervention of Russia and the pro-Hapsburg attitudes of the Slavs and Romanians who objected to their subjection by the Magyars. Then Déak, a monarchist, organised a passive resistance movement against Austrian rule, taking his stand on the concessions of 1848 guaranteeing the Hungarian constitution. Austria's defeat by Prussia at Sadowa forced her to make terms with Magyar nationalism. The Hapsburgs deserted the Slavs who had supported them in 1848 and allowed the empire to be divided between Germans and Magyars. The *Ausgleich* of 1867 established the Austro–Hungarian dual monarchy. But the dual monarchy of the *Ausgleich* was not the settlement demanded by Swift; though Francis Joseph was crowned king of Hungary at Budapest with all the ancient ceremonial, foreign affairs and, by agreement, some financial items were treated as imperial questions. The original reluctance of the Hungarians to participate in a common cabinet increased the effective power of the emperor.[14] As Hungary, with its subjected Slavs, was almost equal to Austria in strength, the partnership was not to Hungary's disadvantage. The Magyar landowners were able to force the German half of the empire to pay disproportionate prices for its food. Magyar influence on foreign policy has already been noted. Ireland, however, would have been overwhelmed under a similar arrangement with England. As J. S. Mill pointed out, 'the most favourable of all combinations of circumstances for the success and permanence of an equal alliance between independent nations under the same crown, exists between Hungary and Austria, the least favourable between England and Ireland'.[15]

Nevertheless, frequent references were made to Austro–Hungarian relations in the 19th-century Irish nationalist press. For example, John O'Mahony, the Fenian head centre, used the Hungarian analogy to demonstrate that Grattan's parliament was a failure insofar as the Irish executive was not responsible to it.[16] In the second half of the 19th century, when Grattan's era seemed a golden age, Déak's demands were sometimes equated with those of the patriots who secured the renunciation act of 1783.[17] Less emphasised was the fact that, as this act of the British parliament made no provision for an Irish ministerial responsibility and merely guaranteed that Ireland should have a sovereign legislature and sovereign judiciary, it did not establish a dual monarchy. In reality it was further from genuine dual monarchy than the system envisaged in the three Home Rule bills.

By 1900 the small Irish separatist population had lost interest in 1782. Most advanced nationalists were in practice republicans, though, like Lalor, they admitted the right of the Irish people to decide their form of government after total independence had been won from England. Before Griffith developed the Hungarian analogy in 1902 he held these orthodox separatist views. Much interest was, however, created by the new programme, opposed alike to parliamentarianism and military insurrection. 'The alternative,' said Griffith, 'of armed resistance to the foreign government of this country is not acquiescence in usurpation, tyranny, and fraud.'[18] Griffith, after the speech to Cumann na nGaedheal, published a series of 27 articles in the *United Irishman*,[19] on the history of Hungary down to the *Ausgleich*, the basis of his famous pamphlet *The Resurrection of Hungary*.

Most of the pamphlet dealt lightly and flippantly with the history of Hungary. Influenced by Swift, Griffith treated Hungary as a Lilliput to satirise current Irish abuses. As T. M. Kettle said, 'it reads like a fairy tale'.[20] Irish religious divisions, west Britons and turncoat nationalists all found their Hungarian analogues. Irish historical characters were equated, where possible, with Hungarians. Many passages were frankly facetious. The final chapters point the moral and demonstrate the new policy for Ireland. Modern advertisers would agree with Griffith's belief that the simplistic and woolly parallel rather than the keen logic of dual monarchism would be more likely to appeal to the masses who were asked to buy the glamour and excitement of foreign revolution.[21] The moral of the book was that separatists could co-operate with constitutionalists if the latter withdrew from parliament and denied the legal validity of the act of union. As a precedent, he cited the republican Kossuth's co-operation with the monarchist Déak.

The basis of Griffith's policy was the 1783 British renunciation act by which, he argued, 'the English parliament renounced all claim or title to govern this country'. As the act was still on the British statute book 'the parliament of Ireland has as legal an existence today as it had in the year 1783'. Hungary, Griffith claimed, had been in exactly the same position after Austria's illegal suspension of the constitution of 1848. But Déak, unlike the Irish parliamentarians Grattan, O'Connell and Parnell whose attendance at Westminster connived at illegality, for 18 years 'refused all compromise and ignored the laws passed for Hungary in defiance of her constitution'. If Ireland had done likewise after 1800 the union would not have lasted five years.

Who was this Déak upon whom Griffith placed so much confidence? Franz Déak was a landowner trained in law whose moderation derived from policy. Unlike Kossuth, he realised in 1848 that the Magyars could not hope to defeat both the Hungarian Slavs and the Hapsburgs. Déak therefore decided on compromise with the latter. Though relatively conciliatory with regard to the Slavs, Déak was still a Magyar supremacist. Again his moderation was based on an idea of expediency which his successors unfortunately did not share. If Slavs are equated with 20th-century Irish Protestants, Déak's example was by no means perfect. A better, if inexact, analogy might be 18th-century Protestant ascendancy Ireland. Griffith's equation of Magyar-dominated Hungary with Grattan's

Protestant-ruled Ireland is perhaps sounder than generally realised.

Griffith's argument was strengthened by quoting Count Beust, author of the Austro–Hungarian *Ausgleich* of 1867, on Gladstone's first Irish Home Rule bill. Beust claimed that while the Hungarian parliament was co-ordinate with the Austrian legislature, Gladstone offered Ireland an assembly whose existence could be terminated in 48 hours by a majority of Westminster MPs. In return for this *opera-bouffe* parliament, said Griffith, Ireland was to renounce her nationality.

Beust, however, considered Ireland's justification for independence weaker than Hungary's. Not only had she no language and literature of her own, but she had also 'given her case away by sending members to the British parliament, thus recognising its authority'. With this, Griffith did not agree. Sending MPs to Westminster was undoubtedly 'a grave political mistake' but 'acceptance of seats in the British parliament by Irishmen cannot render this illegal enactment legal', though Ireland would need to retrace her steps by adopting O'Connell's 'one statesmanlike idea' of establishing a council of 300 to legislate for Ireland.[22] This latter suggestion was worked out in detail in *The Sinn Fein Policy* which had so little reference to the 1782 constitution that O'Hegarty thought that Grattan's parliament had been dropped.[23]

As Hobson has argued, there was no necessary connection between the passive resistance programme and the Hungarian policy.[24] Lalor had maintained that successful passive resistance would achieve more than a mere repeal of the union. Moreover, Griffith's practical policy was based not on a mystical constitution but on the very concrete local government bodies, many of which resulted from the Tory local government act of 1898.

When Griffith originally published *The Resurrection of Hungary* he was careful to demonstrate, in a passage expunged from later editions, that, as he himself opposed any connection between England and Ireland, he could not be considered a follower of Déak. Nevertheless he admitted that many Irishmen did hold these moderate views, which unlike parliamentarianism, were sufficiently forthright and manly to claim the co-operation of Irish separatists.[25] The policy, therefore, was an *argumentum ad hominem,* cunningly designed by a separatist to convert by irresistible logic both parliamentarian and unionist. Hence the importance of the Hungarian analogy which Sweetman wished to exclude. Griffith naturally agreed with the *Donegal Vindicator* which declared that the Irish parliamentary party would 'stultify themselves' if they did not carry out the new Hungarian policy.[26] In 1904 the English Tories, committed opponents of Home Rule, were still in power. Had they won the 1906 general election, it is not impossible that the Irish parliamentary party might in desperation have considered secession as O'Connell had done in similar circumstances.

On the unionist side Griffith was heartened by the suggestion of Standish O'Grady that the Hungarian policy would compel unionists to shift their ground. To Griffith the only claim of unionists to be heard was as part of the Irish nation. In the days of O'Connell, the Fenians, Butt and Parnell the unionists had 'a logical excuse for existence'. If they resisted the Hungarian policy they admitted themselves an English garrison maintained by British armed force. They must now, *pace* O'Grady, 'shift their ground into England'.[27] Griffith was naive if he hoped to make converts by forcing opponents into intellectual corners. O'Grady was at best a very eccentric unionist. Later Griffith was to show more understanding of the unionist outlook.

Another possible advantage of the Hungarian policy was brought out by J. O'Sheehan of London whose pamphlet irritated O'Hegarty and the more advanced men. O'Sheehan believed that the policy was not only constitutionally unassailable but did not yield 'a single iota of Ireland's right to absolute independence'. This greatly strengthened the movement in the face of Irish churchmen 'who ever set their faces against anything savouring of nationality on the ground that it involves disloyalty to the constitution'.[28] Though O'Sheehan failed to take into account the argument that withdrawal of Irish MPs from Westminster would leave English Catholic schools unprotected, Griffith may well have desired to short-circuit the traditional episcopal hostility to extreme nationalism. Neat debating points, however, do not achieve many conversions.

Opinion amongst future Sinn Feiners was divided on the merits of the Hungarian policy. John Sweetman and Charles Dolan were converted by it from parliamentarianism. Sweetman considered the 1783 renunciation act the Irish *Magna Charta*. He saw no reason why separatists and 1782 men could not co-operate in demanding that there should be no voluntary agreement with England till the latter recognised her own obligation. 'I think a Republican could agree with that view without giving up his principles.'[29]

Hobson completely disagreed. The renunciation act had proved valueless in that it was so soon repealed by the British parliament.[30] Here Hobson was in line with modern legists who insist that a British parliament, as a sovereign authority, cannot be bound by the acts of its predecessors.[31] Hobson, moreover, argued that the younger generation had no interest in the old Irish parliament. John Devoy agreed with Hobson that Griffith discussed in excessive detail the final outcome of his policy. To the Irish-American leader the Hungarian analogy when applied to Ireland was unsound. The Fenian rising, the work of a broken remnant, was in no way comparable with the Hungarian movement of 1848–9 which had defeated the Austrians but not their Russian allies. In 1866, said Devoy, Hungary triumphed, not through passive resistance but through force of Prussian arms.[32] Griffith, however, suggested that had Austria not been weakened by Hungarian passive resistance she would have defeated Prussia.[33] The hostility of the subject Slavs was not emphasised by either side.

Of even greater importance was the difficulty, perceived by the parliamentarian T. M. Kettle and the separatist Terence MacSwiney, of organising a movement whose members were working for totally different objectives. As MacSwiney said in 1911, the alliance between men who believe in complete freedom and those who believe in partial freedom must end in deadlock and recrimination. 'Let not the hands of men in the vanguard be tied by alien King, Constitution, or Parliament.'[34] 'Vanguard' has a Leninist ring suggesting a small disciplined cadre rather than the broadly based national movement of Griffith's dreams.

In establishing this movement Griffith was in a dilemma. Sweetman's suggestion that Griffith should himself play the part of Déak shows how little he understood Griffith's purpose. It was not only that Griffith in the early years of the century felt unqualified, 'the Irish Déak must be a man who can *honestly* accept Ireland linked with England just so far as Hungary is linked with Austria as a final settlement'.[35] But Griffith was looking for a leader of an entirely different type, someone perhaps like Sir Thomas Esmonde who had already demonstrated an interest in the 1782 constitution. Esmonde came from an ancient family and held the strategic position of chief whip of the Irish party. Griffith's substitutes, Martyn and Sweetman, were not so satisfactory. Martyn for all his wealth and dramatic flair was an easily satirised eccentric as George Moore showed in *Hail and Farewell*. Sweetman, whose influence on Griffith has been underrated in the past, could also be accused of eccentricity and, worse still, had the look of a loser, having been twice defeated in his attempts to regain his parliamentary seat in 1895. Griffith's personal assumption of the Sinn Fein presidency in 1911 can be interpreted as a defeat for the original Hungarian policy.

O'Hegarty and Terence MacSwiney have suggested that Griffith in the absence of a moderate was forced to pass a self-denying ordinance on himself and accept the limited objective which he had originally suggested to others.[36] Yet the controversies of the preceding chapters demonstrate that Griffith had been criticised for excessive devotion to 1782ism, even in the days when Martyn and Sweetman acted as ostensible Irish Déaks. If, however, Griffith did leave the IRB finally in 1910, there may be a connection between this event and the assumption of the titular Sinn Fein presidency in the following year.

There is another reason for suggesting that Griffith in the end was intellectually converted to the 1782 idea. Nineteenth-century European nationalists did not discard the 18th-century natural rights philosophy but injected 'into it an historical content. They claim this right for the living individual peoples which they believe they have discovered in history.'[37] Griffith, as opposed to that child of the 18th-century Enlightenment, Wolfe Tone, was almost a 19th-century nationalist stereotype. If Ireland possessed no equivalent of the Hungarian iron crown of indubitable antiquity, history must be ransacked to produce an implicit constitution. Pearse was content to start with Wolfe Tone as the first Father of the religion of Irish nationalism, but Griffith must delve deeper. According to an article, probably by Griffith, in the 1909 Irish year book issued by the national council, there had been since Rory O'Connor, who first experienced the Norman invasions in the late 12th century, only five rightful kings of Ireland: Edward Bruce, 'acknowledged and crowned king of Ireland by the nobles and people, 1315–1318'; Henry VIII of England, 'acknowledged king of Ireland by the Irish parliament, 1541'; Charles I, 'acknowledged king of Ireland by the Confederation of Kilkenny, 1642–1649'; James II, 'acknowledged king of Ireland, according to the Irish Constitution, by the Irish parliament, 1689–1691'; and George III, 'acknowledged king of Ireland according to the Irish constitution, 1782–1800'. These brief periods were punctuated by long interregna.[38] The distance between Griffith and Hobson is indicated by the latter's contention that Henry VIII secured recognition by utilising exactly the same corrupt methods which later carried the act of union.[39] To Griffith the 1782 constitution was the constitution refused in the 14th century,[40] and 'the king of England's claims to be king of Ireland by virtue of his being king of England relinquished'.[41] Even if the Irish parliament had denied full Catholic rights, it must be distinguished, Griffith argued, from the Irish constitution which made Ireland a sovereign state. Though this was Griffith's original position he soon became an open admirer of Grattan's parliament, to be distinguished from the vague, metaphysical 1782 constitution. In 1905 he praised that parliament for recognising the Irish nation in its admission of Catholics to the franchise.[42] Griffith eventually considered Wolfe Tone's rebellion something of an impertinence, but even in the first year of the *United Irishman* a critic asked, 'Tone was abreast of the best democratic thought of his age; are you abreast of yours?'[43] Ten years later the same critic complained that Wolfe Tone had been 'quietly removed from the present-day Sinn Fein pantheon'.[44] Griffith stated his matured opinion in *Pitt's Policy*,[45] originally a 1911 series of *Sinn Fein* articles. His thesis was that Pitt, fearing the competition of Irish goods whose production was stimulated by the Irish parliament, carefully fomented the rebellion of 1798 as an excuse for passing the act of union to ensure Ireland's economic servitude. Wolfe Tone thus emerges as a dupe of English imperialism. Griffith would have agreed with the analysis of the union in E. Strauss's Marxist *Irish Nationalism and British Democracy*. Even the republicanism of the United Irishmen was regarded by Griffith as part of Pitt's plan; 'the republican idea found no flaming response in the heart of the Gael, essentially a believer in aristocracy'.[46] Finally, Griffith asserted, strangely in an admirer of Mitchel, that 'Irishmen in their slavery had echoed the English lie that the parliament of Ireland was devoid of virtue'. In Griffith's eyes the tariff autonomy of the 1782 constitution outweighed theoretical limitations of sovereignty. When he asked the popular novelist George A. Birmingham (Rev. J. O. Hannay) to write a futuristic novel on the model of Bellamy's *Looking Backward* to show Ireland as it would have been if no union had occurred, Griffith was obviously thinking of economic development.[47]

It is therefore clear that Griffith did not long, if he had ever really done so, argue the case for 1782 as an orthodox separatist. O'Hegarty, who insisted that Griffith remained a republican at heart,[48] fully understood the essentially conservative cast of Griffith's mind and his place in the 19th-century romantic nationalist tradition. O'Hegarty was fully aware of Griffith's preference for evolutionary rather than revolutionary methods and hatred of the natural rights philosophy and its 'modern radical catch-cries'. Griffith's creed, said O'Hegarty, emphasised 'the rights of nations and the duties of man, the rights of a nation being to freedom and the right to the allegiance and service of all its children, and the duties of man being to fear God and serve his nation'.[49]

O'Hegarty, Hobson and their allies in opposition to Griffith adopted arguments based on totally different premises. Fintan Lalor's theory of revolution called 'moral insurrection' has already been mentioned.[50] In 1907 O'Hegarty quoted Lalor's well-known letter on the subject, in the *Peasant*. 'The difference between it and true military insurrection amounts to nothing more, in practical effect, than the difference between the defensive and the aggressive use of physical force.' Basing his ideology on natural law which he interpreted to prohibit the exercise of any authority over an individual, without the latter's consent, O'Hegarty claimed the right of resistance 'by any and every means of force whatsoever'. The affinity to the 18th-century doctrine which found expression in the American declaration of independence is obvious. But Griffith considered that the slaves owned by the signatories of this document proved it to be mere cant, and cited Mitchel to prove his point. Lalor, however, used natural rights—'the primitive nucleus round which a nation gathers and grows'—as the basis of his national claims. He argued 'that every district, community, or nation of men is owner of itself; and can never of right, be bound to submit to be governed by another people'.

As Griffith foresaw, this argument was open to serious objections from a nationalist viewpoint. While the Irish nation might be discovered in history and could, therefore, claim definite rights, Lalor's theory opened the way to the unlimited application of the self-determination principle. His argument, for example, would allow unionists to claim either that 'the British Isles' formed a natural community with a small minority of Irish malcontents, or contrariwise that north-east Ulster was a community with the right to resist inclusion in an independent Ireland. Sir Lewis Namier has shown that the existence of 'Ulsters' throughout 19th-century Europe produced numerous racial and religious struggles.[51] Today, Lalor's 'primitive nucleus' theory could be used to justify a six county unilateral declaration of independence from a reform-demanding England. Griffith's constitutionalism, as was pointed out, placed unionists in a less impregnable argumentative position unless they were prepared to deny that they were Irish. Lalor's theory, taken to its logical conclusions, has helped to bring about the partition of peoples who with a modicum of tolerance might have been able to live peacefully together.

Lalor believed that his ideas led naturally to a mode of action providing an alternative to mere agitation or military insurrection. First passive resistance would be offered to the 'usurped authority' and when the latter's power began to weaken, 'quiet and peaceable possession of all the rights and powers of government' would be taken and exercised. Lalor thought, unlike Griffith, that such methods would effect more than a simple repeal of the union. If repeal were the object, said Lalor, there was no Irish law fit to serve as a basis for passive resistance. Lalor clearly advocated force to protect the national government; the dual monarchy compromise, contained in the Hungarian policy, was a substitute for force. Lalor's ultimate objective was a republic.

In spite of O'Hegarty's tactical use of Lalor's arguments, few Sinn Feiners appear to have understood their first natural law premise. O'Hegarty's controversy with Frederick Ryan supports this conclusion. Ryan not only believed in the universal rights of man, but put his doctrine into practice as editor of an Egyptian nationalist newspaper and the colleague of W. S. Blunt.[52] When Ryan criticised Griffith's reactionary views, O'Hegarty defended his leader as 'the greatest constructive political thinker since Davis and Mitchel',[53] complaining that 'everybody in Ireland who cannot bind Griffith down to identify the essentials of nationalism with his own pet non-essential goes apart, and from outside pours out a series of malevolent carpings at the man and the movement on side issues'.[54] Such was Griffith's own self-justification. Ryan, however, replied with the corollary of Lalor's 'moral insurrection'. He rejected national independence achieved by 'sneering at the spirit of liberty and humanity throughout the world'.

Griffith's opponents, O'Hegarty, McCullough and Hobson, thus adopted a form of Lalor's ideas, almost ignoring the implications of the natural law foundation. They advocated the offer of passive resistance on broad national grounds, at the beginning of the nationalist campaign. But as British power began to crumble and the relative strength of the Irish increased, open warfare for a republic was anticipated. 'Moral insurrection,' said O'Hegarty, who at this time failed to appreciate Griffith's position, 'differed from the Hungarian policy simply in the fact that it relied upon the Irish nation instead of the constitution granted by England.'[55] In his subsequent *History of Ireland,* O'Hegarty maintained that Grattan's parliament missed its opportunity to unite ascendancy and underground nations.

Both Griffith and his supporters appealed to history. In his endeavours to refute Griffith's friend, H. E. Kenny (*Sean-Ghall*), who argued that Irish republicanism dated from 1790 only and that Davis and Rooney were not republicans,[56] O'Hegarty disclaimed any personal concern about forms of government, but, 'when any section says "work for the King, Lords and Commons, the 1782 constitution", I say that he is raising a contentious issue, the issue of monarchical government'. True nationalism, he considered, required that 'the King, Lords and Commons must be based on some king other than the king of England or any of his relations'.[57] To Griffith, on the other hand, contention had beeen introduced by republicans.

The Sinn Fein league and the IRB supreme council to which O'Hegarty, McCullough, Hobson and Daly all at some time belonged, probably contained a majority of members who, while prepared to utilise passive resistance, believed that a republic must eventually be sought through physical force. Probably the most articulate was Bulmer Hobson who in 1968 could 'still feel the thrill I felt when I first read the writings of James Fintan Lalor'. In 1909 Hobson published a pamphlet *Defensive Warfare* which demonstrated his debt to Lalor.[58] The first step was to boycott the existing government by 'refusing obedience to laws and hampering its action in every possible way'. This was the decisive first step, 'the Rubicon, which once crossed, opens unlimited fields of national action', based

23. Arthur Griffith with Walter Cole (centre)

24. William Rooney

25. Robert Lynd

26. Canon J. O. H

27. Maud Gonne
MacBride

28. William Butler Yeats

29. Standish O'G

30. Officers of the Irish Brigade in the Boer War. Major John MacBride is on the extreme right.

31. Tom Kelly

32. T. M. Kettle

33. Sir Thomas Grattan Esmonde

34. Edward Martyn

35. W. E. Shackleton

36. John Sweetman

37. Sean T. O'Kelly

38. John O'Leary and Major John MacBride, at Fontenoy, Belgium, 1905

39. P. S. O'Hegarty

40. Jack O'Sheehan

41. Bulmer Hobson

42. Sean MacDermott

43. Denis McCullough

44. Patrick McCartan

Catching .
Recruits . .

John Kelly, aged 10, arrested for having "kicked up his feet" and thrown a piece of bread at a woman in the streets of Limerick. He was let out on condition he became a drummer boy in the English Army.

45. Anti-recruiting cartoon from *The Republic*, 20 December 1906.

46. C. J. Dolan

47. Constance de Markievic

48. F. E. Meehan

49. P. A. McHugh

on 'unconquerable courage'. As the government weakens the strength of the national forces is correspondingly increased and they are gradually able to apply stronger methods. 'Ultimately, the relative strengths of the aggressive and defendant peoples has so altered that even the attitude of defence can be gradually abandoned.'[59]

Constitutions, said Hobson, were mere paper and it mattered not a whit whether nationalist activities were legal or illegal, constitutional or unconstitutional. The only test to be applied to any action was its efficacy to achieve its object. Hobson's was a cold, calculating and ruthless doctrine, totally opposed to the views of men like Gandhi and Robert Lynd.

Hobson's views, however, had nothing in common with the 'blood sacrifice' doctrine of 1916. In 1909 Hobson stated quite definitely: 'we must estimate our resources and those of our opponents and only venture into conflict where the chances of war are in our favour. We must not fight to make a display of heroism, but fight to win'.[60] A few days before the Rising in April 1916, Hobson expressed identical sentiments when he told an Irish volunteer audience that 'no man had the right to risk the fortunes of the country in order to create for himself a niche in history'. While recruiting for the IRB between 1914 and 1916, Hobson emphasised the clause in its constitution which insisted that the IRB before starting an insurrection, would await the decision of the majority of the Irish people.[61] Because he refused to identify with the Rising, Hobson lost his position in the nationalist movement. He supported, however, the guerilla tactics used after 1919, believing that Lalor's 'moral insurrection' was virtually 'a manual of instruction in the tactics adopted in the final stages of the struggle which ended with the Treaty of 1921'.[62]

If we accept O'Hegarty's retrospective analysis, Hobson was in the early years of the century exceptional in his attitude. The former, while justifying the Rising of 1916, believed that afterwards, 'there should not have been a shot fired in Ireland, nor a gun bought'. O'Hegarty's subsequent account of the nature of the physical-force ideal prior to 1916 is, however, in striking contrast to the ideas he advocated before 1910 when popularising Lalor's 'moral insurrection'. In 1924 O'Hegarty argued that though physical force had only a subordinate place in pre-1916 separatist theory the idea of a blood sacrifice antedated Pearse's espousal of advanced nationalism. Long before 1916 the IRB supreme council decided in favour of 'a forlorn hope insurrection', if necessary to restore national self-respect.[63]

O'Hegarty's conclusion is difficult to square with Hobson's membership of the supreme council and the IRB oath which demanded the conversion of the Irish people before the application of force. Moreover, attempts to 'weave together' in strict logic the idea that the country should be roused by a sacrificial rebellion and the belief that force should be used to finish off the enemy after the successful application of passive resistance, supported by the whole country, are doomed to failure. It is clear that O'Hegarty, in his 'moral insurrection', derived from Lalor, advocated the latter policy, though even Lalor appears to have had some desire for a sacrificial rebellion. 'Appealing to England's legal and constitutional instinct on the Renunciation Act,' said O'Hegarty in 1907, 'is wasteful and immoral. She is open only to one argument—Force—and we shall have to apply the same force to get either '82 or independence.'[64]

The inner workings of the IRB supreme council are still a closed book. Many and varied doctrines had, no doubt, their advocates. John MacBride who was a member for a time believed that Emmet's epitaph could be written only in blood.[65] Denis McCullough, another member, commenting that 'most, if not all of us believed, that "passive resistance" could only end in armed conflict', pointed out that 'the IRB, in my time, was not wedded or pledged to action in arms only. It was prepared to back or support any man or movement, that had separation from England as its *final* objective.'[66] Sacrificial insurrection may have had supporters. But it would surely have required second sight to anticipate the events of 1916–22 and argue for a sacrificial rebellion, followed by electoral victory and passive resistance breaking into active resistance. These ideas rest on totally different moral conceptions.[67] Griffith's Hungarian policy and Lalor's 'moral insurrection' were both democratic movements in that their success depended on popular approval, while Pearse required an élite or Leninist vanguard. Circumstances altered many opinions. James Connolly, a leader of the 1916 insurrection, in 1896 argued a case almost identical to Hobson's. He suggested that a republican party should come into the open and fight elections to ascertain when the people were ready for insurrection. 'To counsel rebellion,' said Connolly, 'without first obtaining the moral sanction of the people, would be an act of criminal folly which could end only in disaster.'[68] Hobson's report of conversations with Pearse and Connolly before Easter week, when they professed themselves unable to answer Hobson's arguments but still felt a Rising necessary, has the ring of authenticity.[69]

What conclusions can then be drawn? Griffith and the O'Hegarty-Hobson group differed on the question of dual monarchy versus republicanism and passive resistance versus violence. But no enthusiasm was felt for the English monarchy by either side.[70] Monarchy was a unionist party slogan, associated with Irish dependence and, before 1911, the sovereign took an oath against transubstantiation insulting to Catholics. But in spite of these objections Griffith considered that dual monarchy provided an historical basis for Irish nationalism and a platform on which to unite the country. His argument was in places confused and he did not attempt to disentangle the different elements of dual monarchy, the king, lords and commons of 1782, and the Hungarian *Ausgleich*. If dual monarchy had been put in front of the Irish people in its purest form they would have seen that it offered greater independence—post-statute of Westminster dominion status—than the parliamentary party was likely to achieve. The 1782 constitution with its king, lords and commons obscured the central issue and allowed opponents to sneer at a retrogressive desire to retain the wigs and snuff-boxes of the 18th century. Consequently, the Irish people in general, though Asquith's Home Rule bill fell far short of the 1782 constitution, were not tempted to abandon the parliamentarians who 'said moderate things because they believed moderate things'.[71] Before 1914, the latter appeared, moreover, to have an excellent chance of realising their objectives. Separatists, on the other hand, seemed unrealistic in their refusal to countenance any link with England. O'Hegarty and Hobson merely rationalised a very common attitude when they based their policy on Lalor's 'moral insurrection'. The fact that Lalor argued from natural law was not in the end significant, for O'Hegarty was as interested as Griffith in the historical case for Irish nationalism. Republicans went to Lalor to justify a preconceived idea that some violence was necessary in the struggle against England. As Lalor himself said in the article which influenced O'Hegarty, men are not convinced by argument, they convince themselves. After the Treaty, however, O'Hegarty, horrified by the Anglo-Irish War, contended that the answer to Lloyd George in 1920 'should have been the dual monarchy as an irreducible minimum, and nothing else'.[72] It was then too late for such a solution, however reasonable, to pass uncontested in Ireland.

In the controversies which racked the Sinn Fein movement the names of Irish patriots were batted back and forth like shuttlecocks in an endeavour to prove them republicans or monarchists. Both sides used the propagandist expedient of by-passing the actual statements of deceased heroes to discover an implicit harmony with ideas currently advocated. Ireland, like India, suffered from a plethora of political prophets, and the 19th- and 20th-century nationalist tendency to glorify the past confined speculation to fairly narrow boundaries.

But Sinn Fein writers in the pre-1916 period were not academics seeking a thesis of absolute clarity and consistency but propagandists forging verbal tools to redeem the Irish from apparent degeneracy. The actions of a practising politician should not be judged by his rationalisations, but the ideas of an embryo politician may throw light on his subsequent career. A certain general uniformity can be found from a dissection of the writings of the men who were later to play an active part in the Irish revolution. Sean O Faolain is unfair when he claims that Griffith's views, which had a remarkable inner consistency, were completely vague.[73] Though most were forced like O'Hegarty to modify their attitudes when facing practical problems, Bulmer Hobson, and subsequently Griffith, refused to do so. Hobson's views in 1916 placed him in a minority amongst nationalists; six years earlier they were the commonplaces of advanced nationalists. A modification of Griffith's views, rejected in 1910, controlled Ireland's destiny in the Treaty negotiations of 1921. Had separatist Ireland paid more attention to Griffith's belief that ceremonial acceptance of a British monarch descended, *inter alia,* from Brian Boru was a worthy compromise, and that the gun was not the answer to Ireland's internal problems, much future suffering might have been avoided.

9 Economic nationalism

GRIFFITH was a propagandist not an objective student of economic theory; like other nationalist politicians he was compelled to account, in psychologically satisfying terms, for his country's subjection. Ireland's weakness must be shown to lie in foreign rule, not intrinsic inadequacy. As Lalor demonstrated, the argument that, weak or strong, self-government is good in itself, has on its own little appeal for a complacent population. Griffith, therefore, developed an economic policy on the basis of a most optimistic appraisal of Ireland's industrial potentiality. He achieved his object by superimposing the formula of the German economist Friedrich List on the ideas of John Mitchel and Thomas Davis, ghosts haunting Sinn Fein at every turn. From Mitchel, Griffith derived his hatred of the British system of free trade; from Davis he gained his belief in Ireland's abundant geological and physical resources.

Mitchel's contribution to Griffith's economic ideas, though significant, does not require much analysis. The *Jail Journal* is fertile in denunciation of the Manchester school economics. 'Behold, this world is ruled now by Order and Commerce (Commerce, obscenest of earth-spirits, once named Mammon, and thought to be a devil).'[1] Davis was more practical. In a passage selected by Griffith, he saw an analogy in German history. For many years, said Davis, Germany in spite of her coal, water-power and cheap labour had had her markets 'gorged' by England. Her subsequent success was due to her national government which placed tariffs on English goods. Though the German farmer paid a little more for his manufactures he cut down on his poor tax. German manufacturers based on a protected home market soon understood English goods. 'Why not imitate her?'[2]

Davis does hint at possible qualifications on the subject of industrialisation; Fintan Lalor was even more sceptical of the value of manufacturing as opposed to agrarian development; but Griffith under List's influence had no doubts. The latter's greatest work, *The National System of Political Economy*, was published in 1841—four years before Davis's death. In 1885 it became available in translation to Irish readers. In his speech at the first annual convention of the national council Griffith declared himself a follower of Friedrich List, 'the man who thwarted England's dream of the commercial conquest of the world'.[3] List (1789–1846) learnt his protectionist and nationalist philosophy in the United States. Returning to Germany as US consul he endeavoured to spread his new gospel but committed suicide in despair before the full implementation of his policies. From 13 April to 17 August 1907, Griffith published a series of articles, 'the pioneering of Germany', which consisted of long transcriptions from List with relatively little comment.[4]

Griffith's speech at the 1905 convention, published as *The Sinn Fein Policy*, remained the economic doctrine of the movement up to 1918. Although there were new developments during the period, Griffith's economic views were comparatively static. The speech, or pamphlet, can be divided into two parts. The first deals with ultimate economic objectives while the latter outlines an immediate policy to be put into practice by local government bodies.

In the former section Griffith used List's ideas to prove two main contentions; that as the cosmopolitan economics based on Adam Smith were fallacious, economic nationalism was desirable; second, that a nation must develop both industry and agriculture. These two contentions are closely related and consistent with Griffith's rejection of the 18th-century natural rights philosophy. List's views were characteristic of Mazzini and other 19th-century nationalists. 'Between the individual and humanity stands, and must continue to stand, a great fact, the nation.' As the individual was dependent on the nation for maintenance, security and culture, human civilisation was dependent on the existence of individual nations.[5] The task of economics was therefore to preserve and strengthen the nation.

Griffith complacently quoted List's national prerequisites, 'such as we desire to see Ireland'. List emphasised the need for 'a common language and literature', 'manifold natural resources', a large population and defensible frontiers. There should be even development of agriculture, manufactures, commerce and science. Education and culture were to be placed on equal footing with production. Above all a nation needed the power to protect itself and its commerce.

Griffith believed that such a nation would have a soul unlike the type envisaged by Adam Smith. 'True political economy recognises that prompt cash payment, to use Mitchel's phrase, is not the sole nexus between man and man—that there is a higher value than a cash value, and that higher value nationality possesses.'[6]

Griffith's second contention followed from the first. He attacked the theorists and Redmondites who declared that Ireland should concentrate on agriculture. List believed that civilisation progressed naturally from pastoral economy to agriculture, from mere agriculture to agriculture, industry and commerce. Griffith considered likewise that Ireland would have first to reduce her grazing areas and bring them under tillage. He used List to demonstrate that the interests of farmer and industrialist were identical as both were equally important in the development of a complete nation.[7]

The precarious position of an agricultural nation in the world economy was easily demonstrated. It was reliant on poor harvests in agricultural-manufacturing nations and always in competition with other purely agricultural nations. Wars, depressions and the raising of tariffs were almost invariably fatal to its prosperity. In short it was 'always more or less economically and politically dependent on those foreign nations which take from it agricultural products in exchange for manufactured goods'. Finally, the frequently used aphorism, 'an agricultural nation is an individual with one arm who makes use of a foreign arm, but who cannot make use of it in all cases: an agricultural-manufacturing nation is an individual who has two arms of his own always at his disposal'.

List's views on the dependency of agricultural nations had a particular significance for Ireland; Griffith was insistent that political independence alone would not be enough. In modern parlance he feared neo-colonialism as deeply as legislative dependence. He wished therefore to see List's book in the hands of every Irishman.[8]

But how far was List's theory really applicable to Ireland? List's conception of the prerequisites for nationhood was exacting. Not only should a nation possess the power to protect itself, but a large population and considerable natural resources were considered by List essential. A small nation with its own language 'can only possess a crippled literature, crippled institutions for promoting art and science'. Protection of industry in a small state merely fostered private monopoly. 'Only through alliance with some more powerful nations, by partly sacrificing the advantages of nationality, and by excessive energy, can it maintain with difficulty its independence.'[9] Such conclusions, though they anticipated some of the difficulties facing future Irish governments, were totally opposed to the ambitions of Sinn Feiners and Gaelic leaguers. But List, whose life had been spent in an effort to unify Germany, had more to say. The German Zollverein, whose foundation List had encouraged, demanded the surrender of fiscal autonomy by small states to a larger unit. Moreover, List believed that Holland and Belgium—both by the end of the 19th century exceeding Ireland in population—should be merged with Germany. List's explicit references to Anglo-Irish relations were not only acceptable to the most rabid contemporary Orangemen but by the 1970s tacitly endorsed by Irish governments in their free trade agreement with Britain and membership of the EEC. According to the German economist, the union of Britain and Ireland showed the world 'a great and irrefragable example of the efficacy of free trade between united nations'. If all other nations were similarly united 'the most vivid imagination will not be able to picture to itself the sum of prosperity and good fortune which the whole human race would thereby acquire'.[10] British rule in Ireland was to List a 'conquest' remedying the 'territorial deficiencies of the nation'.[11] Any economist believing state regulation more beneficial than free trade between England, Scotland and Ireland, List dismissed as pitiable.[12] As List in another passage speaks of the Irish peasant as a byword in misery[13] it is obvious that he considered Irish suffering a small price to pay for the economic expansion of Britain as a whole. List, moreover, had no use for either Magyar or Indian nationalism, believing that India was doomed to remain economically underdeveloped. Though Griffith published articles demonstrating parallels between the economic exploitation of Ireland, India and Hungary, he may have accepted List's views as applicable to the rest of the underdeveloped world.[14]

Surprisingly few of Griffith's opponents who objected to List's economics mentioned these inconsistencies. Frederick Ryan, however, remarked, 'considering the quarters in which List had ... became a kind of political prophet, it was surely strange to find him proclaiming the Union as a sort of foretaste of the millennium'.[15] Griffith himself, moreover, was unconcerned, accepting no doubt the accuracy of List's general formula while rejecting, as based on a misunderstanding of the facts, the application to Ireland—yet another example of the habit of discovering mystical endorsement in writings diametrically opposed to the desired principle. Griffith's interpretation would, in fact, have weakened List's entire argument.

Griffith thus believed that Ireland's natural resources were large enough to support a very great population. He declared, on one occasion, that had the act of union never been passed, Ireland by 1911 would have had a population of 20,000,000.[16] The Irish parliament, Griffith maintained, would have protected Irish industry and Ireland would have been able to increase her population at the same rate as England. England, however, had deliberately stifled Irish competition and prevented the realisation of Ireland's potentiality. Once English rule was destroyed nothing would prevent

Ireland from taking her rightful place as a great power. Griffith
never doubted the efficacy of protection. He disclaimed any idea
of excluding foreign competition but wished merely to prevent Irish
manufacturers from being 'crushed by mere weight of foreign
capital'. An Irish manufacturer who could produce as cheaply as a
foreigner but charged a higher price was 'a swindler'.[17]

Griffith's optimism, shared by other Irish nationalists, was partly
derived from Thomas Davis and the 'excessively optimistic' survey
of Irish resources published by Sir Robert Kane in the 1840s. In
passage after passage of Griffith's selection of his writings, Davis
declares that Ireland's resources are considerable and that only
industrial knowledge is lacking. Davis believed that Ireland had
sufficient coal to become a manufacturing country. 'We do not
possess as ample fields of flaming coal as Britain, but even of that
we have large quantities,' while in anthracite, easily freed from its
defects by use of vapour, 'we have a manufacturing power that
would supply us for generations'.[18] With water-power, fire-power,
all the essential minerals for peace and war—iron, charcoal and
sulphur—Davis considered that Ireland should be anything but
'poor and paltry'. The great deficiency, he believed, lay in his
country's lack of industrial education.[19] When he compared Ireland
with Prussia, the Young Irelander found everything in favour of
Ireland. It had a more compact territory, the strongest possible
frontier, a military population and means to pay an army. 'Her
harbours, her soil and her fisheries are not surpassed in Europe. . . .
The difference is in knowledge.'[20] Only Prussia's technical skill was
superior to that of Ireland. Griffith's estimate of Ireland's resources
was not dissimilar. He promised investors '400,000,000 tons of coal,
the finest stone in Europe and an inexhaustible supply of peat to
operate on'. In a lecture on Thomas Davis, Griffith's friend William
Rooney also denounced the Irish education system for leaving Irishmen ignorant of the needs and resources of their country.[21]

The second part of Griffith's *The Sinn Fein Policy,* the adum-
bration of a practical programme, also shows the influence of Davis
and Rooney. The actual form of the work is significant. The first
pages attacked the Irish educational system at all levels; List's ideas
were then discussed and followed by specific suggestions. The somewhat surprising separation of education and the rest of the practical
programme is to be found in Davis's opinions cited above. Griffith,
accepting the idea that Ireland's troubles arose from lack of knowledge and know-how, gave education a position of priority at the
beginning of his paper.

At every stage, said Griffith, the existing system of education was
unpatriotic. Primary schools produced recruits for the British army,
secondary schools created a middle class with 'aversion and con-

tempt for industry and "trade" ',[22] and university education was 'regarded by the classes in Ireland as a means of washing away the original sin of Irish birth'.[23] Though the mainly Protestant Trinity College (Dublin University) was condemned in *The Sinn Fein Policy*, Griffith in subsequent more conciliatory days praised a revival of national feeling in the university.[24] In his *Policy*, Griffith proposed the foundation of an education fund, welcoming contributions from overseas Irishmen, the establishment of voluntary schools, in co-operation with those run by the Christian Brothers, and a national university. Eventually a school strike might be attempted, but this would be impracticable until there was an alternative to the existing national schools. Patrick Ford of the *Irish World* accused Sinn Fein of calling on all Irish parents to send their children to Christian Brothers' schools which lacked the accommodation to deal with such numbers.[25]

Belief in the power of education, though shared by earlier German writers like Fichte, owed nothing to List's theory. It might in fact be considered its antithesis. Griffith himself quoted List's passage: 'in every nation will the authority of national language and national literature, the civilising arts and the perfection of municipal institutions, keep pace with the development of the manufacturing arm'.[26] Like Marx, List believed that the educational superstructure of a nation was dependent on an infrastructure of large resources husbanded by state economy. Griffith's revision cut through all difficulties, such as lack of sovereignty and population, by demanding education to mobilise potential resources. The teaching of List which he asked his countrymen to adopt was, in fact, a travesty of List.

Griffith's practical programme attempted to show how a manufacturing arm could be developed without state sovereignty, just as the Gaelic League hoped to make Ireland bilingual in spite of the existing education system. The economic policy was to operate at three levels: the individual; the local government bodies; and a national assembly composed of the general council of county councils, representatives from poor law boards, urban councils, rural councils, harbour commissioners, and the Irish parliamentary party.

The exhortations to the individual were straight-forward. He was to buy Irish goods, cut his alcoholic consumption by half and boycott the recruiting sergeant. Griffith recognised that a general strike against payment of income tax would not be feasible when many income tax payers were unionists. Nevertheless, the two Sinn Fein landowners, Sweetman and Martyn, were continually badgered by opponents sneering at their payment of income tax. There was nothing original in Griffith's propositions, adopted by overseas nationalist politicians from Samuel Adams to Déak. The contemporary Indian Swadeshi movement had a similar programme, and recognised Sinn Fein as an Irish translation of its policy.

Much was expected from the diverse local bodies. In Hungary local councils had played an important part in the development of Déak's policy. All could assist industry by laying out their revenues on Irish goods. Harbour boards, hitherto inefficient, might impose light duties on imported foreign manufacturers and publish a list of Irish receivers. Poor law boards could short-circuit the poor law system which shut up paupers unprofitably in poor-houses and provide remunerative outdoor relief in developments such as afforestation.

These were reasonable suggestions, not dependent on an excessively optimistic view of Ireland's strength. Other more ambitious items demanded a national authority for their implementation. Griffith placed great hopes on the general council of county councils which even under parliamentarian control he recognised as the supreme Irish authority. Tom Kettle might well inquire, 'what will happen if the government suspends the Local Government Act?'[27] The major part played by Sweetman and Esmonde in the establishment of the general council has already been described.

Griffith hoped that the general council could be extended to form a national council of 300 by adding representatives from other local bodies, and the Irish MPs when they withdrew from Westminster. Such a body would then possess great moral influence and the ability to formulate economic schemes for adoption by the local bodies. National arbitration courts, dealing *inter alia* with commercial disputes and based on another idea attributed to Thomas Davis, were suggested, the judges to be appointed by the national assembly. These national courts were intended to gradually supersede British legal institutions. The local body patronage of about 6,000 positions would form the nucleus of a national civil service if used for the benefit of the country rather than the enrichment of corrupt local bosses. Griffith suggested a competitive examination at three levels, requiring a graded knowledge of Irish language, history and resources. Such proposals, useful to nationalists in all countries, belong to Griffith's general theory of revolution rather than to his pure economic policy. Industrial development, dependent as it was on the establishment of a national authority, requires separate treatment.

There is no indication in *The Sinn Fein Policy* that Griffith considered the possibility of miscalculating Ireland's resources. The superabundance of Ireland's natural resources was in fact part of the advanced nationalist credo. The *Gaelic American* once attacked Sir Horace Plunkett for suggesting that Ireland had little coal and the latter was quick to reply that he had been misquoted. Granting the existence of adequate resources, the obstacles, presented by

British misgovernment alone, required removal as a prelude to the full development of Ireland's national stature. Industrial capital was the prime necessity. Griffith invited the entry of Irish-American and foreign capital on commercial terms. He promised an abundant supply of coal, stone and peat: 'the Arigna coal mines, for instance, produce as good coal as the best that Great Britain can produce'. He did not, however, offer iron like Davis and Devoy's *Gaelic American*. Ireland's previous failure to utilise such resources was attributed to the differential rates charged by the Irish railway companies favouring English goods. The French writer, L. Paul-Dubois, agreed that 'all the productive capacity of Ireland is made barren by this inverted-form of protection'.[28] The problem was of long standing. Griffith suggested that the canal system might be revived to enable 'articles such as coal, stone, salt, gypsum, marble, slate' to 'become distributable over a whole country, which the freight of a few miles rendered before unprofitable'. Sweetman, in his 1906 speech to the general council of county councils, later published as a Sinn Fein pamphlet,[29] advocated the purchase of Irish railways and their management by the general council. Griffith's hopes for industrial development through the utilisation of Irish mineral resources seem to have blinded him to the special interests of the Belfast shipbuilding industry, dependent as it was on raw materials from Great Britain. In his final attempt to avert partition in 1914, though offering Ulster substantial safeguards for her linen production, Griffith omitted to provide for ship-building.

A large-scale reform of the banking system and the stock exchange was projected by Griffith to facilitate further the development of industry. The stock exchange was condemned for its failure to quote Irish industry: 'shut out from the natural investment of his money, the small capitalist has been transformed by the *government* stock-brokers of Ireland into a pure speculator—in other words a gambler in shares—and has been fleeced in turn by every species of financial rascal England—fruitful mother—produces'.[30] The banks incurred odium because they lent money to the British government free of interest during the Boer War and periodically bought overvalued British government stock. 'The banks of Ireland then, are willing to lend the money of the Irish people for British purposes, but not for Irish ones.'[31] The remedy was the establishment of a national bank by the Irish assembly, which would, with the support of the public bodies, transact its business through a national stock exchange. This, it was hoped, would soon oust the 'government' stockbrokers.

Griffith's most ambitious ideas were for the formation of an Irish mercantile marine and the establishment of Irish consuls in the European capitals to popularise Irish goods. He believed that a fleet of tramp steamers could easily be financed by the money 'lying idle in our banks' and private investment by Irish shopkeepers and workingmen, in imitation of the Norwegians. The consular service would be supplied by half the money saved when the Irish MPs left Westminster. Profitable markets could be opened up in Argentina, Chile, the USA, Canada, Australia, South Africa, France, Germany, Belgium, Holland, Spain, Russia, Japan, Denmark, Italy and Austro-Hungary. This suggestion was savagely attacked by one of Gavan Duffy's correspondents who pointed out that 'a beggarly little consul on £200 a year' would be able to do nothing to enable Irish goods to compete with the products of foreign countries when it required the full-time services of an able representative to advertise for a single firm. 'It is this futile rubbish which plays the game of the West Briton.'[32]

Such was Griffith's economic policy. It was less optimistic than that of Davis, though like Davis, Griffith had no means of testing the truth of his assumptions by investigation. In summary, several factors important in the development of Sinn Fein must be noted. First, Griffith can hardly be excused for his failure to provide for the heavy industry of the Lagan Valley. Its existence was a justification of List's belief in the great economic advantages of the act of union, as the Lagan Valley depended on free trade with England to obtain its raw materials. Griffith might have argued that Ireland could produce these raw materials and submitted the problem to investigation. He preferred to ignore this and all the other questions introduced by List's theory. The fact that he was able to do so shows how little interest *The Sinn Fein Policy* aroused in the country. Obviously few Irishmen were stimulated to read List for themselves. Sweetman and William Sears, editor of the *Enniscorthy Echo*, however, knew their List.

Secondly, *The Sinn Fein Policy* marks the beginnings of Griffith's adoption of a broader view of nationality. He remarked that 75% of the members of local bodies were elected as nationalists.[33] Though this may be a condescension to a less exclusive terminology, the whole programme is an appeal to non-separatists, for only with their aid would it become practicable. The third related conclusion is that the policy was almost entirely dependent on local governmental bodies and the general council of the county councils. Griffith's interests required that no quarrels should be provoked with any party. The withdrawal of the members from Westminster was not the first step; it was hoped that they would join in behind the general council of county councils. The disadvantages of a multi-branched movement and a clash with the parliamentarians can now be appreciated.

There was little chance of Sinn Fein realising much of its ambitious programme in the years before 1916. The ousting in October 1907 of Esmonde from the chairmanship of the general council of county councils and the latter's declaration in favour of parliamentarianism was, as Ford's *Irish World* gloated, 'a staggering blow' for Sinn Fein.[34] The Sinn Fein annual report for 1908 admitted that 'The General Council of County Councils as the nucleus of a national authority has, of course, become temporarily inoperative, as the General Council surrendered its deliberating functions to the parliamentarian nominees at its annual meeting.'[35] According to Hobson, Griffith's dependence on the general council of county councils was 'all very well if there had been the remotest chance of our getting the Town or County Councils to accept and work the new policy; but to anyone with knowledge of local politics in the provinces at that period this seemed quite out of the question'.[36] Hobson may protest too much. There was no chance of winning over the county councils in opposition to the parliamentarians and UIL, but Griffith's permeation policy might have had some results. The greater militancy of the Dungannon clubs may, moreover, have made some councils more rigid in their parliamentarianism.

Nevertheless Sinn Fein did its best to advertise the programme laid down in Griffith's policy statement. In 1907 credit was claimed for the initiation of a conference of poor law guardians and a decline of 11,130 in figures for British army recruitment. An ambitious list of 15 items was submitted to candidates for local body elections. It is highly significant that a unionist was able to give positive assurances on ten of the questions which were nearly all derived from Griffith's *Sinn Fein Policy*. Four at least were dependent on the general council of county councils. A new item was the demand for 'a general survey of Ireland and the development of its mineral resources'. Griffith thus showed himself willing to put his belief in Ireland's natural resources to the test.[37]

On a small scale Sinn Fein achieved some successes in its economic policy. In 1908 a company was formed, with AE (George Russell) as one of the directors, to establish, on the continental model, a co-operative people's bank providing small loans for industrial and other development.[38] Similar achievements were the publication of the Sinn Fein year book which endeavoured to provide useful information on Irish resources, and even more important, the annual aonach, or trade fair, which attracted a large number of Dublin firms. Sinn Fein also helped to popularise the Irish trade mark, accepted by both unionists and nationalists. Even the far-fetched consular scheme was attempted in a minor way when the national council itself negotiated with the German ambassador on the cattle trade, and President Taft on Irish immigration into the USA. In her Paris days before the establishment of Sinn Fein, Maud Gonne's

L'Irlande Libre had attempted to spread information about Ireland's trading potential.

The impracticability of his programme was not, however, the chief economic criticism received by Griffith from dissident Sinn Feiners and Irish radicals. Many were in fact convinced that Griffith's attitude to social issues was radically defective. In his stimulating Marxist study E. Strauss suggested that Griffith's programme was 'a more self-conscious and articulate version of "Parnellism" ', while James Connolly's ideal of an Irish socialist republic was 'an up-to-date form of the aims for which Michael Davitt had striven and suffered'.[39] Strauss exaggerates the ideological cleavage between Parnell and Davitt and too easily assimilates the opinions of Davitt and Connolly, but his thesis has an element of truth. Griffith was certainly at loggerheads with much Irish radical opinion.

In the early years of the movement there had been much practical co-operation between Griffith and Irish labour. The early *United Irishman* had published articles by the socialist Frederick Ryan and had generally defended the Labour cause. James Connolly was a personal friend of Arthur Griffith. When Connolly stood in 1903 for the Wood Quay ward, Griffith, while criticisng the Labour party as the 'tool of the Pile clique and the whiskey ring', welcomed Connolly's candidature: 'we are not socialists, but we would be intensely gratified to see a man of Mr. Connolly's character returned'.[40] Griffith, himself of working-class origin, clearly sympathised with the poor, especially in the matter of slum housing. He once suggested that Ireland should follow the example of a country providing workers' houses from which eviction was impossible.[41] Griffith, moreover, condemned the Wyndham land act of 1903 on the ground that the favourable terms for landlords amounted to a robbery of the poor.[42] Certain statements indicate a sympathy for the agrarian ideals of James Fintan Lalor. 'There are few people in Ireland,' Griffith once remarked, 'who do not subscribe to Fintan Lalor's theory of the ownership of the soil.'[43] Griffith believed in some control of the land by the whole Irish people and was opposed to the development of a peasant proprietary which like that of France might grow into a new landlordism. In 1913, however, Griffith declared peasant proprietary better than land nationalisation.[44]

In the first years after the establishment of the party, Sinn Feiners in the Dublin corporation through their attacks on slum landlordism and demands for the investigation of tenements owned by members of the corporation became closely identified with Labour in the public mind. P. T. Daly was a representative on the corporation for both the Sinn Fein and labour interests. When Daly and Michael Lehane were disqualified on a technicality from standing in the 1909 election, James Larkin and the Dublin trades council, over which Lehane presided, joined Sinn Fein in taking their part.[45] Daly withdrew from the Sinn Fein organisation after 1910 and became even more closely associated with Larkin in the leadership of the transport and general workers union. O'Hegarty, Hobson and some of the other seceders, though they did not become as closely involved in Labour politics as Daly, showed more sympathy with the left than Griffith. O'Hegarty, who subsequently condemned the socialist 'slabs of doctrinaire jargon' in the 1919 social programme attached to Dail Eireann's declaration of Irish independence,[46] talked some socialism in 1908.[47] Nevertheless, he soon came out in defence of Griffith against a real socialist.

Back in 1909 Griffith had argued that the question of socialism in Ireland should be shelved till after Irish independence. He continued to insist that divisive class issues should not be allowed to dissolve the united nationalist front against England. Griffith's opponents, however, claimed that it was Griffith who had introduced contention by designing an economic policy with an inherent bias against the working class.

Griffith's attacks on Larkin have frequently been described. Larkin was 'the Strike Organiser' who played England's game. To Griffith the Irish 'new unionism' was simply English trade unionism in Ireland. Griffith simultaneously lashed Larkin for being 'the paid servant' of an English union and striking without permission of his Liverpool executive.[48] In denouncing Larkin's 'English-made strike' of 1911 to compel Jacobs biscuit factory to recognise his union, Griffith declaimed against 'doctrinaires whose ultimate message to man is to give up his God, his country, his family and his property and be happy'.[49] Such invective simply utilised the current clichés of anti-socialism. During the great 1913 lock-out, Griffith was strongly opposed to Larkin. Like the clerical authorities, Griffith was particularly incensed by the proposal for transporting the children of locked-out workers to English homes and the black-listing of Irish manufacturers.[50] The former attempt was certainly 'union of hearts' with a vengeance. Griffith's conclusion in late 1913 that the dispute, originating in the attempt of William Martin Murphy, the all-powerful Dublin tycoon, to compel Dublin workers to leave Larkin's union, only continued 'because doctrinaires and idle university professors want to revel in the limelight',[51] hardly did justice to the facts. There was a growing element of paranoia in Griffith's attitude to Larkin. *Irish Freedom's* approach was more balanced. It did not condemn the workers but emphasised the harm that was being done to Ireland. An article by Ernest Blythe was published recommending distributive co-operation as a remedy.[52] In the *Gaelic American* Hobson placed the blame on the employers.[53]

Socialists and radicals naturally lost few opportunities for attacking Griffith. Frederick Ryan, James Connolly, who claimed that the Irish socialist party of 1896 had anticipated the best features of the Sinn Fein policy, W. P. Ryan and others all crossed swords with 'the man who was Sinn Fein'. An anonymous socialist debating with P. S. O'Hegarty in the *Peasant* raised a number of issues often mentioned by other critics.[54] The socialist denounced Sinn Fein economics as an attempt to 'patch up a social structure that irrevocably broke down in the famine year'. To prove his contention that Sinn Fein was a capitalist movement, this critic cited its interest in taxes not paid by the worker, that old bugbear the king, lords and commons of 1782, and the proposals for a national stock exchange and a mercantile marine. The socialist was sceptical of the possibilities of destroying capitalism after independence and inclined towards the union of hearts idea, so much disliked by Griffith, that the interests of Irish and English democracy were identical. Moreover, he contended that Hungary and Germany which Griffith admired, were typical capitalist countries. Sheehy-Skeffington had spoken even more forcefully in his biography of Davitt. 'Irishmen eyes off Hungary, Germany! The people of both countries wear the shackles of social and economic slavery.'[55] Larkin, Connolly and W. P. Ryan agreed in criticising the interest in the king, lords and commons of 1782 as something likely to injure the interests of the workers. In this way the opposition of the socialists reinforced that of the physical-force men.

A particularly significant issue raised by O'Hegarty's opponent was foreign capital. The 'desire to import ready-made capitalists—those grown fat and heavy on the legalised robbery of the workers'—to exploit Irish cheap labour was roundly condemned. James Connolly similarly expressed the irritation of men fighting the notoriously low Irish wages system who heard that 'the National Council has promised lots of Irish labour at low wages to any foreign capitalist who cares to establish in Ireland'.[56] O'Hegarty admitted that he opposed the import of foreign capital, 'and so did almost every Sinn Feiner I know'.[57] Griffith's *Sinn Fein Policy* had not offered cheap labour but extensive natural resources as the bait for foreign capitalists. The widespread criticism suggests a common opinion that behind Griffith's optimistic appraisal of Ireland's mineral potential lay the realisation that low Irish living standards could be made attractive to the foreign investor. Connolly probed deeper into this possibility, insisting that socialists had no sympathy with Griffith's adaptation of List which judged a country's prosperity by the gross national product and ignored the distribution of wealth. By this reckoning, argued Connolly, Ireland in 1847, at the height of the potato famine, could be deemed a wealthy country while Denmark which exported little must be accounted poor.

Connolly's complaint was decidedly unfair in that Griffith had quoted Berkeley and Isaac Butt against the view that mere volume of foreign trade was an index of national prosperity.[58] Like other nationalists Griffith had no difficulty in condemning the food exporters of 1847; those who used foreign goods at the time, he said, were literally starving the farm labourers and small tenants. But Connolly's main contention that Griffith failed to emphasise the need for a juster internal distribution of income is not so easily refuted. Griffith certainly quoted, in his book of extracts, Thomas Davis's view that 'the equal distribution of comfort, education and happiness is the only true wealth of nations',[59] but this was a vague aspiration. Griffith, though not objecting to equality, was distinctly sceptical of the means used in its achievement.

W. P. Ryan of the *Peasant* and Frederick Ryan, associate of the anti-imperialistic English poet, W. S. Blunt, were less inclined to enter theoretical disputes with Griffith, but had no hesitation in pointing out some of the retrogressive consequences of his policies. W. P. Ryan in 1908 lectured the Sinn Fein central branch on its social policy.[60] Many of his criticisms were similar to those of Connolly. Political freedom, said Ryan, would not necessarily lead to social or economic freedom. 'Make the average Irish employer politically free in the morning, and it does not follow for a moment that he will be inclined to treat the Irish employee fairly, to say nothing of bringing him into the business of life and work on co-operative terms.' Workers were therefore sceptical of Sinn Fein's emphasis on independence before social reform. To Ryan, 'the very greatest difficulty in the way of Sinn Fein is the presence in its councils of men who have the most reactionary ideas about property and against co-operation and social evolution on national democratic and practical Christian lines'. The general Sinn Fein reaction to Ryan was unfavourable. Though Hobson expressed basic though not complete agreement with Ryan, Griffith stigmatised the latter's argument as a proposal that Sinn Fein should have a class policy. Ryan's paper replied: 'Social justice is then a "class policy"! Co-operation is "class policy"! The claim that the manual workers of the nation have a right to brighter and sweeter opportunities is a class policy.'

In answer to Frederick Ryan and Francis Sheehy-Skeffington, whom he believed to have derogated nationality to a mere collection of human beings without a soul, Griffith elaborated, perhaps more explicitly than ever before, the doctrine of 'integral nationalism'. 'When we say we love Ireland we do not mean by Ireland the peasants in the fields, the workers in the factories, the teachers in the schools, the professors in the colleges—we mean the soul into which we were born and which was born into us. If this be a metaphysical way of looking at concrete questions we shall remain in the metaphysical along with the unenlightened world that existed before Rousseau and the Manchester school which poor Ryan so implicitly accepted as the repository of the wisdom of all ages. . . . The man who declared that he wanted National freedom in order to promote social reform did not understand the meaning of the nation.'[61]

While Griffith made no secret of his philosophical rejection of socialism, the Sinn Feiners most open to criticism as reactionaries were Martyn, Sweetman, of whom it was said that he 'nominally leads and really satirised the political Sinn Fein movement',[62] and W. E. Shackleton, the Lucan mill owner. The latter's firm was indeed identified with William Martin Murphy's employers' federation. Shackleton's early support may have persuaded Griffith to forget that the *United Irishman* in 1905 had denounced Murphy for using English staff wherever possible in his companies.[63] Most of the Sinn Fein leaders, declared Ryan's paper, 'have no democratic sympathies worth talking about, and have been honest enough not to pretend otherwise'.[64]

More to the point, however, was the frequently voiced complaint that the Sinn Fein policy was appealing increasingly to right-wing elements in Ireland. Griffith's declaration—'I prefer an Irish capitalist to the British government' which was 'the arch-capitalist in Ireland. You will never be able to fight the battle of anti-capitalism out in Ireland till you have cleared the British from the field'[65] was open to the same objection as the 1782 policy. If Irish capitalists were to be used against the British government they would insist on a prior assurance of their status after independence. Griffith by his 'opening to the right' was virtually compelled to give this assurance. The columns of the *Irish Nation and Peasant* were filled with condemnations of this development, especially when certain manufacturers and merchants of 'the English garrison' had been supported by Sinn Fein.[66] Frederick Ryan was particularly outspoken: 'We have Mr. Griffith telling the Irish landlords that their best chance of retaining their privileges against Irish democracy lies in Home Rule! In other words political freedom is not to be sought as a means of social liberation and the uplifting of the people, but as a means of preserving the anti-social privileges of a class. A sort of clerical-tory nationalism is to rise on the ruins of the old *United Irishman.'*

Ryan considered that Griffith's defence of the Spanish government's execution of Francisco Ferrer, an educational secularist, was symptomatic of his new attitude. The Ferrer case, like the the Spanish Civil War of the 1930s, neatly polarised clericalist and secular-liberal viewpoints. It seems, moreover, that Ryan was correct in his belief, at the time of the *Sinn Fein* daily, that Griffith's attempt to conciliate the conservatives was ultimately futile. 'The pathos of it all is that the landlords and reactionaries all round look askance at these performances, they have their own leaders and papers which they trust, and whilst they make some use of Sinn Fein to sow confusion they will scarcely bother to maintain it.'[67] As Strauss demonstrated, Griffith for most of his career was 'equally rejected by the businessmen of Ulster and by the small-town traders and merchants of the South'.[68]

A few years after his death, Griffith was accused of 'denouncing "the English economics" of *laissez-faire'*, while accepting 'the *fait accompli* of capitalism, which his glorified heroes, Davis and Mitchel, had denounced as "the English system" '.[69] To many modern left-wing analysts this criticism might appear to ignore the Fascist alternative to both *laissez-faire* liberalism and socialism. Categorising Griffith as a Fascist is an oversimplification, though his ideas do have something in common with the proponents of the corporate state. The clearest statement of Griffith's final position was made in a *Sinn Fein* article in answer to his critics during the lock-out of 1913.[70]

Reiterating his support for protection against free-trade England whom he regarded as the cause of most of the social evils inside her territories, Griffith rejected the idea of class war. 'I deny that Capital and Labour are in their nature antagonistic—I assert that they are essential and complementary the one to the other.' Socialism therefore was no remedy; it was not capitalism but the abuse of capitalism that oppressed the workers. 'Not in the destruction of the Capitalist, but in his subjection to the Law of the state, interpreting the conscience and interest of the Nation, will Labour be delivered from its oppression and restored to all its rights.' The nation insisting on a reasonable wage for the worker and a fair profit to capital would say to labour: 'For I am the Nation—your father and the father of capital also, and in my house my children shall not oppress the other—it shall not be a house divided against itself.' Griffith did, however, admit that in the past Irish labour had done more for Ireland than Irish capital.

As a precedent, Griffith cited the ancient civil code of Ireland which fixed the payment of workers, 'not on competitive but on absolute lines'. The value of completed work was socially appraised and payment was made accordingly. In the absence of Irish feudalism, the artisan could rise to high social status; the gilds had considerable influence on the government. Griffith's views on this subject appear to have owed something to Thomas Davis's *Udalism & Feudalism*, 'one of the most interesting things Davis ever wrote'.[71]

Griffith on this subject appears close to Connolly's insistence on the ancient Gaelic love of equality and democracy.

On a more practical level, Griffith cited the New Zealand industrial conciliation and arbitration act which since its passage in 1894 had been a source of radical inspiration not only in Australasia but also in Canada, the USA, Britain and other countries. The chief feature of the New Zealand system was the power of the arbitration court to make compulsory awards binding on both parties. Though the New Zealand act was at first regarded as one of the most socialistic pieces of legislation in history—the American H. D. Lloyd's *A Country without Strikes* was the typical reaction of many admirers—criticism intensified on the left when depressed conditions made the court an instrument of employers rather than workers. By 1913 the New Zealand militant unionists who admired, and who in some cases knew James Larkin personally, were in revolt against the New Zealand industrial arbitration system. However, when Griffith used New Zealand to support a policy Sinn Fein had been suggesting for some time, he adopted an argument which still possessed some appeal for moderate labour men. In September 1913 Griffith had praised Connolly, 'the man in the leadership of the Transport Union with a head on his shoulders', for accepting the idea of a conciliation board to prevent strikes.[72] Though rebuffed by Griffith, Seamus O hAodha asked, after Griffith's 1913 exposition of 'Sinn Fein and the Labour question', 'why he should preach socialism in practice and attack it in name'.[73] The Sinn Fein leader, moreover, felt vindicated when the Irish Catholic hierarchy accepted the arbitration idea. This he hoped would silence 'the political soft-heads who bonded themselves together to resist "every proposal coming from Sinn Fein—good or bad" '.[74] To meet the immediate difficulty that Ireland, unlike New Zealand, had no national authority to impose awards, Griffith suggested that the parliamentary party, which still possessed the confidence of the country, should take on this responsibility.[75] Such a proposal was certain to alienate not only the physical-force men but socialists who had reason to doubt the sympathy of many bourgeois parliamentarians.

Though critics insist that the compulsory arbitration system, which without preventing strikes still exists in Australasia and elsewhere, has Fascist undertones, Griffith's espousal of the idea does give more plausibility to his apparently reactionary and ultra-nationalistic economic policy. In future periods of galloping inflation some means, perhaps a prices and incomes policy, of defending community interests against unregulated capital and militant labour must be considered.

Time has dealt ironically with Griffith's economics. Strauss argued that Griffith's programme had been fully adopted by the Irish Free State after the latter's death,[76] but it is doubtful if the early attempts by Griffith's successor W. T. Cosgrave to implement the 'tariff personality'[77] won by Griffith in the 1921 Treaty were more than half-hearted.[78] After 50 years of independence, Ireland has negotiated a free trade agreement with England and joined the EEC. Irish opponents of the EEC stigmatise it as 'Redmondism'. Foreign capital has been admitted in significant proportions, but its critics utilise arguments not unlike those employed by Griffith against England. On the other hand, coal and other resources have been better exploited, often with foreign capital, since the economic breakthrough of the late 1950s associated with the name of Dr. T. K. Whitaker. The successful public corporation, Bord na Mona, has followed the suggestions of Griffith and Thomas Davis in exploiting Ireland's turf resources.

Perhaps in the last resort, as Francis Hackett, once a contributor to *Sinn Fein,* recognised, Griffith's economics were ultimately based on 'that lofty intransigence which declines to make terms with society as it is. The tragedy of Ireland has made him vengeful as well as sorrowful. His pride demanded a popular consecration, a spirit in regard to England that had in it the scorn of Swift, the stiff neck of John Mitchel, the serpent wisdom of Nietzsche. . . . He would not recognise in existing agricultural Ireland the fulcrum that was to be found there. He preferred to flash lightning from his heights . . . his antagonism to England is really a sort of individual antagonism. Like Mitchel and Parnell, Arthur Griffith stands outside the movement of the whole people. . . . A voice crying in the wilderness he has carried his wilderness with him. The economics of Ireland were secondary to his hatred of England, stones of wrath in a Ulysses battle against the Manchester Cyclops.'[79]

Racial pride was thus the motivating power behind Griffith's ambitious programme for economic development. Like Parnell, another protectionist, who hated the English for despising him as Irish,[80] Griffith required proof of his conviction that the Celtic races were inherently superior to the Saxon English, a people fit only for slavery.[81] National power through rapid industrial advance appeared the unavoidable acid test of such Celtic pre-eminence.

CONCLUSION

The passing of Non-Violent Sinn Fein

IN the preceding pages we have traced the growth of the Sinn Fein movement from small beginnings in 1891 to its precarious existence on the eve of the Rising. In 1910, Hobson, O'Hegarty and their allies broke away from Griffith's organisation and started a new paper, *Irish Freedom*. This monthly, published by the Wolfe Tone clubs, preached an uncompromising doctrine of republicanism. They had finally discarded the 1782 constitution and shattered the basis of Griffith's campaign for unity. Not only did the extremists withdraw, but the moderates now placed their confidence in the Irish parliamentary party, which, holding the balance of power in the house of commons, appeared certain to produce a Home Rule bill. Sinn Fein was thus split on both sides. This fact alone would have accounted for the decay of Sinn Fein branches in the country. At this stage, it seemed that the movement had lost the will to live. Sinn Fein, however, struggled on to provide a vital basis for the 1917 post-Rising reorganisation.

There are two allied conclusions which throw much light on the character of Sinn Fein during this early period. Neither has received adequate attention from writers whose conceptions of the movement have been formed by post-1916 Sinn Fein.

In the first place, Griffith originally had no intention of forming a political party in the accepted sense of the word; in the second, and this arose from the first, he never wished to fight the parliamentary party in the constituencies. Unlike post-1916 Sinn Fein, the early movement was based on local government bodies, many of which owed their existence to the act of 1898, and not on parliamentary representation. It is not difficult to see why. In 1900 the separatists, enervated by the long reign of Parnell, had no prospects or policy other than force which then, as now, had little appeal for the 'silent majority'. The reunion of the Parnellite and anti-Parnellite parties and the formation of a strong outside organisation in the United Irish League might have begun a new active period, during which separatists could offer conditional support to the parliamentarians. Instead, the century opened with the South Mayo by-election where the nominee of the United Irish League opposed the separatist absentee candidate, Major John MacBride. Though the preceding decade had seen contests between rival parliamentary parties, this was the first time that parliamentarians and anti-parliamentarians came into head-on collision. From the viewpoint of national strategy, such a contest was to be avoided at all costs; but, unfortunately for the cause of Irish cohesion, the inexorable pressures of events in 1900 rendered conflict unavoidable. The result was a crushing and humiliating defeat for the separatists, which not only made the divorce between them and the parliamentarians absolute, but also fostered the belief amongst the latter that the strength of non-parliamentarian nationalists was negligible.

Griffith developed his Hungarian policy as an attempt to achieve national unity by what Basil Liddell-Hart might have termed the strategy of the indirect approach. Griffith realised that an attack on the parliamentary machine was doomed to immediate failure, but knew that many of his separatist supporters wished to make that attack. As a compromise, Griffith initiated a campaign of propaganda which encouraged the Irish local governmental bodies to begin a movement of passive resistance against British rule, and argued simultaneously that the parliamentary party should return to Ireland as its leader. The adhesion of parliamentarians in general was necessary to implement the policy, but conversion of the whole Irish representation at Westminster was not the first essential step. Griffith desired notable converts who would be willing to start a new national movement with the compromise objective of the 1782 constitution. Griffith himself was to be an *eminence grise,* supplying public propaganda while giving advice and criticism behind the scenes. There was no place in his scheme for a new political party or parliamentary contests. As the parliamentary party, especially after the Liberal victory of 1906, remained unmoved, Griffith's admirers demanded that he should himself form a political party with branches in the country to fight parliamentarians. The national council, then a loose Dublin organisation with somewhat petty objectives,[1] was, accordingly, extended and provision made for affiliating country branches. Such was the origin of the Sinn Fein organisation. Lack of money and executive disapproval prevented it contesting parliamentary seats during this period, barring the by-election at North Leitrim in 1908, an exceptional case forced on Sinn Fein by its opponents.

At this stage the controversy over the 1782 constitution deepened. Followers of Hobson and O'Hegarty felt that as separatists formed a majority in the movement, it should become avowedly republican in its objective. They supported the initial offer of passive resistance, but believed that when this had demoralised the British government, physical force should take its place to win a republic. Griffith, on the other hand, still hoping to convert the parliamentarians and liberal unionists, insisted that no man, who was not prepared to demand more than a dual monarchy status for Ireland, should be excluded from the movement. This meant in effect that the movement would be non-violent. After passive resistance had achieved a certain degree of success, nationalists were committed to negotiating with the British government on the basis of the 1783 renunciation act instead of driving out the enemy by physical force. Ostensibly, the controversy did not concern declared objectives—the aim of Sinn Fein was stated vaguely as independence—but personnel. Could separatists co-operate with dual monarchists?[2] In India in 1920, Gandhi, distinguishing between true non-co-operation and violent 'Sinn Feinism', similarly appealed even to the advocates of physical force to give non-violence a fair trial.[3] The Irish issue can be demonstrated diagrammatically.

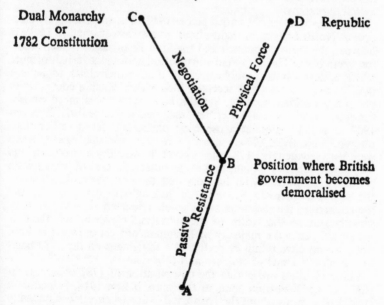

Dual Monarchy C — Negotiation — Physical Force — D **Republic**
or
1782 Constitution

B **Position where British government becomes demoralised**

Passive Resistance

A

All Sinn Feiners could start from 'A' offering passive resistance. No constitutional argument is necessary at that stage. When 'B' is reached passive resistance has successfully demoralised the British government. Here an insuperable difficulty arises. The dual monarchists will now begin negotiations with the British government while the physical-force men are changing from passive to active resistance to win a republic. Can we expect the different sections to shake hands and then part; the dual monarchists to the conference table; the separatists to the barricades? Such a situation is in theory unthinkable. No co-operation is apparently possible on that basis. Griffith, it is true, suggested that the separatists might accept 1782[4] as a stepping-stone, and later campaign for a republic. This would necessarily have been a peaceful campaign, and as such unattractive to the republicans. Assuming that Britain believed that there was a vital difference between a dual monarchy and a republic, she would be given time to marshal her demoralised forces. Moreover, the republicans would have to fight their own countrymen who had made the settlement with Britain. In the Austro–Hungarian empire the republican followers of Kossuth had achieved little after the *Ausgleich*. The issue was therefore perfectly plain: there was no middle way. Sinn Fein would have to decide whether it aimed at a dual monarchy or a republic.

That question was not settled before 1917. The impending by-election at North Leitrim brought about a hasty amalgamation in 1907 between the national council and the Sinn Fein league (which stood for a republic). The Sinn Fein constitution adopted a verbal formula which allowed both republicans and dual monarchists to believe that the organisation had accepted their views. Such a compromise obviously decided nothing, yet the controversy was more or less dropped. Griffith and his critics remained unreconciled. Between 1907 and 1910, conflict arose over particular issues rather than ultimate objectives. There are two reasons for this. First, there were very few genuine 1782 men except the wealthy and pugnacious Sweetman, Charles Dolan, and some others, several of whom were probably separatists who had decided to limit their objectives in the national interest. Second, the lack of support given by the the country to the movement as a whole relegated all revolutionary speculations to the realm of metaphysics. Nevertheless, there is little doubt that the majority of Irishmen, not yet enrolled in Sinn Fein, would have infinitely preferred a settlement on the 1782 basis to a protracted war of violence and terrorism.

The difficulties preventing the co-operation of 1782 constitutionalist and physical-force man in the years before 1914, helped at a later date to bring about the Irish Civil War. In an almost uncanny way the theory of 1910 became the reality of 1921. Griffith, negotiating with England for something like the 1782 constitution, was opposed by de Valera, apparently prepared to use more force to win a republic. By then, however, O'Hegarty was a staunch Griffith-ite, Hobson excluded from the nationalist movement, and Mac-Dermott executed. Griffith's original programme, though open to objection in detail, was at least a serious attempt to achieve Irish independence without partition and without bloodshed. It might have succeeded.*

Griffith's ideas have been dissected in previous chapters. It has been shown that though originally an orthodox separatist, his opinions gradually changed as he worked out his new policy. The common belief that Griffith remained a republican at heart, merely accepting the dual monarchist idea as a means to the end of national cohesion, does not stand examination. His mature thought formed a coherent whole. Thomas Davis and John Mitchel were his tutors. It seems that the actual content of Mitchel's writings, as opposed to his spirit and style, influenced Griffith hardly at all. On both the questions of republicanism and physical force, Griffith took a line sometimes diametrically opposed to that of Mitchel; and on some subjects where Mitchel had introduced qualifications to mitigate the severity of an opinion, Griffith preached the same doctrine in its bleak purity. The influence of Davis was of a different order. From him Griffith learned to respect Grattan's parliament, and this respect was due mainly to the fact that it had possessed the potential authority to protect Irish industry. Davis and Griffith were no exceptions in an age that regarded political economy and political science as synonymous. They differed from the majority of their countrymen in their belief that economy must be national, not cosmopolitan. Discussion about theoretical systems of government left Griffith cold. His was a power philosophy where the power envisaged was industrial. He relinquished his early republicanism without regret for he considered it irrelevant as an objective, disagree-ing here with Mitchel. In this respect the Treaty of 1921 accorded fully with Griffith's earlier views. Griffith's contemporaries were puzzled because he was neither a socialist nor a *laissez-faire* liberal. Was he therefore an early advocate of the corporate state? It would be a harsh judgment to call Griffith a Fascist, but an ambivalence between authoritarian and democratic tendencies in his thinking undoubtedly exists.

This ambivalence comes out clearly in his views on religion. Though himself a Catholic, Griffith's attitude to Protestantism was not one of mere toleration but positive appreciation. Like most nationalists he felt unbounded respect for the religion of so many great Irishmen. Moreover, in his earlier days he had toyed with anti-clericalism. In an early *United Irishman* controversy between

*As late as 1927 Kevin O'Higgins still believed that the dual monarchy idea would help to end partition.

Griffith and Fr. P. F. Kavanagh, the priest, because of Griffith's support of the Emperor Julian, who attempted to revive paganism, had bracketed him with 'the infidel Gibbon'.[5] Griffith soon outgrew this phase. An Orangeman complained in 1907 that Griffith's paper which had once described the Vatican as the 'bane of Ireland' was now drawing closer to Rome.[6] In his treatment of foreign affairs he demonstrated a different nature. The notorious cases of Dreyfus and Ferrer saw Griffith ranged with the persecutors. In his introduction to the *Jail Journal* he attacked the whole liberal philosophy with a ferocity which made Mitchel, in the following pages, sound tepid. This tendency was at work in the efforts to compromise with unionism. It is significant, though at first sight paradoxical, that the attempted alliance strengthened the clerical aspect of his policy. He began to draw towards—though he did not explicitly use religious terminology—the idea of safeguards for Protestants as a community. The IRB constitution, on the other hand, aimed at the complete separation of church and state and the freedom of the individual: 'In the Irish Republic there shall be no state religion but every citizen shall be free to worship God according to his conscience and perfect freedom of worship shall be guaranteed as a right and not granted as a privilege.'[7] This ideal was embodied in the republican proclamation of 1916. In such a constitution the individual would be secured in his rights against the encroachment of all associations and there would, therefore, be no need to give guarantees to any church. To offer safeguards, on the other hand, to Protestants as a group, would be to compromise a basic democratic ideal and make national unity impossible of attainment. Any hint of safeguards to Protestant churches, as appeared in the present Irish constitution before the referendum of 1972,* implied a position of pre-eminence for the Catholic church—a situation which most unionists are committed to resist. Thus, in practice, no safeguard would have proved sufficient. Griffith's ideas led logically to this *impasse* for which he must bear some responsibility. His rejection of liberalism and individual rights prevented him from accepting the IRB secular objective as well as its doctrine of physical force and republicanism. His very respect for Irish Protestants might have led him to advocate the constitutional recognition of their churches. Yet in matters like common education and mixed marriages, Griffith was unable to reassure potential Protestant allies.

It has been shown that most aspects of Griffith's thought led to a mild corporate state where the individual became a means to the higher life of the body politic. In his perfect community, labour and

*It is significant that George Gavan Duffy, who tended to support Griffith in the early period, was one of the few Irish judges who attempted to interpret the Irish constitution in a specifically Catholic sense.

capital would submit to governmental regulation; and that would mean, in the case of Ireland, hard work and sacrifice from both classes while industrial power was developed to what W. W. Rostow has called the 'take off' stage. Consequently, Griffith, assuming Ireland's fiscal autonomy, did not care about forms of government and titles.

Although Griffith's basic thought was consistent, it must not be supposed that all ideas thrown out during his journalistic career were in total harmony. The tactic of non-violence, for example, is difficult to square with the ideal of a corporate state. Nevertheless, even in Gandhi's movement, which had much in common with early Sinn Fein, there was a germ of authoritarianism. Nor must it be thought that Griffith was the only real spokesman for the Sinn Fein movement. Not only did men so vocal as Hobson and O'Hegarty differ from him in fundamentals, but the movement often carried Griffith in directions he had no desire to go. Therefore an assessment of the early movement as a whole must be attempted.

Sinn Fein after 1910 appeared so moribund that its subsequent re-organisation on a national basis was partly due to the fact that unionist newspapers wrongly used its name as a contemptuous epithet for the Rising of 1916. It would, however, be unhistorical and unjust to dismiss Sinn Fein as a complete failure before 1916.

The first solid achievement of early Sinn Fein was negative, but not for that reason unimportant. In spite of all temptations, it never compromised the basic ideal that independence must be won in Ireland and not bargained for at Westminster. In 1909 the only hope for Sinn Fein influence appeared to lie in an alliance with William O'Brien's All-for-Ireland League. The passage of a Home Rule bill seemed so imminent that even Griffith may have considered the policy of doctrinaire abstention no longer expedient. The majority of Sinn Fein, led by Hobson and O'Hegarty, refused to countenance any alliance with O'Brien except on an unequivocally abstentionist basis, and the matter was, accordingly, dropped. The future was to justify the undeviating upholders of principle, and early Sinn Fein, instead of joining the dreary ranks of Irish nationalist movements which have sacrificed all to expediency and failed, lived to provide a basis for the national Sinn Fein organisation of 1917. Without this basis the later movement might well have degenerated into anarchy.*

Not only did early Sinn Fein prepare the ground for subsequent organisation, but it instituted a forum for nationalist debate and thus generated a capital fund of ideas which was constantly drawn upon in the troubled years after 1916. For the first time separatists

*General Macready owned a copy of *The Resurrection of Hungary* and marked the dates of each proposal as it was carried out.

had been able to discuss their views in public, and in diversity of opinion Sinn Fein compared favourably with earlier nationalist movements. Though the ideas of Griffith tended to predominate, he was up to 1916 confronted by the critical younger men who generated a modicum of intellectually creative tension. The most important idea advocated by Sinn Fein during this period was Griffith's doctrine that the cornerstone of Irish independence was 'tariff personality'—based, if necessary, on individual consumer preference.

A third achievement of Sinn Fein, not very highly regarded by separatists and virtually ignored by parliamentarians who continued to stigmatise the movement as physical force, was its technique of non-violent resistance. This was not merely the unrealised theory of Griffith, but an idea which appealed to several thoughtful minds. Robert Lynd was the most articulate exponent of the theory which was defended by George Gavan Duffy in controversy, while Griffith devised the practical programme to put it into action. Even P. S. O'Hegarty was converted after 1916.

Finally, the very fervour and virulence of early Sinn Fein propaganda helped to revolutionise a significant minority of young Irishmen who were indoctrinated with a passionate desire for political liberty. Many inferiority complexes, fostered by Ireland's long dependency and frustration, were burnt out by Griffith's flaming invective. To be assured that he was worthy of freedom, while the Anglo-Saxon was fit only for slavery, was an original but not unwelcome experience for the Irishman. No critic ever denied Griffith's effectiveness as a propagandist; a whole nationalist generation was indebted to his intellect. Even after the 1916 Rising, as the files of *Nationality* demonstrate, Griffith continued to urge his old programme in its entirety. There were frequent references to Hungary, Parnell, List and even Grattan. The Sinn Fein election victory of 1918 was celebrated by a republication of Griffith's editorial on Dolan's 1908 defeat.

Sinn Fein had suffered the worst of its misfortunes in reaching its lowest ebb in 1916. Ill-luck and some errors of judgment lay in the past, partial success in the future. The massive structure of the parliamentary party which then dominated the Irish scene, was soon to crumble to dust, leaving its despised rival room to construct a flawed but more enduring edifice. But the building might well have been stronger had it incorporated, instead of rejecting, some of Griffith's most significant proposals. Perhaps, as Davitt suggested at the inception of the movement, Sinn Fein asked too much of human nature. If so, Griffith was in good company. Mahatma Gandhi made even greater claims on the integrity of the average Indian, and like Griffith, lived to see his beloved fatherland partitioned with bloodshed. Even if Gandhi's non-violence delayed Indian independence for a generation,[8] the Mahatma would have considered the time well spent had it helped to improve the character of the Indian people.[9] In the modern world nationalism, as Tolstoi, Gandhi and even Arthur Griffith on occasions perceived, can only be justified when it leads to a higher objective, the brotherhood of man.

EPILOGUE

Calculated violence in the Anglo-Irish War and after

It was ironical that Griffith, for a considerable part of the Anglo-Irish War, found himself nominally presiding over the application of Hobson's policy, while the latter was excluded from all influence in the movement. This book would be incomplete without some attempt to survey the ideas thrown up by successful Irish guerilla leaders who have stimulated revolutionaries in other countries. Books like Robert Taber's *War of the Flea*[1] have tried to generalise from experience in many countries, but have often neglected the illuminating memoirs of three key officers of the IRA, Dan Breen,[2] Ernie O'Malley[3] and Tom Barry.[4] Griffith's relations with these officers were not close. Contemporary readers of Gandhi's *Young India* were left in no doubt about the Mahatma's critical attitude to Irish violence.[5] But what was the case for physical force in the Anglo-Irish War from the viewpoint of its protagonists?

In the absence of memoirs by Michael Collins the accounts of Breen, O'Malley and Barry together give considerable insight into the tactics adopted by the Irish revolutionaries and their bearing on modern problems. As Taber says, the British showed in Cyprus that they had learnt nothing from their experiences in the war of Irish independence.[6] Meanwhile the modern IRA consciously borrows tactics from the Cypriot General Grivas, himself perhaps influenced by Tom Barry.[7] It appears that the lessons of history are more readily appreciated by revolutionaries than by the forces of counter-insurgency.

The Irish rebellions of 1798, 1848 and 1867 made relatively little contribution to the theory of revolution except to illustrate the fact that a rebellion may be totally crushed but live on as a mythology which can subsequently be utilised by more determined revolutionaries. It is, however, interesting to note that Wolfe Tone, who tried unsuccessfully in 1798 to provide liaison between the forces of the French Revolution and the Irish insurrection, made some scattered suggestions for a type of guerilla warfare bearing some resemblance to the much-vaunted thoughts of Chairman Mao. The Irish rebels, said Tone, should avoid pitched battles and towns till they had built up solid support in country areas. Then they should attempt to hold a strong provincial centre and use it as a base for attacking the capital.[8] After the failure of the rebellion, Joseph Holt and Michael Dwyer adopted these tactics on a small scale.[9] Other unsuccessful Irish 19th-century insurgents suggested similar methods which they were unable to effect in practice.

The Irish insurrection of 1916, involving in different ways Breen, O'Malley and Barry, appeared at first sight another total failure in dislodging British control of Ireland. Yet by 1922 British troops had retired from all but the six north-eastern counties of Ireland.

Of the three future guerilla leaders, Dan Breen alone was associated with the nationalist movement prior to 1916. He was born in 1894 to a large working-class family in Tipperary, a county with a long history of political and agrarian unrest. Brought up by a widowed mother, Breen was influenced by a nationalist schoolmaster but started work at odd jobs when fourteen. Eventually he became a railway linesman. He joined the Irish volunteers when they were formed in his district and also the secret IRB. Associated with Sean Treacy, another legendary figure of the revolution, Breen was one of a small minority of Irish volunteers in the district who refused to support the War. Bitterly disappointed at the failure of the 1916 Rising to extend to the country, Breen and Treacy were determined not to miss a future opportunity for striking a blow against Britain.

By 1916, however, neither Tom Barry nor Ernie O'Malley had made contact with Irish nationalism. Barry heard of the Rising when serving with the British army in Mesopotamia. Hailing from the West Cork area, Barry, four years younger than Breen, came from a similar background. Unlike Breen, however, he had no knowledge of Irish nationalism and joined the British army to see the world and experience war. The 1916 Rising, when he heard of it, made a considerable, if delayed, impression on him. When Barry returned to Ireland in February 1919, the Anglo-Irish War had already begun and an ex-British soldier with four years' experience was a godsend to the insurgent cause.

The 1916 Rising also decisively influenced Ernie O'Malley. In background O'Malley was very different from Breen and Barry. He came from an affluent Mayo Catholic family which later moved to Dublin. His early years brought him velvet suits, a succession of governesses and a familiarity with the local gentry, both Catholic and Protestant. The O'Malley family was completely pro-British and first contact with Irish traditions came from a nanny. When the 1916 Rising took place O'Malley, then a medical student in

Dublin, was toying with the idea of following in the steps of his elder brother, a British army officer. In the first days of the insurrection Ernie was torn between the conflicting suggestions that he join the loyalists in the defence of pro-British Trinity College or that he engage in some distant sniping at British forces. After deciding in favour of the latter, O'Malley, unknown to his parents, joined the post-Rising Irish volunteers and read methodically the basic texts of Irish nationalism, such as the writings of Wolfe Tone and Fintan Lalor.

If Tom Barry's chief value to the movement was his military experience, O'Malley's ability, in his brother's uniform, to impersonate a British officer and buy much needed arms, helps to explain why he was chosen by the Dublin volunteer headquarters to act as their organising agent in the country in 1918. As he himself admits, and as the more practical Tom Barry complained,[10] O'Malley was at the outset a very bookish soldier, always conscious of the background difference, which he hoped to transcend, between himself and his men. *On Another Man's Wound* is self-conscious, literary and introspective. It abounds in descriptive purple passages. In the middle of a gun-fight O'Malley is aware of the 'strong sweet smell from the clover'. On two occasions he admits his inability to shoot down an enemy within easy range. Eventually, however, as divisional commander, he orders the reprisal execution, which he describes in detail, of three British officers. O'Malley was the only one of these three leaders to be captured by the British. His description of the torture of prisoners by the British[11] would now appear commonplace to demonstrators and militant radicals in many countries.

General Tom Barry, who wrote even later (1949) after the Anglo-Irish War than O'Malley (1936) has a style in marked contrast to his brother officer whom he quotes without approval. The two men appear to have clashed on the occasion of their only meeting during the Anglo-Irish War. In Barry's book there are no references to Dostoyevski, the *Mahabharata*, Villon, and no descriptions of dangerous but romantic journeys to visit the burial places of heroes of the ancient Irish epic, the *Tain Bo Cuailnge*. Instead Barry concentrates on the guerilla strategy and tactics of his command which operated almost entirely within his native area of West Cork. *Guerilla Days in Ireland* contains a number of detailed explanations for military decisions which may be based on notes made at the time. His chief concern is the correctness of his decisions and the responsibility for the lives of his men.

Dan Breen, whose book, *My Fight for Irish Freedom,* was published first in 1924, is more of a swashbuckler than either Barry or O'Malley. As befits the man credited, not very accurately, with opening the campaign of violence at the Soloheadbeg ambush of January 1919 when two members of the Royal Irish Constabulary were shot, Breen is particularly aware how dramatic, if gory, incidents can stir up a hitherto apathetic population.[12] He demonstrates effectively how the men of Soloheadbeg began as pariahs but ended as heroes, able to command the motor cars and houses of most Irish Catholics. Breen operated in both South Tipperary and Dublin. Throughout his book he shows hostility to the political leaders of the movement who disliked violence.[13] He respected both O'Malley, with whom he co-operated in several attacks on police barracks in Tipperary, and Tom Barry, though he hardly knew the latter. In the end Breen, Barry and O'Malley took the anti-Treaty side in the Irish Civil War. All appear to have been largely motivated by the resentment of soldiers in the field against politicians at the capital who had consistently let them down. All disliked the new conflict and none gives any serious account of it.

Their resentment against politicians was symptomatic of the tension between the political and military wings of the movement. Griffith, who had favoured non-violence and a settlement with Britain short of independence, was deputy leader of the government, and during de Valera's long absence in America in 1919 and 1920, the nominal head of state. Barry's memoirs have little to say about Griffith, but Breen, without mentioning names, complains that certain political elements were consistently opposed to an aggressive policy.[14] He is, however, not entirely fair in his assertion that Dail Eireann never accepted responsibility for the actions of the IRA.[15] O'Malley does mention Griffith by name as an opponent of force and doubtful in his separatism. He also deplores his influence on Collins.[16] Griffith, who apparently succeeded in preventing certain violent IRA projects,[17] played Archbishop Makarios to Breen's General Grivas in Cyprus. The exact number of political Sinn Feiners opposed to violence is uncertain but contemporary discussion indicates that it was considerable.*

Michael Collins, the best-known figure in the Irish revolution, should have been well placed to integrate the political and military wings of the movement. Not only was he a member of the Dail but in addition minister of finance in the Irish government. He also controlled the Irish volunteers who had an executive independent of the Dail. Cycling daily to his office in a business suit, Collins ran a ruthless system of intelligence which penetrated the very heart of Dublin Castle, the nerve centre of British administration in Ireland. He organised the systematic elimination of those detectives who knew the Irish leaders personally. As a result, neither Collins

---

*In 1920, Sir John Anderson ordered that Griffith and the moderates should be left unmolested.

nor any other member of the volunteer headquarters staff was ever arrested by the British who were compelled increasingly to rely blindly on raids of buildings based on occasional tip-offs from a decreasing number of informers.

Outside Dublin Collins's touch was less certain. Communication with volunteer, or IRA, units in the country was extremely hazardous as British forces frequently searched trains and stopped cars. Barry, recognising this fact, nevertheless regretted that Collins and the other headquarters men never visited his area.[18] O'Malley, whose duty it was to make the liaison, was also critical of this failure, especially on the occasion when Collins and the chief-of-staff, Richard Mulcahy, ridiculed President de Valera's ignorance of the Irish military situation.[19] Tom Barry, who once visited Dublin for briefing, was compelled to travel disguised as a tubercular medical student and evaded arrest only by the skin of his teeth. As a guerilla leader accustomed to dealing with the enemy at gun point, Barry resented Collins's sneer that he was 'a windy beggar' after the latter had, by acting drunk, casually bluffed his way past a British road block.[20] The country guerillas also complained of the inability of Dublin to supply them with sufficient arms and ammunition. Ultimately, Collins aligned with Griffith in signing the Treaty. Though they disliked his caustic tongue and opposed him in the Civil War, Barry, Breen and O'Malley all venerated Collins as a national leader.

Before analysing their contributions to the theory and practice of guerilla warfare the main actions of the three leaders can be summarised. O'Malley's work as organiser of country volunteer units began in 1918 and was briefly interrupted by the general election which enabled the IRA to assert itself as the military arm of a lawfully constituted government. O'Malley was active in Coalisland, Offaly, South Roscommon, Clare, Donegal and North Dublin. Sometimes he traded a few inaccurate shots with the police. Generally he found his duties difficult. It was often hard to instill fighting spirit into nominal volunteers whose leaders were totally averse from the necessary paper-work but prepared to falsify enrolment figures. The older men who maintained a despotic regime over their sons were not sympathetic to the movement. Above all, O'Malley found it difficult to transcend his upper-class background when dealing with country folk. There were some mitigating features. The clergy with their puritanical ways encouraged young men to join the volunteers as a diversion. In spite of his notorious localism the Irish countryman showed considerable fighting spirit when roused from his lethargy by some successful exploit. O'Malley nevertheless gained a reputation for being a slave-driver.[21]

Reacting against the attacks on the regular, if militarised, Royal

Irish Constabulary (RIC), the British government increased the troop build-up and recruited additional police from hard-bitten ex-soldiers in England. The arrival of the unruly 'Black-and-Tans' in March and the Auxiliaries, a body of ex-officers, in July 1920, intensified the struggle. O'Malley was sent to Tipperary where he participated in a number of attacks on police barracks alongside Breen, Sean Treacy and their commandant, Seamus Robinson. Breen's narrative overlaps with O'Malley's at this point. After a period in County Cork, O'Malley was sent to Kilkenny, where the IRA was feeble, in an attempt to capture the Auxiliary headquarters at Inistioge. Instead, O'Malley was himself tamely arrested in his billet and remained in captivity till his escape from Kilmainham gaol in February 1921. His last assignment before the Truce was command of the new second southern division which was an attempt to centralise the brigades in Limerick, Tipperary, Kilkenny and Waterford. Tom Barry, believing that a brigade was the natural unit for guerilla warfare, considered this development premature,[22] and O'Malley himself admitted that it was difficult to build up divisional loyalty. He was also handicapped as an outsider without experience as commander of a local brigade.[23]

Dan Breen's activity in the Anglo-Irish War is more quickly summarised. The Soloheadbeg ambush, in which he participated with Treacy and Robinson, not only forced the group onto the run but greatly embarrassed the political leadership—probably led by Griffith—which attempted to persuade these activists to emigrate.[24] The daring rescue of Sean Hogan at the railway station of Knocklong resulted in the death of two more policemen. Breen and Treacy then appear to have been used by Collins in Dublin in the elimination of the 'G' division detectives. Breen participated in the unsuccessful attempt to assassinate the viceroy, Lord French, at Ashtown and then returned with his friends to Tipperary where the third brigade carried out a number of successful attacks on police barracks. Back in Dublin, Breen and Treacy escaped a raiding party which attempted to arrest them at 'Fernside', the house of a sympathiser. It has been argued, not very convincingly, that Breen's account of a gun battle with numerous soldiers, many of whom he killed, is exaggerated.[25] Soon afterwards while Breen was recovering in hospital, Sean Treacy was cornered and shot dead in a Dublin street after despatching two of his attackers. Breen seems to have spent much of the remaining period before the Truce with the brigade in Tipperary which was now supplied not only with dugouts but motor transport.

Tom Barry's exploits were on a grander scale. Barry approached a local volunteer leader in Bandon, County Cork, in mid-1919 and was put on to intelligence work against the British. In May 1920 he was asked, as a result of his British army experience, to organise the training of the West Cork brigade. Shortage of arms and the total inexperience of most volunteers encouraged Barry to arrange a series of week-long training courses at different locations in the brigade area. Only officers could be put through, but these were to pass their training on to the men. The courses were nothing if not practical. The first lesson taught defensive precautions against surprise by the British. The course ended with an attempt to ambush a British unit before the precious rifles were handed over to the new trainees. Barry believed that after his intensive course the men were capable of engaging regular troops from any army in the world.

Barry was appointed to command the brigade flying column, formed on the instruction of headquarters. The training camps, through which 150 men eventually passed, became instant flying columns which could remain for relatively long periods in action against the British. Most of the volunteers retained their normal jobs and acted in an auxiliary role only.

In November 1920 Barry achieved a legendary success which was also a copybook exercise in guerilla warfare. For some time the new British Auxiliaries had terrorised the district and created an aura of invincibility. At Kilmichael Barry's column ambushed and totally wiped out two lorries containing eighteen Auxiliaries and captured their rifles, thirty revolvers and a considerable amount of ammunition. After the battle, which cost the lives of three members of a column of thirty-six, Barry put the somewhat shaken volunteers through five minutes of brisk arms drill.[26] In the next months Barry fought a number of similar short engagements. Barracks were attacked and sometimes destroyed, the pro-British town of Skibbereen was held up, and the efforts of increasingly large British forces to surround IRA units were easily evaded. One of the most impressive break-outs occurred at Crossbarry in March 1921 when Barry's column of 104 men, stimulated by the music of bagpipes, aggressively fought their way out of a trap against forces outnumbering them three to one on the spot. British tactics in this instance recall the 'oil slick' techniques used in Vietnam and elsewhere to flush out guerillas by extending lines of regulars from a series of strong points. It has, however, been caclulated that one guerilla can account for ten to a hundred regulars in such a campaign.

Did Breen, Barry and O'Malley contribute significantly to the theory of guerilla warfare? Taber considers the Irish terrain, a word regarded as pretentious by Barry, to have been ideal for guerilla fighting. The small scale of operations, and the fact that the IRA was fighting a political war, greatly assisted by Black-and-Tan atrocities, ensured the success of the Irish cause even though there was little novelty in the tactics used by the guerillas.[27] Professor

Hayes-McCoy suggests that Irish guerilla tactics in 1919–21 recapitulated the use of the Irish countryside by Hugh O'Neill's war against Queen Elizabeth, and numerous other examples in the not-so-distant past.[28]

The interest aroused by Mao,[29] Che Guevara[30] and others has made the basic ideas thrown up by guerilla struggles relatively familiar. A guerilla, we hear, is a fish swimming in the sea of the population. By converting the masses to his political objectives he becomes unassailable against the forces of counter-revolution whose contradictions he is able to exploit. The chief contradiction is the inability of the guerilla's opponents to deal with him without further alienating the general population. Guerilla groups are small and mobile, making sallies from remote provinces where they have plenty of cover rather than concentrating on major cities or attempting to hold clearly-defined areas. Major engagements are avoided but pressure on the foe is continuous. Mao particularly recommends short engagements of five minutes. Above all, as Taber, following Tom Barry, insists, the guerilla wins by continuing to exist.[31] Arms must be obtained from the enemy. Warfare is learnt through warfare. The guerilla forces are like a net, spread out to take in the people, drawn in to concentrate and destroy the enemy.

Mao's three stages of revolutionary war help to explain some of the complexities of the Irish Revolution. Strategic defence is guerilla warfare proper. In this first stage, 'territory is nothing, attrition everything'. The second stage is an equilibrium of power where the guerillas control certain liberated areas but cannot destroy the enemy in its strongholds. Finally, comes the strategic offensive when the guerillas have increased their strength to divisional level and can conclude the war by pitched battles against regular forces.

Much of the confusion involved in waging and interpreting the Anglo-Irish War appears to lie in a misunderstanding of the stages of popular war which are in fact based on ordinary commonsense. The 1916 Rising failed because it was a city-based insurrection which anticipated the stage of strategic offensive. Similarly, the attempt, criticised as futile by Tom Barry, to organise Irish armed divisions before the Truce was based on a similar misunderstanding of the existing progress of revolutionary conflict. This was less excusable in view of the fact that Fintan Lalor in the late 1840s had explained carefully the need for a graduated development from passive resistance to guerilla warfare before anything like a pitched battle could be attempted. Like Che Guevara, Lalor believed that the peasant should be revolutionised by land distribution. The British land acts after 1903 had somewhat weakened the agrarian potential of Ireland. Barry suggests, however, that his brigade, by billeting in the houses of large landowners, burning them as reprisals, and confiscating for redistribution the lands of wealthy informers, began the levelling process.[32] O'Malley was well-read in Lalor's ideas which should have been generally known by the Irish leaders. All through the Anglo-Irish War period, however, there appears to have been an unrealistic belief in the possibility of a simultaneous rising of the whole people leading to a pitched battle. As late as 1918, Breen's associate, Sean Treacy, expected a war of pikes and trenches.[33] Only gradually, according to O'Malley, did the volunteer headquarters accept the need for a series of small engagements.[34] The belief that Collins signed the Treaty because he believed that the IRA was finished, indicates that the Irish leader may not himself have been fully aware of the potential of guerilla war. When in mid-1921 Tom Barry told a sceptical de Valera that the IRA could last another five years[35] he showed a confidence that has been partially justified by experience in other countries.

Apart from the attempt to foist a premature divisional structure on the IRA brigade system, there were three other factors obscuring the essential guerilla development of Ireland. One was the dependence of many units on Dublin for arms. When he asked an ineffectual unit with characteristic acerbity, 'What the hell does a lot of lousers like you want arms for?'[36] Michael Collins unconsciously underlined the lesson that good brigades captured their own weapons from the enemy. Yet right up to the Truce there were grandiose plans for buying arms, to be landed in Barry's area from abroad. Had the war continued, increased British troops spread over even wider areas would surely have provided even more opportunities for seizure of arms and equipment. As Grivas pointed out in Cyprus, numbers have little meaning in guerilla warfare where the counter-revolutionary forces soon reach saturation point.[37]

Another problem was the extreme localism, clearly brought out by O'Malley, of the Irish countryman. It is surprising to find that Barry's brigade was, in spite of its leader, mainly restricted to its own area of West Cork and that an attempt to find billets in the next division was criticised as poaching by the local IRA commandant.[38] When under extreme pressure, Barry considered withdrawal over a wider area, and had the war continued it would have been necessary to move further afield, especially as there were many counties where the IRA was too inactive to take the pressure off West Cork. It is obvious, however, that outside their home localities, flying columns would have operated with uncertain knowledge of the terrain and might have been less popular with the surrounding populations.

A third difficulty lay in the desire of Irish leaders like Griffith to slow down militancy in some areas in the hope that the political organs of passive resistance would have a chance to develop.[39] In the immediate military context Griffith was probably wrong, but if he was thinking of the ultimate conciliation of Protestant Ulster, he may well have been right.

Such considerations lead to the vital question of the Irish guerilla's ability, in Mao's words, to swim like a fish in the sea. Here Breen's experience was perhaps the most illuminating. The Soloheadbeg ambush may have been a blow acting as a 'catalyst'[40] and in line with the dictum of Lalor—whom O'Malley says was often quoted at the time—'Somewhere, somehow, and by someone a beginning must be made'.[41] Compare with Mao's 'one spark can light a prairie fire'. But Breen and his friends were originally shunned by former allies and sometimes other volunteers. They were refused shelter even in the outhouses of apparently reliable nationalists. Nevertheless, the fact that no one was prepared to play the informer indicates the existence of revolutionary potential which could be stimulated by the continued aggressiveness of a very small number of determined men. As Che Guevara, whose mother was a Lynch,[42] and Regis Debray have pointed out in opposition to Mao, it is not necessary to wait till all the conditions required by revolution are present; they can be created. Breen was particularly alive to the importance of spectacular, if unsuccessful, action. The attempted assassination of the viceroy at Ashtown was, he believed, the turning point:

The people were beginning to appraise the situation. In private many defended our standpoint. The great majority of our countrymen were taking their bearings. Some of them were shocked at the daring force-tactics, but it was becoming obvious to all that we meant business and that it was their duty to stand by us.[43]

The death of Martin Savage in the attempt provided the spectacular funeral which always has an enormous effect on Irish opinion. But even more important was the arrival of the Black-and-Tans in March 1920, a little more than two months after the Ashtown affray. As Breen realised, 'the frightfulness of the Tans proved to be a boomerang against those who had cast it'.[44] As in Ulster today, the use of soldiers to do police work always antagonises the population, especially when they resort to indiscriminate ruthlessness.[45] Breen was quickly proved correct in his suggestion to Sean Treacy that 'if the fight for freedom were once started, the whole country would rally to our cause'.[46] According to Breen, the reluctant headquarters staff of the volunteers was compelled to follow the more aggressive members of the rank and file. Barry, however, is less critical of the volunteer higher command which he maintains never acted to impede the aggression of local units.[47]

The experience of Barry and O'Malley confirms that of Breen. All were perfectly aware of the need to win the total loyalty of the civilian population. Barry was careful when he ordered the destruction of a road bridge or the cutting of a road to provide an alternative route suitable for a horse and cart but not an armed lorry. Because 'the ordinary people were the bastion' on which the movement was built he did not blow up railway lines whose destruction would have had military advantages but would also have created shortages and unemployment. In a real crisis he admits that this would have been done. Barry nevertheless recalls that in 1921 he was sufficiently immature to question the emphasis President de Valera placed on the feelings of the people and their response to increased British terrorism and economic pressure.[48] In the Irish Civil War, which Barry tried to bring to an earlier end, the anti-Treaty forces were less solicitous of public opinion.

There was, however, a darker side to the problem of public acquiescence. Like other revolutionaries the Irish guerillas used terrorism against spies and informers and shot prisoners in reprisal for IRA men executed by the British. Barry, Breen and O'Malley devote considerable space to justifying these actions which provided propagandist ammunition for the British government and shocked otherwise sympathetic observers like Gandhi. Today such terrorism appears, apart from Mao's movement in China, an indispensable aspect of guerilla warfare, adopted by EOKA in Cyprus, the Vietcong and numerous other revolutionary movements. Since the Anglo-Irish War, where the British used only occasional observer planes (one of which was burnt by the IRA), the utilisation of bombers dropping everything from nuclear bombs to napalm on civilian populations makes it more difficult to draw a moral distinction between the means adopted by established governments and their revolutionary opponents. Taber and others argue that terrorism is relatively selective.[49] The critical Brian Crozier admits that 'terrorism directed solely against the occupying power can be devastatingly effective'.[50] Certainly Barry, Breen and O'Malley deny the execution of any but British troops (as definite reprisals) or active spies and informers on their behalf. Normally, captured soldiers were well treated and released. The Irish leaders would have been in general agreement with Che Guevara who, though opposing indiscriminate terrorism and the elimination of unimportant enemies, believed assassination effective against notorious foes.[51]

It is obvious from the preceding account that those Irish revolutionary leaders in the 1919–21 period who reflected on their practical experience were fully aware of the principles later popularised by writers and practical revolutionaries like Mao and Che Guevara. Though Barry's book was not published till 1949 and may have been partially influenced in its construction by subsequent events elsewhere, the Irish revolution and its writings had an immediate effect on revolutionaries in other countries. In India, Nehru and Gandhi, who apparently met Dan Breen in 1931,[52] discussed Irish tactics in the 1920s; revolutionaries in Morocco tried to enlist the services of both Breen and his Auxiliary opponents;[53] in Israel leaders of the Irgun and Stern group studied Irish revolutionary writings.[54] There is, as O'Malley recognised when he heard the headquarters staff discussing Clausewitz and guerilla precedents from Cuba and the Boer War, a limit to the use of analogies from other countries,[55] especially when the theorists have little communication with the areas of greatest activity. However, modern developments would have demonstrated to O'Malley that lack of arms should not necessarily inhibit the guerilla, and would surely have inspired the Irish revolutionary movement with greater confidence in its ability to hold out indefinitely against Britain. Treaty negotiators like Michael Collins might have been more sceptical about Lloyd George's ultimatum backed by an immediate and terrible war; and the Irish Civil War might have been avoided if its opponents had realised the impossibility of again 'swimming in the sea' of the general population as the united movement had so successfully done.

What relevance have 1919–21 precedents to the present revolutionary situation in Ulster? Both wings of the modern IRA are well versed in both the writings of the Anglo-Irish War and more recent examples of guerilla activity. Many aspects of conflict in northern Ireland repeat the lessons of the past. The IRA guerillas are able to swim in the sea of the Catholic population, both sides of the border. The shooting of British soldiers and some of the bomb explosions recall the early activities of Dan Breen and Sean Treacy which, though unpopular at first, were subsequently accepted by the general population. The reaction of the British troops and their deliberate efforts to quell opposition by calculated ruthlessness are too obviously reminiscent of the Black-and-Tans to require further comment. The Derry massacre of January 1972 suggests that Britain has learnt little from her widespread experience in wars of colonial liberation. The fortuitous abolition of the death penalty in Britain has saved the government from even grosser errors. Again, the IRA has been able to exploit the contradictions of the British government, unable to avoid the appearance in Catholic eyes of being simply the agent of the repressive Protestant ascendancy.[56]

Allowing for these obvious similarities, there are, however, some very obvious contrasts between Ulster in the 1970s and the 1919–21 situation. To apply Mao's metaphor,* in the six counties of northern Ireland the IRA guerilla must swim in a solution consisting of two parts of Protestant oil to one of Catholic water. Barry, Breen and

*As Conor Cruise O'Brien has effectively done in *States of Ireland*, London, 1972.

O'Malley operated mainly in areas where Protestants were a small minority, and their writings show clearly the polarisation of the two communities. Though in 1919–21 the IRA was fighting for a secular republic, based on the ideas of eminent Protestant nationalists in the past, and though it was prepared to defy the Catholic bishop of Cork who attempted to excommunicate the guerillas, many Protestants in the south appear to have genuinely feared for their religion. Barry, who in childhood had considered it no sin to steal from a Protestant, blamed British divide-and-rule tactics. He rightly judged it useless to inform a Protestant, condemned to death for espionage by the IRA but justifying his actions on religious grounds, of the many Protestant nationalists venerated by the Republicans.[57] A similar polarisation of communities in Ulster today explains why the IRA will only be able to swim in a third of the sea while very different organisms will occupy the oily remainder. This alone suggests that the original non-violence of the Civil Rights movement, which has many parallels with Griffith's early Sinn Fein, might still be the best policy.

The communal divisions of Ulster inhibit guerilla action in other ways. In previous campaigns the IRA was able to follow, albeit unsuccessfully, the standard policy of avoiding the main cities and striking rapidly in country areas. Inability to relieve pressure on Catholics threatened by Protestants in Belfast and Derry split the IRA. The new provisionals, rejecting the less violent but socially more radical policies of the officials, were committed to the defence of the static 'no go' areas in the major cities of Belfast and Derry. The ease with which the barricades were removed by British troops indicates the failure of their policy. The IRA faces its own contradictions and time alone will decide the outcome. The indiscriminate bomb campaign by hitting friend and foe alike is a measure of the difficulty of guerilla tactics in a divided community. These tactics would probably have been rejected by Breen, Barry and O'Malley, not to mention Che Guevara. Though it will probably prove impossible to destroy the IRA completely, especially if the British continue to repeat all their old errors, lasting peace is unlikely to come to the area before the advent of a new type of fish, able to swim in both Catholic water and Orange oil.

In spite of all his weaknesses, Arthur Griffith had a positive and sympathetic approach to the problems of his aggressively unionist fellow-countrymen. It may well be time for Irish nationalists to give him his proper place in tradition and think seriously about his non-violent answer to the reconciliation of Irish races and creeds. Irish nationalists in Ulster might reflect on the words of Mahatma Gandhi, probably more relevant to the Irish situation today than they were to that of 1920. The Mahatma did not counsel acceptance of oppression but offered an active and courageous method of reconciling hitherto antagonistic groups upon whose unity depends the future greatness of Ireland:

We can if we will, refrain, in our impatience, from bending the wrong-doer to our will by physical force as Sinn Feiners are doing today. . . . The purer the suffering the greater the progress. Hence did the sacrifice of Jesus suffice to free a suffering world.[58]

Throughout the world force appears to have obtained its objectives with expedition, but subsequent generations may discover that such heroic achievements were from the outset dangerously flawed.

Appendix:
Sinn Fein executive members

1905–6:

President:	E. Martyn
Vice-Presidents:	J. Sweetman and A. Griffith
Hon. Secretaries:	W. L. Cole and M. O'Hanrahan
Hon. Treasurers:	M. J. Lord and P. O'Carroll
(Various committees).	

1906:

President:	E. Martyn
Vice-Presidents:	J. Sweetman and A. Griffith
Hon. Secretaries:	W. L. Cole and M. O'Hanrahan
Hon. Treasurers:	P. O'Carroll and T. J. Sheehan

Resident

Mrs. Wyse Power
Miss M. Murphy
Miss Macken
Ald. T. Kelly
P. T. Daly, TC
J. J. Reynolds, TC
S. T. O'Kelly, TC
Henry Dixon
J. P. Kenny
W. E. Shackleton
T. S. Cuffe
P. Hughes.

Non-Resident

S. MacManus (Donegal)
P. O'Flaherty (Galway)
Fr. W. Harpur, CC (Wexford)
P. S. O'Hegarty (London)
W. Roche (Cork)
Fr. M. O'Connolly (Ballaghadereen)
B. Hobson (Belfast)
Patrick Hughes (Dundalk)
Jas. Wood (Castlebar)
Richard Bonner (Derry)
Thomas Martin (London)

1907:

President:	E. Martyn
Vice-Presidents:	A. Griffith and J. Sweetman
Hon. Secretaries:	W. L. Cole and S. T. O'Kelly
Hon. Treasurers:	P. O'Carroll and T. J. Sheehan

Resident	*Non-Resident*
T. Kelly	Fr. O'Connolly (Ballaghadereen)
P. T. Daly	Fr. W. Harpur (Wexford)
T. S. Cuffe	Fr. L. Kieran, PP (Monaghan)
D. O'Healy	Jas. Wood, DC (Castlebar)
W. O'Leary Curtis	Jas. O'Flaherty, DC (Loughrea)
R. C. Bonner	P. S. O'Hegarty (London)
W. E. Shackleton	B. Hobson (Belfast)
P. Hughes	P. Hughes, DC (Dundalk)
S. Deakin	S. MacManus (Donegal)
Mrs. Wyse Power	R. Brennan (Wexford)
M. J. Lord	Eamon O'Neill, UDL (Kinsale)
Miss Macken	T. Martin (London)

1908:

President:	J. Sweetman
Vice-Presidents:	A. Griffith and B. Hobson
Hon. Secretaries:	S. T. O'Kelly and W. L. Cole
Hon. Treasurers:	J. A. Deakin and Mrs. Wyse Power

Resident	*Non-Resident*
T. Kelly	J. O'Flaherty
P. T. Daly	Fr. W. Harpur
S. Milroy	C. J. Dolan
F. J. Lawless	W. Sears
Miss M. Murphy	Fr. L. Kieran
H. Holahan	W. Ganly
W. O'L. Curtis	P. Hughes
S. OhIcedha (S. O'Hickey)	Fr. M. O'Connolly
Mrs. M. Moloney	P. S. O'Hegarty
D. O'Healy, TC	D. McCullough
W. E. Shackleton	G. Gavan Duffy
R. C. Bonner	R. Lynd
	S. McManus.

1909:

	(Figures represent votes)
President:	J. Sweetman
Vice-Presidents:	A. Griffith (50) and B. Hobson (29)
Hon. Secretaries:	S. T. O'Kelly (36) and T. S. Cuffe (31)
Hon. Treasurers:	J. A. Deakin and Mrs. Wyse Power

Resident	*Non-Resident*	
T. Kelly (49)	J. O'Flaherty (Galway)	(50)
P. T. Daly (47)	Fr. W. Harpur (Wexford)	(46)
S. Milroy (42)	C. J. Dolan (Leitrim)	(43)
F. J. Lawless (34)	W. Sears (Wexford)	(41)

Resident	*Non-Resident*	
Miss M. Murphy (34)	Fr. L. Kieran (Monaghan)	(40)
H. Holahan (31)	W. Ganly (Longford)	(38)
M. D. Clare (30)	P. Hughes (Louth)	(39)
Geo. McGrath (30)	Fr. M. O'Connolly (Mayo)	(37)
W. L. Cole (28)	P. S. O'Hegarty (London)	(36)
C. de Markievicz (24)	D. McCullough (Antrim)	(35)
D. O'Healy (24)	G. Gavan Duffy (London)	(30)
W. E. Shackleton (22)	Robert Lynd (London)	(29)

1910:

President:	J. Sweetman
Vice-Presidents:	A. Griffith and T. Kelly
Hon. Secretaries:	Mrs. Wyse Power and W. L. Cole
Hon. Treasurers:	P. O'Keeffe and J. Doyle

Resident	*Non-Resident*
S. Milroy	Fr. O'Flannagan
Miss M. Murphy	Fr. L. Kieran
T. S. Cuffe	G. Duffy
C. de Markievicz	J. O'Flaherty
G. McGrath	P. S. O'Hegarty
M. D. Clare	F. Lawless
J. A. Brennan	W. Sears
P. T. Daly	P. Hughes
M. Foley	G. Nicholls
S. L-Eirbhain (S.Irvine)	S. Etchingham
The O'Rahilly	P. Kehoe
C. Murphy.	

1911:

President:	A. Griffith
Vice-Presidents:	Mrs. Wyse Power and T. Kelly
Hon. Secretaries:	Seaghan O Dubhghaill and C. Murphy
Hon. Treasurers:	P. O'Keeffe and P. Morgan

Resident	*Non-Resident*
T. S. Cuffe	P. Hughes (Dundalk)
S. Milroy	J. O'Flaherty (Loughrea)
C. de Markievicz	Fr. Harpur (Campile)
The O'Rahilly	W. Sears (Enniscorthy)
'John Brennan'	Frank Lawless (Swords)
P. S. Breen	Sean Etchingham (Gorey)
Miss Murphy	P. O'Malley (Connemara)
Jas. Doyle	Fr. M. K. O'Connolly (Carracastle)
M. Foley	Fr. M. O'Flanagan (Loughglynn)

Resident	Non-Resident
J. Whelan	P. Kehoe (Riversdale)
S. Irvine	George Nicholls (Galway)
E. Ceannt	

1912:

President:	A. Griffith
Vice-Presidents:	T. Kelly and Mrs. Wyse Power
Hon. Secretaries:	E. Ceannt and T. O'Shea
Hon. Treasurers:	P. Morgan and P. O'Keeffe

Resident	Non-Resident
C. de Markievicz	F. Lawless (Swords)
T. S. Cuffe	P. Hughes (Dundalk)
J. Whelan	W. Sears (Enniscorthy)
P. S. Breenan	J. O'Flaherty (Loughrea)
G. McGrath	P. O'Malley (Connemara)
'John Brennan'	S. Etchingham (Gorey)
S. Milroy	Fr. O'Flanagan (Loughglynn)
Ald. Macken	P. McCann (Cashel)
W. L. Cole	G. Nicholls (Galway)
C. Murphy	Fr. M. K. O'Connolly (Carracastle)
The O'Rahilly	P. Kehoe (Wexford)
J. Doyle	Fr. W. Harpur (Campile).

Under the caption 'Week by Week' the following brief account of the 1917 Sinn Fein convention was published in the issue of *Nationality* for 3 November 1917:

Our space is not adequate to publish a full report of the Sinn Fein Convention, and accordingly it will be separately issued, as rapidly as possible. Under the revised constitution the Governing Body of Sinn Fein will consist of the seven officers and 24 Executive members elected by the Convention, with one representative chosen by the Sinn Fein Branches in each Parliamentary Constituency. The officers and Executive members elected at the Convention last week were as follows: President, Eamon De Valera; Vice-Presidents, Arthur Griffith (1,197 votes), and Father O'Flanagan, C.C. (780); Hon. Treasurers, W. Cosgrave, M.I.P. (537), and Laurence Ginnell, M.I.P. (491); Hon. Secretaries, Austin Stack (857), and Darrell Figgis (510); Executive members, Eoin MacNeill (888), Cathal Brugha (685), Dr. Hayes (674), Sean Milroy (667), Countess Markievicz (617); Count Plunkett, M.I.P. (598); Piaras Beaslai (557); Joseph McGuinness, M.I.P. (501); Finian Lynch (475); Harry Boland (448); Dr. Kathleen Lynn (425); J. J. Walsh (424); Joseph McDonagh (421); Father Matt Ryan, P.P. (416); Father Wall, C.C. (408); Mrs. Thomas Clarke (402); Diarmuid Lynch (390); David Kent (385); Sean T. O'Kelly, T.C. (367); Dr. T. Dillon (364); Mrs. Joseph Plunkett (345); Sean McEntee (342); Ernest Blythe (340); Michael Collins (340).

References

Chapter I. Literary Prelude 1890–1900 PAGES 3–16

1. ALLAN WADE, ed., *The Letters of W. B. Yeats,* London, 1954, p. 193.
2. *United Ireland,* 12 October 1891. Though there were a number of poems on the death of Parnell, Yeats's was placed at the head of the leader column.
3. W. B. YEATS, *The King of the Great Clock Tower,* Dublin, 1934, p. 29.
4. CONOR CRUISE O'BRIEN, 'Passion and Cunning: An Essay on the Politics of W. B. Yeats', in A. N. Jeffares and K. C. W. Cross, *In Excited Reverie: A Centenary Tribute to William B. Yeats, 1865–1939,* London, 1965, pp. 216–20.
5. JOHN O'LEARY, *Some Recollections of Fenians and Fenianism,* London, 1896, p. 2.
6. MARCUS BOURKE, *John O'Leary: A Study in Irish Separatism,* Tralee, 1967, p. 179.
7. *Ibid.,* pp. 180–92.
8. O'BRIEN in Jeffares & Cross, p. 213. See also E. R. R. Green, 'Charles Joseph Kickham and John O'Leary', in T. W. Moody, ed., *The Fenian Movement,* Cork, 1968, p. 88. O'Leary's creed was 'really more suitable for an artist than for a man of action'.
9. ELIZABETH COXHEAD, *Daughters of Erin: Five Women of the Irish Renascence,* London, 1965, p. 19.
10. WADE, *Letters of W. B. Yeats,* pp. 108 and 110.
11. *Ibid.,* p. 165.
12. P. BRADLEY, Introduction to William Rooney, *Poems and Ballads,* Dublin, 1901, XIII–XIX.
13. *Irish Freedom,* Dublin, 15 December 1911.
14. *Ibid.,* November 1910, quoted from Arthur Griffith, Preface to Rooney's *Poems & Ballads,* IX.

15. See Bourke, pp. 200–7.
16. MAUD GONNE MACBRIDE. *A Servant of the Queen*, Dublin, 1950, p. 167. 'The parliamentary party was dead before Parnell, and should have been buried with him.'
17. P. COLUM, *Arthur Griffith*, Dublin, 1959, p. 24.
18. *Sinn Fein*, 7 October 1911.
19. 'Lucan' (P. S. O'Hegarty) in *Irish Freedom*, November 1910.
20. PADRAIG O MUIREAGAIN in *Sinn Fein*, 9 November 1912.
21. Minutes of the Celtic Literary Society, National Library of Ireland, MS 200, p. 1. James Doyle, J. R. Whelan, J. Murphy, J. Clegg, J. Ryan and J. Doran were present.
22. BRADLEY, Introduction to Rooney's *Poems and Ballads*, XX.
23. *Sinn Fein*, 9 November 1912.
24. BRADLEY, XX.
25. Minutes of Celtic Literary Society, p. 2 (3 February 1893).
26. MACBRIDE, *A Servant of the Queen*, p. 89.
27. Celtic Minutes, p. 9.
28. O'LEARY, *Recollections*, p. 30.
29. BRADLEY, XIII.
30. Celtic Minutes, p. 72 (O'Donnell elected 30 November 1894).
31. *United Ireland*, 5 October 1893.
32. *Ibid.*, 28 October 1893.
33. Celtic Minutes, p. 29.
34. G. A. LYONS, *Some Recollections of Griffith and his Times*, Dublin, 1923, p. 3.
35. O MUIREAGAIN, *Sinn Fein*, 9 November 1912.
36. Celtic Minutes, p. 116.
37. COLUM, *Griffith*, p. 32.
38. Rooney's essay on Davis was published for the first time by the *Gaelic American*, 18 January 1908.
39. See *Daily Independent*, 15 December 1893, for full report of debate.
40. Celtic Minutes, p. 21 (30 November 1894).
41. *Ibid.*, p. 131 (25 January 1896).
42. 2 October 1896.
43. YEATS, *Autobiographies*, London, 1956, p. 205.
44. See Diarmuid O Cobhthaigh, *Douglas Hyde*, Dublin, 1917, pp. 39, 45 and 58. Canon Hannay, who according to his own account, obtained the 'undeserved honour' of a place in the central governing board of the Gaelic League, gives some interesting examples in support of his contention 'that there was a great deal that was ridiculous about this enthusiasm for a language which many of the most ardent revival enthusiasts did not know'. See George A. Birmingham (J. O. Hannay), *Pleasant Places*, p. 185, *passim*. Hannay's appoint-

ment was an attempt to maintain the unsectarian character of the League by electing one of the few sympathetic Protestant ministers.

45. A. DENSON, *Letters from AE*, London, 1961, p. 30 (30 August 1898).
46. COXHEAD, *Lady Gregory*, London, 1966, p. 114.
47. *Irish World*, 21 April 1900.
48. *Sinn Fein*, 2 August 1902.
49. *Irish World*, 14 July 1900.
50. EIBHLIN NI MHURCHU, *Siúlach Scéalach*, Dublin, 1968, p. 59.
51. *Irish World*, 11 April, 1908.
52. *Gaelic American*, 20 June 1908.
53. *Sinn Fein*, 23 January 1911. See C. Wittke, *The Irish in America*, Louisiana, 1956, p. 73, and Alice E. Smith, 'The Sweetman Irish Colony', *Minnesota History*, IX (1928).
54. *Gaelic American*, 11 April 1911 (East Wicklow and North Meath). See also *Irish World*, 27 April 1895. F. S. L. Lyons, *The Irish Parliamentary Party, 1890-1910*, London, 1951, p. 49, ft. 1.
55. *Sinn Fein*, 28 January 1911.
56. BOURKE, *John O'Leary*, p. 207, and C. C. O'Brien in Jeffares & Cross, p. 216.
57. G. A. LYONS, *Some Recollections*, p. 7.
58. BOURKE, *O'Leary*, p. 217.
59. WADE, *Yeats's Letters*, p. 289 (to Lady Gregory, 1 November 1897): 'I am afraid Miss Gonne will have a bad time in America. O'Leary has heard from there that the Irish parties, opposed to hers, have been busy circulating the spy story. They have made it most detailed, including machinations against Ireland by an imaginary brother.'
60. *Irish World*, 30 October and 27 November 1897.
61. *Fainne an Lae*, 20 and 27 August 1898.
62. COLUM, *Arthur Griffith*, London, 1959, pp. 45-6.
63. *Irish Freedom*, November 1910, and W. O'Brien and D. Ryan, eds., *Devoy's Postbag*, II, Dublin, 1953, 347 (29 May 1902).
64. G. A. LYONS, p. 7.
65. COLUM, *Griffith*, p. 50.
66. *United Irishman*, Dublin, 4 March 1899.
67. OLIVER ST. JOHN GOGARTY tells the story.
68. BOURKE, *O'Leary*, p 232.
69. *Sinn Fein*, 2 September 1911.
70. WADE, *Yeats's Letters*, p. 304 (to Lady Gregory, 6 November 1898), and see also pp. 421-2 (to Lady Gregory, January 1904).
71. YEATS, *Autobiographies*, p. 416.
72. WADE, *Yeats's Letters*, p. 353 (to Griffith, 16 July 1901).

73. *Irish World*, 2 February 1901.
74 G. A. BIRMINGHAM, *Pleasant Places*, p. 187, T. MacSwiney, *Principles of Freedom*, Dublin, 4th Irish edition, 1964, p. 102.
75. MACBRIDE, *A Servant of the Queen*, p. 278.
76. COXHEAD, *Daughters of Erin*, p. 48.
77. *Irish World*, 28 July 1900.
78. COLUM, *Griffith*, p. 59.
79. WADE, *Yeats's Letters*, p. 338 (to Lady Gregory, 12 April 1900).
80. *Irish World*, 2 February 1901.
81. WADE, *Yeats's Letters*, p. 351 (to Lady Gregory, 21 May 1901).
82. BIRMINGHAM, *Pleasant Places*, pp. 187–8; H. E. Kenny (*Sean-Ghall*) to A. S. Green, 9 May 1915, A. S. Green papers, National Library of Ireland, MS 15082(3) and H. E. Kenny to William Bulfin, 20 January 1907, *William Bulfin Papers*, National Library of Ireland, MS 13810(13).

Chapter II. Sinn Fein United PAGES 17–36
 1. *United Irishman*, 15 March 1900, quoted by P. S. O'Hegarty, *A History of Ireland under the Union*, London, 1952, p. 637.
 2. *United Irishman*, 6 October 1900.
 3. P. S. O'HEGARTY, *Ireland under the Union*, p. 639.
 4. MAUD GONNE MACBRIDE, *A Servant of the Queen*, p. 303.
 5. *United Irishman*, 1 December 1900.
 6. LIAM DE ROISTE in *Cork Evening Echo*, 26 August 1954.
 7. *Ibid.*, 28 August, 1954.
 8. *United Irishman*, 1 November 1902.
 9. *United Irishman*, 22 November 1902, quoted in O'Hegarty, *Ireland under the Union*, p. 642.
10. *United Irishman*, 29 November 1902.
11. ALLAN WADE, *Yeats's Letters*, p. 338 (to *Freeman's Journal*, 20 March 1900 and *Daily Express*, 3 April 1900).
12. G. A. LYONS, *Some Recollections of Griffith and his times*, p. 55. In later editions of *A Servant of the Queen* (earliest 1938), Maud Gonne's description of the scene is expurgated. While Lyons cites Griffith as the prime mover of the affair, Maud Gonne characteristically claims that she was the leader, as the others were shy and unknown. This seems correct. See also *United Irishman*, 23 May 1903.
13. A. DENSON, *Letters from AE*, p. 47 (to W. B. Yeats, May 1903).
14. *United Irishman*, 18 April 1903.
15. *Ibid.*, 30 May 1903.
16. W. B. Yeats, Edmond Martyn, Fr. O'Connolly, Fr. P. F. Kavanagh, Anna Parnell, Liam de Roiste, Dr Mark Ryan, Seamus MacManus, Seamus O'Sullivan and Mrs. Wyse

Power, were members (*United Irishman*, 30 May 1903, and O'Hegarty, *Ireland under the Union*, p. 644).

17. O'HEGARTY, *Ireland under the Union*, p. 644.
18. *United Irishman*, 16 July 1903.
19. *Ibid.*, 8 August 1903.
20. *Ibid.*, 2 July 1904.
21. *Ibid.*, 16 July 1904.
22. *Ibid.*, 23 July 1904, quoted by O'Hegarty in *Ireland under the Union*, p. 648, to illustrate his thesis—largely correct—that Griffith, starting as a physical-force, IRB man was forced by necessity to play the part of Déak and limited his own views.
23. *Irish World*, 12 February 1876.
24. *United Irishman*, 18 March 1905.
25. *United Irishman*, 28 February 1903. See also Mrs. R. M. McEvatt, 'Thomas Martin and the Founding of Sinn Fein', *The Capuchin Annual 1970*, Dublin, pp. 97–113. This article is based on the Thomas Martin letters, MS 15790, included in the *William O'Brien Papers* in the National Library of Ireland. The following have been used in the above narrative:
    T. M. Healy to Martin, 27 July 1904.
    R. D. O'Hart to Martin, 21 July 1904.
    A. Griffith to Martin, n.d. July [1904].
    W. L. Cole to Martin, 29 December 1904.
26. Three men, Collins, Keating and Twohey were present but seem to have played little further part in the movement. The words 'Sinn Fein' were coming into general use, though Maire Butler suggested them to Griffith.
27. *John Sweetman's Papers*, in possession of family, Griffith to Sweetman, no date.
28. W. L. Cole to T. Martin, 29 December 1904, *William O'Brien Papers*, MS 15790.
29. *United Irishman*, 18 March 1905. Not necessarily by branches; individuals might be united by a central body.
30. *Ibid.*, 9 December 1905, containing all the following description.
31. *George Gavan Duffy Papers*, National Library of Ireland. P. S. O'Hegarty to Gavan Duffy, 11 April 1907.
32. *United Irishman*, 2 May 1903.
33. BULMER HOBSON, *Ireland Yesterday and Tomorrow*, Tralee 1968, pp. 1–4.
34. The following direct quotations from Denis McCullough are taken from a statement made to the present writer on 14 October 1957. See also Fr. F. X. Martin, ed., *Leaders and Men of the Easter Rising: Dublin 1916*, London, 1967, pp. 97–9.

35. *Bulmer Hobson Papers*, National Library of Ireland, Minute of Dungannon club.
36. *Ibid.*, 22 March 1905.
37. HOBSON, *Ireland Yesterday and Tomorrow*, pp. 8, 10, 13 and 19
38. HOBSON, *Dungannon Club Manifesto to the Whole People o Ireland*, 1905.
39. HOBSON, *Ireland Yesterday and Tomorrow*, pp. 9, 10, 25–7.
40. *United Irishman*, 21 October 1905.
41. HOBSON, *Ireland Yesterday and Tomorrow*, pp. 8 and 21 Martin, ed., *Leaders and Men*, p. 100, and Dublin Student Dungannon Club, *Manifesto to the Students of Ireland*, Dublin 1906.
42. HOBSON, *Ireland Yesterday and Tomorrow*, pp. 23–4.
43. The Irish national club (a Fenian body watched by Scotlan Yard) was the nucleus of London Cumann na nGaedheal On 28 September 1903 an executive was formed for Londo at Chancery Lane. Michael MacWhite of the national clu was elected president with O'Hegarty secretary. See Mar Ryan, *Fenian Memories*, Dublin, 1945, p. 201.
44. *P. S. O'Hegarty Papers*, report of 1905 Cumann na nGaedhea convention.
45. *Ibid.*, 'Minutes of Dungannon Club (in O'Hegarty's hand 25th April 1906'.
46. MARK RYAN, *Fenian Memories*, p. 205.
47. *P. S. O'Hegarty's Papers*, 'Minutes of London Executiv National Council, 24 October 1906'.
48. *Sinn Fein*, 8 September 1906.
49. *Ibid.*, 7 September 1907.
50. *George Gavan Duffy Papers*, Hobson to Gavan Duffy, 1 May 1906, and see 'Monarchy or Republic', by a convert from unionism in *Sinn Fein*, 18 May 1907.
51. *Peasant*, 13 July 1907.
52. *P. S. O'Hegarty Papers*, 'Minutes of Dungannon Club, 28 September 1906'. In July 1906 O'Sheehan read a paper defending 1782 to the Dungannon club (later published as pamphlet, *Constitutionalism and Sinn Fein* by national counci (*P. S. O'Hegarty Papers*, 'Minutes of Dungannon Club, 15 July 1906').
53. *Ibid.*, 'Minutes of National Council Executive London, 24 October 1906'. Hobson, writing to Gavan Duffy, had been doubtful about the earlier arrangement. 'As to having Griffiths [*sic*] and Cole at the Meeting, I am in your hands— do as you think best—but what if they preach the '82 Renunciation Act etc., and I separation—the only thing which I could honestly advocate—we would not be much good to a

mixed crowd that wants converting. . . .' (*George Gavan Duffy Papers*, Hobson to Gavan Duffy, 23 October 1906).

54. *P. S. O'Hegarty Papers*, 'Minutes of Dungannon Club, 7 December 1906'.

55. *Ibid.*, (Minutes of National Council Executive, London, 7 December 1906. *Ibid.*, 9 January 1907).

56. Its last issue was 16 May 1907, many of its contributors joined the staff of the *Peasant*. It was an expensive production and did not pay its way.

57. Mitchel's words, 'We must have Ireland not for certain peers or nominees of papers in College Green, but Ireland for the Irish', used to head the leader column of the *United Irishman*. When *Sinn Fein* began after Fr. Conor's libel action in 1906 the words were dropped. *Republic*, 20 December 1906.

58. O'HEGARTY, *The Victory of Sinn Fein*, Dublin, 1924, p. 30.

59. *George Gavan Duffy Papers*, O'Hegarty to Gavan Duffy, 5 February 1907.

60. *Ibid.*, O'Hegarty to Gavan Duffy, 10 February 1907.

61. HOBSON, *Ireland Yesterday and Tomorrow*, p. 10.

62. *Sinn Fein*, 2 February 1907.

63. *George Gavan Duffy Papers*, O'Hegarty to Gavan Duffy, 5 February 1907.

64. W. O'BRIEN and D. RYAN, eds., *Devoy's Postbag*, II, 359 (13 June 1908). Griffith was reluctant to leave his paper.

65. *Peasant*, 9 March 1907. *George Gavan Duffy Papers*, O'Hegarty to Gavan Duffy, 9 April 1907.

66. *Ibid.*

67. 1908. See O'Hegarty, *Victory of Sinn Fein*, p. 162.

68. The facts in this paragraph are taken from Denis McCullough's statement to the present writer and Hobson's statement to Bureau of Military History, *Bulmer Hobson Papers*, National Library of Ireland. It will be noted that a class issue was present; Martyn and Sweetman being men of substance and position.

69. *Peasant*, 13 April 1907.

70. *Ibid.*, 27 April 1907. Sean MacDermott became paid secretary. Hobson's minor position might have been due to his absence in America.

71. *Ibid.*, 11 May 1907.

72. *P. S. O'Hegarty Papers*, 'Minutes of Dungannon Club', 26 May 1907.

73. *George Gavan Duffy Papers*, O'Hegarty to Gavan Duffy, 11 April 1907. Three priests and W. E. Shackleton, a prosperous Protestant mill owner in Lucan, were members of the executive.

74. D. McCullough in his statement, shows that the members

of the Sinn Fein league on the Supreme Council IRB gained experience working together and so formed a 'bloc' against the older members.

75. Statement made to present writer, 7 October 1957. There is no reason to doubt its accuracy.

76. *Peasant*, 27 July 1907. Writing to Gavan Duffy, 14 August 1907, Griffith proved over-sanguine: 'Sir Thomas Esmonde's action has been misrepresented in the press. I will win him out all right. Wait a few days.'

77. *P. S. O'Hegarty Papers*, D. McCullough to P. S. O'Hegarty, 9 July 1907.

78. *Sinn Fein*, 17 August 1907. £270 was realised from this source —nearly half the total election fund.

79. *George Gavan Duffy Papers*, O'Hegarty to Gavan Duffy, 22 August 1907. Gavan Duffy did not go over.

80. *Sinn Fein*, 7 September 1907. See constitution adopted in 1907. This states the same compromise though more explicitly: 'That we will not make any voluntary agreement with Great Britain until Great Britain keeps her own compact which she made by the Renunciation Act of 1783', and then quotes it in full.

81. J. O'SHEEHAN, *Constitutionalism and Sinn Fein*, national council pamphlet, 1907, p. 15.

82. *Peasant*, 26 December 1908. See also O'Hegarty, *Ireland under the Union*, p. 652.

83. HOBSON, *Ireland Yesterday and Tomorrow*, p. 12.

84. Dr. Patrick McCartan describes the arguments used in connection with the amalgamation as 'hair splitting'. Letter to present writer, 23 July '57.

85. *Gaelic American*, 7 September 1907.

Chapter III. Redmond Confronted, 1900–14 PAGES 37–58

1. OLIVER ST. J. GOGARTY, *It Isn't this Time of Year at All!* London, 1954, p. 191.

2. These charges were repeated on both sides of the Atlantic. Michael Conway, an ex-Parnellite MP, who became a Sinn Feiner in New York claimed inside information. See *Gaelic American*, 7 September 1907.

3. *Irish Daily Independent*, 27 February 1895, *Irish World*, 16 November 1901.

4. JEFFARES AND CROSS, *In Excited Reverie*, p. 223.

5. *United Irishman*, 25 November, 2 and 9 December 1899.

6. T. M. KETTLE, ed., *Irish Orators and Oratory*, p. 426.

7. *United Irishman*, 17 February 1900.

8. *Freeman's Journal*, 19 February 1900.

9. *United Irishman*, 10 and 17 February 1900.

10. For details see F. S. L. Lyons, *The Irish Parliamentary Party*, p. 88, etc.

11. *Irish World*, 9 March 1901.

12. *United Irishman*, 24 February 1900.

13. *Ibid.*, 17 February 1900.

14. *Ibid.*, 24 February 1900.

15. *Freeman's Journal*, 21 February 1900.

16. *Ibid.*, 21 and 26 February 1900.

17. *Ibid.*, 22 February 1900, and *United Irishman*, 24 February 1900.

18. 27 July 1907.

19. 10 March 1900.

20. *Freeman's Journal*, 1 March 1900.

21. *Irish World*, 9 March 1901, and John MacBride to mother, 13 March 1901, *William O'Brien Papers*, MS 13770, acc. 2512.

22. *Peasant*, 11 May 1907.

23. *United Irishman*, 20 and 27 January 1906.

24. A. S. Green to J. O. Hannay, 1 March 1907, *J. O. Hannay Papers*, no. 394. P. S. O'Hegarty (Sarsfield) reviewing Mrs. Green's *Irish Nationality*, declared, 'By God, this is a book! The best book that has ever been done in English on Irish history'. *Irish Freedom*, 15 June 1911.

25. *Sinn Fein*, 29 June 1909 (Dolan's resignation). *Gaelic American*, 20 July 1907. For analysis of the pledge issue as it affected the parliamentary party see Lyons, *The Irish Parliamentary Party*, pp. 117–20. For Dolan's mental process see Patricia Lavelle, *James O'Mara: A Staunch Sinn Feiner, 1873–1948*, Dublin, 1961, p. 84. P. A. McHugh to John Redmond, 29 and 25 June 1907, *Redmond Papers*, National Library of Ireland, MS 15203(6).

26. *Sinn Fein*, 29 June 1907.

27. *Irish World*, 17 August 1907.

28. *Gaelic American*, 20 July 1907.

29. P. A. McHugh to John Redmond, 1 July 1907, and John Redmond to P. A. McHugh, 2 July 1907 (copy), *Redmond Papers*, MS 15203(6).

30. *Gaelic American*, 20 July 1907 and 14 February 1908.

31. *Ibid.*, 11 April 1908.

32. *Leitrim Guardian*, 2 January 1908, quoted by *Gaelic American*, 25 January 1908.

33. *Gaelic American*, 25 January 1908.

34. *Ibid.*, 25 January 1908.

35. *Ibid.*, 17 August 1907. For James O'Mara, son of the Irish parliamentary party trustee, Stephen O'Mara, see Lavelle,

James O'Mara: A Staunch Sinn Feiner, 1873–1948, pp. 69–9C for North Leitrim.

36. *Gaelic American*, 2 November 1907.
37. *Irish World*, 27 July 1907; *Gaelic American*, 3 August 1907 and 4 January 1908.
38. *Freeman's Journal*, 14 November 1907; *Gaelic American*, 3C November 1907; *Irish World*, 17 August 1907, and F. S. L Lyons, *John Dillon: A Biography*, London, 1968, pp. 23 and 289.
39. *Irish World*, 17 August and 27 July 1907.
40. *Gaelic American*, 31 August 1907.
41. *Ibid.*, 10 August 1909.
42. *Ibid.*, 31 August 1909.
43. *Ibid.*, 24 August 1907, and *Sinn Fein*, 3 August 1907.
44. *Gaelic American*, 14 September 1907.
45. *Ibid.*, 27 July 1907 (Patrick McCartan's report).
46. *Ibid.*, 3 August 1907, report in *Independent*, 3 December 1906.
47. *Ibid.*, 2 March 1907 and 15 August 1908.
48. McHugh to Redmond, 1 July 1907, *Redmond Papers*, MS 15203(6). *Freeman's Journal*, 15, 21 and 22 February 1908. After declaring their freedom from ecclesiastical opinion the parliamentarians then claimed that Mgr. Dolan was on their side.
49. *Gaelic American*, 16 May 1908.
50. *Ibid.*, 19 February 1908.
51. Though the *Freeman's Journal* tended to play down the disorder, there was no real disagreement on the facts of the by election in the *Freeman*, *Sinn Fein* and the unionist *Irish Times*. The *Freeman*, 20 February 1908, for example, admits the presence of the Belfastmen.
52. *Irish Times*, 21 February 1908. Dolan read the telegram at a meeting. As the incident was not referred to by the *Freeman* it appears genuine. For other intercepted telegrams from Meehan to AOH presidents calling for aid, see *Sinn Fein*, 22 February 1908.
53. 17 February 1908.
54. *Irish Times* and *Freeman's Journal*, 18 February 1908. The *Irish Times* claims that there were stones as well as eggs and that the reception accorded to Sinn Fein was not spontaneous but had been carefully prepared beforehand.
55. *Ibid.*, 20 February 1908.
56. *Ibid.*, 21 February 1908.
57. *Ibid.*, 22 February 1908.
58. *Gaelic American*, 7 March 1908.
59. *Irish World*, 28 March 1908.

50. Arthur Griffith, a pencil sketch, 1915

51. Padraig Pearse

52. James Connolly

53. Sean Milroy

54. Eamon Ceannt

55. John Redmo

56. William T. Cosgrave

57. Michael (The) O'Rahilly

58. Eoin MacN

). Arthur Griffith and members of the O'Donovan Rossa funeral committee, Dublin, 1 August 1915. This section from a large group includes Eamon de Valera; and Thomas MacDonagh, Edward Daly, Thomas J. Clarke and Michael O'Hanrahan who were executed in 1916.

60. Arthur Griffith and Desmond Fitzgerald, Dublin, 1918.

61. Arthur Griffith with (from left) J. J. Walsh, Mrs. Griffith and Mrs. Wa
at Croke Park, during the truce, 1921.

Arthur Griffith and Eamon de Valera in London, for de Valera's meeting with Lloyd George, July 1921.

63. Irish plenipotentiaries at Hans Place, London, December 1921 (from left, seated): Arthur Griffith, Eamon Duggan, Michael Collins, and Robert Barton. Standing: Erskine Childers (secretary), George Gavan Duffy and John Chartres (a member of the secretariat).

64. The plenipotentiaries leaving London, on their way to Dublin, December 1921. Gavan Duffy is on the extreme left, Griffith in the centre with Collins on his immediate left.

65. Arthur Griffith arriving at University College, Dublin, for the
Treaty debate, 14 December 1921.

66. Removal of the remains of Arthur Griffith from St. Vincent's private nursing home, 96 Lr. Leeson Street, Dublin, to the City Hall for the lying-in-state, 12 August 1922.

67. At the burial of Arthur Griffith in Glasnevin cemetery, Dublin.

60. *Irish People,* quoted in *Gaelic American,* 4 April 1908.
61. All figures from *Freeman's Journal,* 24 February 1908.
62. 24 February 1908.
63. 21 March 1908. *Irish World,* 30 March and 6 April 1907 (quoting *Leader,* 9 and 16 March and *Freeman's Journal,* 9 March) and *Irish World,* 28 March 1908.
64. *Irish Times,* 24 February 1908. For attempts to head off Meehan, see McHugh to Redmond, 29 June 1907, *Redmond Papers,* 15203(6).
65. *Sinn Fein,* 29 February 1908.
66. *Gaelic American,* 21 March 1908.
67. 29 February 1908.
68. *Irish Times,* 24 February 1908.
69. *Freeman's Journal,* 24 February 1908, and *United Irishman,* 7 January 1905.
70. *Gaelic American,* 28 March 1908 and 1 September 1910.
71. *Ibid.,* 11 April 1908.
72. *Ibid.,* 9 May 1908.
73. *Ibid.,* 4 July and 15 August 1908.
74. DIARMUID O COBHTHAIGH, *Douglas Hyde,* p. 47
75. *Gaelic American,* 27 May and 15 July 1911.
76. A. DENSON, *Letters from AE,* p. 114 (AE to Arthur Balfour, 1 June 1916).
77. *Gaelic American,* 16 July 1910, for an attempt to answer this criticism. See also George's letter to *Nation* quoted in *Irish World,* 5 August 1882.
78. *Irish Nation and Peasant,* 8 October 1910.
79. *Gaelic American,* 29 January 1910.
80. *Irish Nation and Peasant,* 15 October 1910.
81. *Gaelic American,* 5 and 12 February and 15 October 1910, and O'Brien & Ryan, eds. *Devoy's Postbag,* II, 393 (McCullough to Devoy, 2 April 1910). *Sinn Fein,* 25 July 1914, and *Gaelic American,* 24 December 1910.
82. *Sinn Fein,* 21 October 1911, 17 February and 23 March 1912. See also Hobson in *Gaelic American,* 21 December 1912. 'Ireland in reality holds the winning cards in her hand if only her people could be made to see it, if only she had statesmen instead of party politicians.'
83. *Sinn Fein,* 15 July 1911.
84. *Maoriland Worker,* Wellington, 12 and 26 May 1911.
85. *Sinn Fein,* 7 October 1911.
86. *Irish Freedom,* 1 October 1912.
87. *Sinn Fein,* 14 October 1911.
88. *Ibid.,* 4 February and 28 July 1911.
89. *Ibid.,* 27 April 1912.

90. *Ibid.*, 20 April 1912.
91. *Ibid.*, 6 April 1912.
92. *Ibid.*, 11 May 1912 and *Gaelic American*, 18 May 1912.
93. *Sinn Fein*, 27 July 1912.
94. *Ibid.*, 31 August 1912.
95. *Gaelic American*, 20 April 1912 (Hobson article).
96. *Sinn Fein*, 30 November 1912.
97. P. COLUM, *Griffith*, p. 125.
98. *Sinn Fein*, 14 October 1911, 6 April 1912, 20 December 1913 (Citing 1828 and 1868 threats).
99. *Irish Freedom*, 15 December 1910.
100. *Sinn Fein*, 24 August 1912.
101. *Ibid.*, 20 December 1913.
102. *Ibid.*, 7 March 1914. 'The most noteworthy feature of the Unionist campaign is the vindication it has shown of the Sinn Fein policy, for we find that not by Sinn Fein, but by *the threat of it* a Government (and a strong Government as governments are reckoned strong in Britain) has been held up and made to stop and consider what steps they can take to get out of a dilemma.'
103. *Ibid.*, 28 March 1914.
104. *Ibid.*, 9 May 1914. Letter to daily press.
105. *Ibid.*, 18 April 1914.
106. *Ibid.*, For Hobson on partition, see *Irish Freedom*, August 1914.
107. *Sinn Fein*, 2 March 1912.
108. *Ibid.*, 11 February, 18 March, 6 April 1911.
109. A. GRIFFITH, ed., *Thomas Davis—the Thinker and Teacher*, Dublin, 1922, p. 172.
110. *Sinn Fein*, 18 October 1913 (etc.), and Griffith to Hannay (October 1906), *J. O. Hannay Papers*, Trinity College, Dublin, no. 351. See also no. 291.
111. *Sinn Fein*, 8 August 1914.
112. F. S. L. LYONS, *John Dillon*, p. 426.
113. *Gaelic American*, 26 October 1912.

Chapter IV. Sinn Fein Divided, 1908–16 PAGES 59–73
1. *United Irishman*, 12 July and 18 June 1902.
2. F. K. SCHILLING, 'William O'Brien and the All-for-Ireland League', 1956, p. 61 (Unpublished thesis, Trinity College, Dublin).
3. *William O'Brien Papers*, O'Brien to Dunraven, 28 December 1907, National Library of Ireland, MSS 8554/9.
4. SCHILLING, p. 63.

5. See contrast between *Sinn Fein*, February 1909 and *United Irishman*, 28 January 1905.
6. *Sinn Fein*, 10 October 1908.
7. It was an evening paper, thus avoiding competition with *Freeman's Journal*, etc.
8. *George Gavan Duffy Papers*, Sweetman to Gavan Duffy, 29 October 1909.
9. *Ibid.*, O'Hegarty to Gavan Duffy, no date 1908.
10. *John Sweetman Papers*, Griffith to Sweetman, 1 July 1908.
11. P. S. O'HEGARTY, *Sinn Fein—an Illumination*, Dublin, 1919, p. 37.
12. *George Gavan Duffy Papers*, P. S. O'Hegarty to Gavan Duffy, 23 October 1909.
13. *Ibid.*, Sweetman to Gavan Duffy, 29 October 1909.
14. *Gaelic American*, 5 February 1910.
15. See Marcus Bourke, *The O'Rahilly*, Tralee, 1967, p. 38, and *Gaelic American*, 16 January 1909.
16. SCHILLING, p. 82. He corrects the date given by O'Brien.
17. WILLIAM O'BRIEN, *The Irish Revolution and How It Came About*, London, 1923, p. 67.
18. *Sinn Fein*, 4 May 1907.
19. *Ibid.*, 5 September 1908, and *Gaelic American*, 28 December 1907 and 1 February 1908.
20. *George Gavan Duffy Papers*, J. Brady to Gavan Duffy, 9 December 1909 and Gavan Duffy to Brady, 10 December 1909 (Copy).
21. Brady claimed that 'to say that Mr. William O'Brien or any other prominent Irishman had anything whatsoever to do with the origin of my suggestions or proposals, is wholly unfounded, (*Sinn Fein*, 1 January 1910, and see also *Irish Independent*, 1 January 1910), but Schilling shows his plan's similarity to O'Brien's own conception of the United Irish League as 'an extra parliamentary body to control the parliamentary party'. Schilling, p. 81.
22. The following description is based on the accounts given in *Sinn Fein*, 30 December 1909; *Irish Nation and Peasant*, 1 and 8 January 1910; *George Gavan Duffy Papers*, W. Sears to Gavan Duffy, 22 December 1909; Anne Marreco, *The Rebel Countess: The Life and Times of Constance Markievicz*, London, 1967, pp. 109 and 124; W. O'Brien and D. Ryan, eds., *Devoy's Postbag*, II, 301; McCartan to Devoy, 31 March 1910. Statement by P. S. O'Hegarty to Mr. Sean O Luing, c. 1950.
23. The following were present: Sweetman, Griffith, T. S. Cuffe, S. T. O'Kelly, Mrs. Wyse Power, Tom Kelly, P. T. Daly,

W. L. Cole, D. O'Healy, F. J. Lawless, M. P. Clarke, C. W. Magrath, H. Holahan, Miss Murphy, Countess Markievicz, S. Milroy, S. Nichols, P. Hughes, J. O'Flaherty, W. Sears, D. McCullough and B. Hobson, *Sinn Fein,* 30 December 1909.

24. See Mitchel on Meagher, M. J. MacManus, ed., *Thomas Davis and Young Ireland,* Dublin, 1945, pp. 77 and 84. See also (Davis) *Gaelic American,* 23 October 1909.

25. *Irish Nation and Peasant,* 15 January 1910.

26. *Ibid.,* 3 February 1910.

27. *Ibid.,* 12 February 1910. Even the editor, W. P. Ryan, who was responsible for the O'Brien negotiation disclosures, claimed that his action was not directed against compromise but the secrecy with which the negotiations had been undertaken (5 February 1910).

28. *Irish Nation and Peasant,* 15 February 1910.

29. *Ibid.,* 10 September 1910.

30. *George Gavan Duffy Papers,* Memorandum 24 February 1910.

31. *Ibid.,* Milroy to Gavan Duffy, 5 March 1910.

32. W. O'BRIEN and D. RYAN, *Devoy's Post Bag,* II, 390, McCartan to Devoy, 31 March 1910.

33. *P. S. O'Hegarty Papers,* programmes of national council meetings.

34. *Ibid.,* Minutes of National Council London Executive, 26 May 1908.

35. *Gavan Duffy Papers,* O'Hegarty to Gavan Duffy, 25 September 1909.

36. *Ibid.,* Gavan Duffy to Brady, 15 January 1910.

37. *Gavan Duffy Papers,* O'Hegarty to Gavan Duffy, 9 August 1910.

38. *Ibid.,* Gavan Duffy to O'Hegarty, no date.

39. *Ibid.,* Gavan Duffy to O'Hegarty, 10 September 1910.

40. The private meeting of the Convention was held in the Sinn Fein rooms in Harcourt Street.

41. *Sinn Fein,* 8 October 1910.

42. BULMER HOBSON, *Ireland Yesterday and Tomorrow,* p. 12.

43. MARCUS BOURKE, *The O'Rahilly,* p. 38.

44. *Irish Freedom,* July 1913, and *Sinn Fein,* 31 May 1913.

45. *Sinn Fein,* 13 May 1911.

46. *Gaelic American,* 8 July 1911.

47. *Ibid.,* 29 July and 26 August 1911.

48. *Sinn Fein,* 9 November 1912.

49. *Gaelic American,* 18 October 1913 (Hobson).

50. *Ibid.,* 24 December 1910.

51. *Sinn Fein,* 9 March 1912.

52. *Gaelic American,* 30 March 1912.

53. HOBSON, *Ireland Yesterday and Tomorrow*, p. 12.
54. *Gaelic American*, 1 October and 12 November 1910.
55. *Ibid.*, 25 January 1913.
56. *Irish World*, 16 March 1907, etc., for remarks in this vein.
57. *Sinn Fein*, 1 July 1911.
58. *An Bearna Baoghail*, Christmas 1912, p. 12.
59. *Sinn Fein*, 27 November 1913.
60. *Ibid.*, 13 September 1913.
61. *Ibid.*, 29 November 1913.
62. *Ibid.*, 30 December 1913.
63. BOURKE, *O'Rahilly*, p. 72.
64. *Gaelic American*, 13 December 1913.
65. *Ibid.*, 30 May 1914.
66. BOURKE, *O'Rahilly*, p. 83.
67. *Ibid.*, p. 100.

Chapter V. The Party Machine PAGES 74–88
1. *United Irishman*, 9 December 1905. Further details will also be taken from this source.
2. *Ibid.*, 20 January 1906.
3. *Memoirs of Desmond Fitzgerald, 1913–1916*, London, 1968, p. 30.
4. *United Irishman*, 20 January 1906; *Irish Press*, 5 July 1961 (Sean T. O'Kelly memoirs); *Gaelic American*, 9 February 1907.
5. *Irish World*, 1 February 1908.
6. *Gaelic American*, 1 February 1908. Merchant's Quay, Usher's Quay and North Dock were won.
7. *Ibid.*, 6 February 1909.
8. *Annual Register*, 1909, p. 276.
9. *Irish World*, 17 July 1909. Sean T. O'Kelly memoirs in *Irish Press*, 6 July 1961.
10. *Irish Press*, 3 July 1961, and *Gaelic American*, 28 November 1908 (P. T. Daly's report).
11. ALLAN WADE, *Yeats's Letters*, p. 591 (Yeats to Ernest Boyd, 20 January 1915).
12. *Sinn Fein*, 9 August 1913.
13. WADE, p. 612 (Yeats to Lady Gregory, 11 May 1916).
14. *Sinn Fein*, 1 March 1913.
15. SHAW DESMOND, *The Drama of Sinn Fein*, 1923, p. 128.
16. *Sinn Fein*, 8 September 1906.
17. *Ibid.*, 5 September 1908.
18. Dublin, Galway, Cork, Wexford, Leitrim, Louth. *Sinn Fein*, 28 August 1909.

19. *George Gavan Duffy Papers,* O'Hegarty to Gavan Duffy, 9 August 1910, and Gavan Duffy to O'Hegarty, 10 September 1910.
20. BULMER HOBSON, *Ireland Yesterday and Tomorrow,* p. 12, O'Brien and Ryan, *Devoy's Postbag,* II, 394.
21. *Sinn Fein,* 8 September 1906.
22. *Ibid.,* 7 September 1907.
23. *Annual Register,* 1908.
24. *Ibid.,* 28 August 1909.
25. *Sinn Fein,* 28 August 1909.
26. HOBSON, *Ireland Yesterday and Tomorrow,* p. 36.
27. *Sinn Fein,* 7 September 1907, published reports for the year 1906–1907, the only complete financial statement when the total revenue was £234.10.1. Over half that sum (£122.9s.4d.) had been 'received through appeals in *Sinn Fein';* while the sale of pamphlets (£39.2s.8d.) alone realised more than the revenue from affiliations (£32). In that year there were only 57 branches formed and 12 in the process of formation. As there is no mention of any other type of income from the branches in that year, i.e. subscriptions and local collections, it must be assumed that either no attempt was made to collect such contributions or that the word 'affiliation' applied to all forms of revenue from the branches. This uncertainty is not easily resolved. Further, the report of 1909 declared that the revenue from affiliations for the previous year had dropped by £35. If affiliation meant only branch affiliation fees, that was a fall of 50% (£66 to £31). Moreover, the 60 branches of 1907 contributed more than 128 branches in 1909. These discrepancies make analysis difficult.
28. Griffith to William Bulfin, n.d. 1904, *William Bulfin Papers,* National Library of Ireland, MS 13810 (12), and M. Chavasse, *Terence MacSwiney,* Dublin, 1961, pp. 23–4.
29. *Gaelic American,* 15 August 1908.
30. *George Gavan Duffy Papers,* Hobson to Duffy, November 1906. *Gaelic American,* 1 August 1908 and 7 August 1912.
31. *George Gavan Duffy Papers,* n.d., 1908, O'Hegarty to Gavan Duffy. O'Hegarty in his organisation seems to have responded to the situation in the same way as Griffith. By 1909 there was only one branch in existence. *Ibid.,* O'Hegarty to Gavan Duffy. No date, 1909.
32. *Sinn Fein,* 28 January 1911, received £2.17.6d. for recruitment work from the *late* Davis branch in London.
33. *Sinn Fein,* 2 April 1910.
34. W. O'BRIEN and D. RYAN, *Devoy's Post Bag,* P. McCartan to Devoy, 31 March 1910.

35. At least one member of the National Council Executive of 1909, W. E. Shackleton, subsequently supported the parliamentarians. (Communication from son).
36. P. S. O'HEGARTY, *Sinn Fein—An Illumination*, p. 39.
37. D. MACARDLE, *The Irish Republic*, Dublin, 1951, p. 232.
38. SHAW DESMOND, *The Drama of Sinn Fein*, p. 132. See also D. Macardle, *The Irish Republic*, pp. 230–3.
39. There were, of course, the constituency representatives at the quarterly meetings, but these would probably not have much experience.
40. O'HEGARTY, *The Victory of Sinn Fein*, p. 175, and Michael Laffan, 'The Sinn Fein Party, 1916–1921', *Capuchin Annual* 1970, pp. 227–35.
41. *The Irish Nation and Peasant*, 19 June 1909.
42. *Sunday Independent*, Dublin, 12 August 1945.

Chapter VI. Revolutionary Perspectives PAGES 91–8

1. See Robert Taber, *The War of the Flea: A Study of Guerilla Warfare Theory and Practice*, London, 1970, pp. 90–8.
2. JEAN LACOUTURE, *Ho Chi Minh*, London, 1968, p. 12.
3. FENNER BROCKWAY in *Peace News*, quoted in *Irish Independent*, 20 July 1957.
4. B. R. NANDA, *The Nehrus*, London, 1962, p. 90, and J. Nehru, *An Autobiography*, London, 1953, p. 99.
5. M. Q. SIBLEY, ed., *The Quiet Battle: Writings on the Theory and Practice of Non-Violent Resistance*, New York, 1963, pp. 135–55.
6. NEHRU, *Autobiography*, p. 84: 'If Gandhiji's argument for the suspension of civil resistance was correct, our opponents would always have the power to create circumstances which would necessarily result in our abandoning the struggle.'
7. See *Tolstoi's Writings on Civil Disobedience and Non-Violence*, New York, 1968.
8. D. G. TENDULKAR, *Mahatma, Life of Mohandas Karamchand Gandhi*, Bombay, 1951, II, 418–20. Quoted in *All Men are Brothers: Life and Thoughts of Mahatma Gandhi as told in his own Words*, Paris, 1958, p. 175.
9. HANS KOHN, *Nationalism: Its Meaning and History*, Princeton, 1955, pp. 149–50.
10. SIR LEWIS NAMIER described the Magyar system in international politics as 'a marvellous machine which through a multitude of wheels and levers made one of the smallest nations in Europe into a great power'. See *Vanished Suprem-*

acies: Essays on European History, 1812–1918, New York, 1963, p. 119.

11. *Gaelic American,* then banned in India, remarked (1 February 1908) that 'if the Indians in India would only show half the tenacity and courage in fighting for their independence that they are showing in resisting the humiliations imposed on them in South Africa, India would be free in five years'.

12. M. K. GANDHI, *An Autobiography or The Story of my Experiments with Truth,* Ahmedabad, 1966, p. 239. In 1920 Gandhi said: 'I isolate this non-co-operation from Sinn Feinism, for, it is so conceived as to be incapable of being offered side by side with violence. But I invite even the school of violence to give this peaceful non-co-operation a trial. It will not fail through its inherent weakness.' See Nehru, *Autobiography,* p. 84.

13. *Sinn Fein,* 4 August 1906 quoted the *Amrita Bazar Patrika,* Calcutta, 9 June 1906, which praised Griffith's Sinn Fein policy: 'What we have to do now is to keep this scheme before us as our model and utilise so much of it for our regeneration as it is possible for us to do.' The *Bande Mataram,* Calcutta, declared of Sinn Fein that 'Heaven itself seems to have pointed out to us in the year of Swadeshi, the real way . . .' The *Mahratta,* Poona, insisted that 'Swadeshi' was an exact translation of 'Sinn Fein'. See *Sinn Fein,* 5 January and 7 August 1907. According to Nehru in the same year, Sinn Fein 'is a most interesting movement and resembles very closely the so-called Extremist movement in India. Their policy is not to beg for favours but to wrest them. They do not want to fight England by arms, but "to ignore her, boycott her, and quietly assume the administration of Irish affairs" . . . Among people, who ought to know, this movement is causing . . . consternation. They say that if its policy is adopted by the bulk of the country, English rule will be a thing of the past.'

14. *Sinn Fein,* 2 March 1907.

15. *P. S. O'Hegarty Papers,* Minutes of the National Council London Executive, 27 November 1908.

16. *Irish Nation and Peasant,* 27 August 1910; P. S. O'Hegarty, *The Victory of Sinn Fein,* p. 163.

17. *Sinn Fein,* 12 June 1909 ('Sinn Fein and Physical Force') and the Irish Year Book (issued by the national council) 1909 ('The Ethics of Sinn Fein'). The latter was first published in *Sinn Fein.* For estimate of Lynd see R. A. Scott-James, *Fifty Years of English Literature, 1900–1950,* London, 1951, p. 53.

18. *Sinn Fein,* 19 June 1909.

19. See George Catlin, *In the Path of Mahatma Gandhi*, London, 1948, p. 259. Tilak interpreted the passage in a diametrically opposed sense.

20. For a discussion of Gandhi's ambiguities on the issue see Paul F. Power, *Gandhi on World Affairs*, London, 1960, pp. 55–65; M. Gandhi, *All Men are Brothers*, pp. 92, 102–3; Nehru, *Autobiography*, p. 99. Nehru and the younger men, however, approved of Sinn Fein tactics of withdrawal from parliament rather than abstention from elections in 1920, 'but in such matters he [Gandhi] was adamant'.

21. *Gaelic American*, 6 February 1909.

22. E. KEDOURIE, *Nationalism*, London, 1966, pp. 59 and 63.

23. DANIEL CORKERY, 'Davis and the National Language', in M. J. MacManus, ed., *Thomas Davis and Young Ireland*, pp. 14–23. See also Corkery's *The Fortunes of the Irish Language*, Cork, 1968, p. 116.

24. *United Irishman*, 15 May 1902.

25. A. DENSON, *Letters from AE*, p. 40, AE to W. B. Yeats, April 1902

26. See Thomas Kinsella, ed. and trans., *The Tain*, Oxford, 1970, p 197.

27. HUGH SHEARMAN, *Not an Inch: A Study of Northern Ireland and Lord Craigavon*, London, 1942, p. 15.

28. S. O FAOLAIN, ed., *Memoirs of Theobald Wolfe Tone*, London, 1937, pp. 24, 52, 70. See also Patrick Byrne, *Lord Edward Fitzgerald*, Dublin, 1955, p. 143, and Frank MacDermot, *Theobald Wolfe Tone*, Tralee, 1969, p. 62, for rejections of Tone's original republicanism. For the orthodox separatist case against this viewpoint see P. S. O'Hegarty's review of MacDermot's *Tone* in the *Dublin Magazine*, October–December 1939, pp. 66–72.

29. See Gandhi, *An Autobiography*, p. 338: 'Amongst the many misdeeds of the British rule in India, history will look upon the Act depriving a whole nation of arms as the blackest.' For Davis see Arthur Griffith, ed., *Thomas Davis: The Thinker and Teacher*, Dublin, 1922, pp. 15, 66–7, 81–3 and 171–2. This selection of Davis's writings, in that it was made by Arthur Griffith himself, is particularly valuable for a study of Sinn Fein.

30. L. FOGARTY, ed., *James Fintan Lalor: Patriot and Political Essayist*, Dublin, 1947, p. 144, quoted from *Nation*, 8 May, 1847.

31. D. V. TAHMANKAR, *Lokamanya Tilak*, London, 1956, p. 264.

Chapter VII. Parnell and Sinn Fein PAGES 99–110
1. *Sinn Fein,* 27 April 1912; *Gaelic American,* 14 March 1908
2. In the 1860s 'nationalist and fenian had become synonymous terms'. T. W. Moody, 'The New Departure in Irish Politics 1878–9', in T. W. Moody and H. H. Cronne, eds., *Essays in British and Irish History in Honour of J. E. Todd,* London 1899, p. 307.
3. Engels to Marx, 29 November 1869, quoted in N. Mansergh, *The Irish Question, 1840–1921,* London, 1965, pp. 94–5.
4. *Sinn Fein,* 20 December 1913. For Sean MacDermott, *Gaelic American,* 1 June 1907.
5. *Sinn Fein,* 29 June 1907.
6. *Ibid.,* 21 February 1914.
7. *Ibid.,* 29 June 1907. See also R. B. O'Brien, *Life of Charles Stewart Parnell,* London, 1910, p. 120.
8. *Sinn Fein,* 29 June 1907.
9. MICHAEL DAVITT, *The Fall of Feudalism in Ireland,* London 1904, p. 310.
10. *Gaelic American,* 13 July 1907, and Lavelle, *James O'Mara* p. 78.
11. F. SHEEHY-SKEFFINGTON, *Michael Davitt, Revolutionary Agitator and Labour Leader,* London 1908, p. 72.
12. J. L. HAMMOND, *Gladstone and the Irish Nation,* London, 1938, pp. 321, 724 and 727.
13. R. B. O'BRIEN, *Parnell,* pp 362 and 367.
14. *Gaelic American,* 25 January 1908.
15. *Ibid.,* 18 July 1908.
16. *United Ireland,* 10 October 1891.
17. *Gaelic American,* 23 November and 13 July 1907.
18. T. W. MOODY, ed., *The Fenian Movement,* Cork, 1968, p. 42.
19. M. HURST, *Parnell and Irish Nationalism,* London, 1968, p. 57. 'In choosing a nominal constitutionalism as the basis for operations, Parnell did just what intelligent nationalist leaders in similar situations had done, did and were to do.'
20. *Gaelic American,* 10 August 1907.
21. *Ibid.,* 23 November 1907.
22. See obituary number of *United Ireland,* Dublin, 10 October 1891. Parnell, it claimed, was 'the only Irish chief for two hundred years fit to stand on an Irish bill beard to beard, foot to foot, mind to mind, eye to eye with the Englishmen'.
23. In 1876 Sir Julius Vogel of New Zealand was forced to appeal to Parnell to ensure the passage of the colonial stock act. See R. M. Burdon, *The Life and Times of Sir Julius Vogel,* Christchurch, 1948, p. 161.
24. *Sinn Fein,* 7 October 1911.

25. L. PAUL-DUBOIS, *Contemporary Ireland* (Translated by T. M. Kettle), Dublin, 1911, p. 125.
26. *Gaelic American,* 2 June 1907.
27. *Ibid.,* 4 December 1909.
28. *Ibid.,* 6 July 1907; *Sinn Fein,* 29 June 1907.
29. *Gaelic American,* 13 July 1907. For Fr. Yorke, *ibid.,* 21 August 1907 (quoted from San Francisco *Leader*). For Dilke, Hammond, *Gladstone and the Irish Nation,* p. 150.
30. *Gaelic American,* 19 December 1908.
31. MAUDE GONNE MACBRIDE, *A Servant of the Queen,* London, 1938, p. 87.
32. D. A. THORNLEY, 'The Irish Home Rule Party and parliamentary obstruction, 1874–87', *Irish Historical Studies,* XII, March 1960, pp. 50 and 56.
33. *Gaelic American,* 30 November 1907 (Dolan).
34. O'BRIEN, *Parnell,* p. 537.
35. *Gaelic American,* 4 December 1909 (Sweetman), etc.
36. *Sinn Fein,* 29 June 1907.
37. HURST, p. 68.
38. *Sinn Fein,* 29 June 1907.
39. *United Irishman,* 12 and 14 May and 2 June 1900 (Controversy between 'Cuguan'—Griffith—and Fr. P. F. Kavanagh).
40. *Gaelic American,* 23 November 1907.
41. O'BRIEN, *Parnell,* p. 539.
42. *United Irishman,* 8 April 1899.
43. *Gaelic American,* 19 November 1910 (letter in Dublin *Independent*).
44. *Ibid.,* 20 July 1907.
45. C. C. O'BRIEN, *Parnell and his Party,* p. 349.
46. *Gaelic American,* 12 September 1908.
47. *Sinn Fein,* 28 January 1911.
48. For a full discussion of this question, see R. P. Davis, 'Imperial Federation and Irish Home Rule' in 'The Irish-Catholic Question and New Zealand Society, 1868–1922', unpublished Ph.D. thesis, University of Otago, Dunedin, 1968, pp. 397–428.
49. O'BRIEN, *Parnell,* p. 367.
50. ARTHUR GRIFFITH, 'Pitt's Policy' in *The Resurrection of Hungary,* Dublin, 1918, p. 105, and *Sinn Fein,* 27 December, 1913.
51. *Gaelic American,* 11 August 1906.
52. HURST, p. 85.
53. Griffith does not appear to have emphasised Parnell's economics but did comment favourably on Isaac Butt's somewhat similar views, *Sinn Fein,* 22 August 1908.

54. GRIFFITH, *The Resurrection of Hungary*, Dublin, 1918, p. 118.
55. GRIFFITH, Introduction to John Mitchel, *Jail Journal*, Dublin, 1913; XIV, *Sinn Fein*, 25 October 1913; *Irish Freedom*, September 1913.
56. *United Irishman*, 13 August 1904. For review of Childers, 'the first Englishman who has written a book in favour of Home Rule without unconsciously insulting Irishmen', see *Sinn Fein*, 9 December 1911.
57. *Sinn Fein*, 15 July 1911.
58. JOHN MITCHEL, *The Last Conquest of Ireland (perhaps)*, Dublin, 1861, p. 307.
59. D. W. GREENE and SEAN O TUAMA, 'Long Ago, but not so far away', pt. 1, broadcast on Radio Telefis Eireann, television, 13 November 1970.
60. Quoted in *Gaelic American*, 18 January 1908.
61. SIR HORACE PLUNKETT, *Ireland in the New Century*, London, 3rd ed., 1909, p. 6.

Chapter VIII. Republicanism and Dual Monarchy PAGES 111–26

1. A. GRIFFITH, ed., *Thomas Davis—the Thinker and Teacher*, p. 113.
2. *United Irishman*, 25 March 1848.
3. J. MITCHEL, *Jail Journal*, 1854, p. 99.
4. JOHN O'LEARY, *Recollections of Fenians and Fenianism*, London, 1896, I, 122.
5. It was changed several times. One version is given in *Bulmer Hobson Papers:* 'In the presence of God, I . . . do solemnly swear that I will do my utmost to establish the national independence of Ireland, and that I will bear true allegiance to the Supreme Council of the Irish Republican Brotherhood and Government of the Irish Republic and implicitly obey the constitution of the Irish Republican Brotherhood and all my superior officers and that I will preserve inviolable the secrets of the organisation.'
6. W. K. HANCOCK, *Survey of British Commonwealth affairs*, London, 1937, I, 101.
7. P. H. PEARSE, *Ghosts*, Dublin, 1915, p. 6.
8. HANCOCK, *Survey of British Commonwealth affairs*, I, 104.
9. The Irish parliamentary party was prepared to compromise with some form of Home Rule and partnership in the British Empire but did not give up the theoretical right to full dual monarchy status or the right to win independence by arms.
10. Quoted by P. S. O'HEGARTY, *Ireland under the Union*, p. 648.

11. O'LEARY, *Recollections of Fenians and Fenianism*, London, 1896, p. 27.
12. L. FOGARTY, *James Fintan Lalor*, 1918, pp. 78–9.
13. *Gaelic American*, 12 December 1908.
14. See A. J. P. Taylor, *The Hapsburg Monarchy*, London, 1964, pp. 146–8.
15. J. S. MILL, *England and Ireland*, London, 1868, p. 34.
16. *Irishman*, 26 May 1860.
17. *Ibid.*, 4 August 1866.
18. GRIFFITH, *The Resurrection of Hungary*, Dublin, 1904, p. 2.
19. 21 January to 2 July 1904.
20. *New Ireland Review*, February 1905. T. M. Kettle, 'Would the Hungarian policy work?'
21. *John Sweetman Papers*, no date, 1904.
22. GRIFFITH, *The Resurrection of Hungary*, pp. 86, 89, 91 and 92.
23. *Peasant*, 13 July 1907.
24. BULMER HOBSON, *Ireland Yesterday and Tomorrow*, p. 9.
25. GRIFFITH, *The Resurrection of Hungary*, 1904, p. 95, pp. 82–96, consist of the final article *United Irishman*, 2 July 1904. When *The Resurrection of Hungary* was published in 1918 this passage was removed—a clear indication of Griffith's change of views.
26. *United Irishman*, 17 September 1904.
27. *Ibid.*, 28 January 1905.
28. J. O'SHEEHAN, *Constitutionalism and Sinn Fein*, Dublin, 1907, pp. 2 and 15.
29. *Gaelic American*, 11 April 1908.
30. HOBSON, *Ireland Yesterday and Tomorrow*, pp. 10 and 19.
31. See for example, E. C. S. Wade and G. G. Phillips, *Constitutional Law*, 6th ed., London, 1960, p. 43.
32. *Gaelic American*, May 1908.
33. *Sinn Fein*, 2 December 1911.
34. TERENCE MACSWINEY, *Principles of Freedom*, Dublin, 4th ed., 1964, pp. 77–8. Originally in *Irish Freedom*, 1911.
35. *United Irishman*, 23 July 1904.
36. P. S. O'HEGARTY, *Ireland under the Union*, p. 652; MacSwiney, *Principles of Freedom*, p. 78.
37. HANCOCK, *Survey*, I, 97.
38. *Leabhar na hEireann, The Irish Year Book* (issued by national council), 1909, p. 267.
39. *Gaelic American*, 19 October 1912.
40. *United Irishman*, 13 August 1904.
41. *Ibid.*, 11 March 1905.
42. *Ibid.*, 13 August 1904.
43. *Ibid.*, 26 August 1899.

44. *Irish Nation and Peasant,* 27 November 1909.
45. The general argument of *Pitt's Policy* was that England had made a great mistake by refusing partnership with Ireland in 1800. This partnership, Griffith maintained, would have given Ireland a share in the British empire, and increased her population and industrial power proportionately with England. The dual monarchy of England and Ireland would consequently have been too strong to fear the industrial competition of Germany which began in the last quarter of the 19th century.
46. GRIFFITH, *The Resurrection of Hungary,* 1918, p. 110.
47. *Ibid.,* p. 116, and Griffith to Hannay, 27 February 1906 *Hannay Papers,* no. 257.
48. O'HEGARTY, *The Victory of Sinn Fein,* Dublin 1924, p. 30.
49. O'HEGARTY, *Sinn Fein—an Illumination,* p. 30. The resemblance to Mazzini is obvious.
50. *Irish Felon,* 1 July 1848. John Mitchel expressed general agreement with this policy of Lalor. See R. M. Henry, *The Evolution of Sinn Fein,* p. 53, for Mitchel's views on passive resistance. O'Hegarty outlined Lalor's article in the *Peasant* 13 July 1907.
51. LEWIS NAMIER, *Vanished Supremacies,* pp. 166–7.
52. *Irish Independent,* 14 January 1955.
53. *Irish Nation and Peasant,* 6 November 1909.
54. *Ibid.,* 20 November 1909.
55. *Peasant,* 13 July 1907.
56. *Ibid.,* 29 June 1907.
57. *Ibid.,* 20 July 1907.
58. HOBSON, *Ireland Yesterday and Tomorrow,* p. 41.
59. HOBSON, *Defensive Warfare,* Belfast, 1909, pp. 21 and 52.
60. *Ibid.,* p. 52.
61. *Bulmer Hobson Papers,* Statement to Bureau of Military History.
62. HOBSON, *Ireland Yesterday and Tomorrow,* p. 41.
63. O'HEGARTY, *The Victory of Sinn Fein,* p. 165.
64. *Peasant,* 27 July 1907.
65. *Gaelic American,* 1 April 1911.
66. Statement to present writer.
67. 'On one side was the dogmas of the undying republic, won by the blood of the martyrs, living in its own right, needing no ratification by popular vote, but needing only resolution and arms . . . Here in germ was the party state. But on the other hand was nationalistic democracy, equally resolute for Irish independence, but admitting the right of the Irish people to choose the symbolism and forms of government in which

that independence would express itself.' Hancock, *Survey*, I, 104.

68. *Shan Van Vocht*, 2 October 1896.
69. HOBSON, *Ireland Yesterday and Tomorrow*, p. 74.
70. Even a supporter of Griffith, Seamus MacManus, believed that a 'foreign king offered to us by force . . . might be borne with as a necessary evil—provided our people only formally acknowledge him. If they ever showed him that heart homage which is due only to a king of their own, they would be untrue to themselves and untrue to Ireland.' *United Irishman*, 3 September 1904.
71. ROBERT LYND, *Ireland a Nation*, London, 1919, p. 56.
72. O'HEGARTY, *The Victory of Sinn Fein*, p. 579.
73. SEAN O FAOLAIN, *Constance Markievicz*, London, 1967, p. 74. 'Griffith had many ideas as to what he meant by such words as Liberty. He had more ideas than most. The trouble was that they were always vague.'

Chapter IX. *Economic Nationalism* PAGES 127–44
1. JOHN MITCHEL, *Jail Journal*, Dublin, 1854, p. 289.
2. A. GRIFFITH, *Thomas Davis—the Thinker and Teacher*, p. 198. No source is given.
3. GRIFFITH, speech at convention (*United Irishman*, 9 December, 1905). Later published as *The Sinn Fein Policy*. See *The Resurrection of Hungary* (collected writings, 1918), p. 142.
4. *Sinn Fein*, 13 April to 17 August 1907.
5. GRIFFITH, *The Sinn Fein Policy*, in *The Resurrection of Hungary*, p. 142. Quoted from F. List, *National System of Political Economy*, translated Sampson Lloyd, London, 1885, p. 174. (Hereafter cited as *National System*).
6. *Ibid.*, (F. List, *National System*, p. 175).
7. GRIFFITH, *The Sinn Fein Policy*, p. 144. F. List, *National System*, p. 179.
8. GRIFFITH, *The Sinn Fein Policy*, p. 142.
9. F. List, *National System*, p. 175.
10. *Ibid.*, p. 123.
11. *Ibid.*, p. 176.
12. *Ibid.*, p. 272. He compared the Union of England, Scotland and Ireland with the Zollverein and the American Union. The 1966 free trade agreement between Great Britain and the Republic of Ireland is an interesting application of this view.
13. *Ibid.*, p. 418.
14. *United Irishman*, 21 January 1905, quotes article by Kossuth

on economic suppression of Hungary by Austria, with Ireland
and England substituted for Hungary and Austria. The
article refers to British economic imperialism in India. List
National System of Political Economy, p. 270, declared that
'all Asiatic countries of the torrid zone will pass gradually
under the dominion of the manufacturing commercial nation
of the temperate zone'.

15. Lecture on List to Young Ireland Branch, UIL (*Irish Nation
    and Peasant*, 2 April, 1910). 'By List's own doctrine Ireland
    was too small a nation for protection. For he laid down in
    his book that in small nations protection becomes mere
    private monopoly.'
16. GRIFFITH, *Pitt's Policy*, p. 138. In *The Sinn Fein Policy*, he
    argued that a mercantile marine would soon bring the Irish
    population to its 1845 level (8,000,000).
17. GRIFFITH, *The Resurrection of Hungary*, p. 152.
18. GRIFFITH, ed., *Thomas Davis—the Thinker and Teacher*, p. 16.
19. *Ibid.*, p. 151.
20. *Ibid.*, p. 161.
21. GRIFFITH, *The Sinn Fein Policy*, p. 152. Rooney's lecture was
    first published by the *Gaelic American*, 18 January 1907.
22. GRIFFITH, *The Sinn Fein Policy*, p. 139.
23. *Ibid.*, p. 140.
24. *Irish World*, 6 December 1912. L. Paul-Dubois, *Contemporary
    Ireland* (translated T. M. Kettle, 1911), p. 368, condemns it as
    'one of the worst systems of education ever devised; a system
    so bad that if England had wished to "kill Ireland's soul"
    when she imposed it upon the sister isle, she could not have
    discovered a better means of doing so'.
25. *Irish World*, 3 August 1907.
26. GRIFFITH, *The Sinn Fein Policy*, p. 147.
27. T. M. KETTLE, *New Ireland Review*, February 1905, 'Would
    the Hungarian policy work?'
28. *Gaelic American*, 22 June and 24 August 1912. See as well
    L. PAUL-DUBOIS, *Contemporary Ireland*, Dublin, 1911, p. 32
    for a discussion of the railway problem.
29. J. SWEETMAN, *The Purchase of Railways by the Nation*, Dublin
    1906.
30. GRIFFITH, *The Sinn Fein Policy*, p. 158.
31. *Ibid.*, p. 159. See Paul-Dubois, *Contemporary Ireland*, p. 32
32. GRIFFITH, *The Sinn Fein Policy*, p. 151. George Gavan Duffy
    Papers, The O'Donnell to Gavan Duffy, no date 1910.
33. GRIFFITH, *The Sinn Fein Policy*, p. 155.
34. *Irish World*, 9 November 1907.
35. *Sinn Fein*, 22 August 1908.

36. Hobson, *Ireland Yesterday and Tomorrow*, p. 20.
37. *Sinn Fein*, 7 September 1907 and 11 January 1909.
38. *Ibid.*, 15 August 1908.
39. E. Strauss, *Irish Nationalism and British Democracy*, London, 1951, p. 223.
40. *United Irishman*, 10 January 1903.
41. *Sinn Fein*, 25 October 1913.
42. *United Irishman*, 18 April 1903.
43. *Ibid.*, 19 November 1904.
44. *Sinn Fein*, 27 December 1913.
45. *Gaelic American*, 6 February 1908.
46. P. S. O'Hegarty, *A History of Ireland under the Union*, p. 727.
47. *Peasant*, 10 October 1908.
48. J. D. Clarkson, *Labour and Nationalism in Ireland*, New York, 1925, p. 268.
49. *Sinn Fein*, 30 September 1911.
50. *Ibid.*, 6 December 1913.
51. *Ibid.*, 27 December 1913.
52. *Irish Freedom*, November 1913.
53. *Gaelic American*, 27 November 1913.
54. *Peasant*, 21 November 1908.
55. Francis Sheehy-Skeffington, *Michael Davitt*, p. 71.
56. *Irish Nation and Peasant* (now title of *Peasant*), 23 January 1909.
57. *Peasant*, 26 December 1908.
58. *Sinn Fein*, 22 August 1908.
59. Griffith, ed., *Thomas Davis—the Thinker and Teacher*, p. 199.
60. *Peasant*, 26 December 1908.
61. *Irish Nation and Peasant*, 2 January 1909; and *Sinn Fein*, 26 April 1913.
62. *Irish Nation and Peasant*, 4 September 1909.
63. Arnold Wright, *Disturbed Dublin*, London, 1914, pp. 157–9; *United Irishman*, 14 October 1905.
64. *Irish Nation and Peasant*, 20 February 1909.
65. *Ibid.*, 3 July 1909. (Robert Lynd).
66. *Ibid.*, 20 February 1909.
67. *Ibid.*, 27 November 1909.
68. Strauss, *Irish Nationalism and British Democracy*, London, 1951, p. 219.
69. Clarkson, p. 267, New York, 1925.
70. *Sinn Fein*, 25 October 1913.
71. J. M. Hone, *Thomas Davis*, London, 1934, p. 61.
72. *Sinn Fein*, 27 September 1913.
73. *Ibid.*, 6 December 1913.
74. *Ibid.*, 28 February 1914.

75. *Sinn Fein,* 27 September 1913.
76. STRAUSS, *Irish Nationalism,* p. 218.
77. W. K. HANCOCK's illuminating phrase.
78. See, for example, Joseph Johnston, *The Sickness of the Irish Economy,* Dublin, 1957, p. 6.
79. F. HACKETT, *Ireland—A Study in Nationalism,* New York, 1918, p. 328.
80. R. B. O'BRIEN, *Parnell,* p. 39.
81. P. COLUM, *The Road Round Ireland,* New York, 1930, p. 304.

Conclusion: The Passing of Non-Violent Sinn Fein   PAGES 147–55
1. One of these was to lower the cost of burial at Glasnevin cemetery.
2. 'The Sinn Fein platform is, and is intended to be, broad enough to hold all Irishmen who believe in Irish independence, whether they be republicans or whether they be not. Republicanism as republicanism has no necessary connection with Irish nationalism; but numbers of Irishmen during the last 116 years have regarded it as the best form for an independent Irish government. What the form of an Irish national government should be is an interesting but not a material question. It is the thing itself, regardless of its form, Ireland wants.' (*Sinn Fein,* 18 May 1907).
3. PANDIT NEHRU, *An Autobiography,* p. 84. (Quotes Gandhi's *Doctrine of the Sword,* 1920).
4. It is difficult to see how the 1782 constitution could help either at the start of the movement or at the time of settlement except as a legal myth akin to Sorel's myth of the general strike which might never take place.
5. *United Irishman,* 23 June 1900.
6. *Gaelic American,* 9 February 1907. (Article by Lynd).
7. *Bulmer Hobson Papers,* The constitution of the IRB (Amended, Clause 18).
8. MICHAEL EDWARDES, *The Last Years of British India,* London, 1963, p. 57, takes this view. 'As long as civil disobedience remained non-violent, it did not greatly worry the government.'
9. *All Men are Brothers,* p. 119. 'Through realisation of freedom of India I hope to realise and carry on the mission of the brotherhood of man.' This view owes much to Mazzini whom Griffith also quoted.

Epilogue references

Epilogue: Calculated Violence in the Anglo-Irish War and After
    PAGES 159–72

1. ROBERT TABER, *The War of the Flea: A Study of Guerilla Warfare, Theory and Practice,* London, 1969.

2. DAN BREEN, *My Fight for Irish Freedom* (1st. ed., 1924), Tralee, 1964.

3. ERNIE O'MALLEY, *On Another Man's Wound* (1st. ed., 1936), London, 1961.

4. TOM BARRY, *Guerilla Days in Ireland* (1st. ed., 1949), Tralee, 1968.

5. *The Collected Works of Mahatma Gandhi,* Government of India, Ahmedabad, 1965, XVII, 488 and XVII, 218–20 and 131–4.

6. TABER, pp. 116–7.

7. *Irish Independent,* 8 December 1970.

8. O FAOLAIN, ed., *The Autobiography of Theobald Wolfe Tone,* p. 108.

9. G. A. HAYES-MCCOY, 'The Conduct of the Anglo-Irish War' in Desmond Williams, ed., *The Irish Struggle, 1916–1926,* London, 1966, p. 60.

10. O'MALLEY, p. 93, and BARRY, p. 146.

11. O'MALLEY, pp. 203–12, etc.

12. There had been a number of raids for arms in 1917 and 1918, mainly in the south of Ireland at places such as Cork, Macroom, and Tralee. In November 1918 Donnchadha MacNeilus nearly killed an RIC sergeant while attempting to resist arrest in Cork city. Had he not escaped, and had his victim died, MacNeilus might have been executed. It was the conjunction of Soloheadbeg and the Dail Declaration of Independence which invested the action of Breen, Treacy and their comrades with particular importance. For details of early violence, see FLORENCE O'DONOGHUE, *No Other Law,* Dublin, 1954, pp. 44–5.

13. BREEN, pp. 27, 48, 96, 102, 120, 161. Breen demonstrates the opposition between the two wings of the movement by quoting O'Malley's objection to villagers who called him a Sinn Feiner: 'O holy mackerel, do you hear what they are calling us, "Bloody Sinn Feiners"?'

14. BREEN, p. 161.

15. BREEN, p. 96. In early 1921, de Valera as president of the Dail accepted responsibility for the war and though the Dail did not actually pass a resolution to this effect its consent was implicit.

16. O'MALLEY, pp. 193–4. 'Griffith had seen the development of the military aspect with misgiving.'

17. P. S. O'HEGARTY, The Victory of Sinn Fein, pp. 47–8. 'I believe that the shooting and the ambushing and the savagery and moral collapse which they generated, sickened his soul and then his body.' See also COLUM, Arthur Griffith, p. 212. Griffith believed that the IRA should be used mainly as police.

18. BARRY, p. 171.

19. O'MALLEY, p. 273.

20. BARRY, p. 164.

21. O'MALLEY, p. 135, etc.

22. Barry, p. 149.

23. O'MALLEY, p. 317.

24. BREEN, p. 48.

25. BREEN, pp. 134–7. See also RICHARD BENNETT, The Black and Tans, London, 1964, p. 87. Bennett whose book has a strong anti-Irish bias provides a totally inaccurate quotation from Breen. His criticism of Breen is supported by no evidence.

26. BARRY, pp. 44–7.

27. TABER, pp. 94–8. Taber appears to base his conclusions on Bennett.

28. HAYES-MCCOY, in The Irish Struggle, p. 65.

29. See MAO TSE-TUNG, Selected Military Writings of Mao Tse Tung, Peking, 1966, pp. 77–186 ('Problems of Strategy in Guerilla War'), and Fremantle, ed., Mao Tse-Tung: An Anthology of His Writings, New York, 1971.

30. CHE GUEVARA, Guerilla Warfare, London, 1970.

31. TABER, p. 24. 'The guerilla's mere survival is political victory, and BARRY, p. 26, 'Strange as it may seem, it was accepted in West Cork that the paramount objective of any Flying Column in the circumstances then prevailing, should be, not to fight but to continue to exist.'

32. BARRY, p. 77.

33. HAYES-MCCOY, in The Irish Struggle, p. 61.

34. O'MALLEY, pp. 98 and 108.

35. BARRY, p. 175. Barry considered himself over-optimistic an

excluded the possibility of holding out against large-scale reinforcements. After the Treaty, Collins denied he had feared Lloyd George's 'immediate and terrible war'. See MICHAEL COLLINS, *The Path to Freedom*, Cork, 1968, p. 31.

36. BARRY, p. 167.
37. TABER, p. 113.
38. BARRY, p. 145.
39. O'MALLEY, p. 152 (July to August 1920).
40. TABER, p. 34.
41. O'MALLEY, p. 51.
42. E. R. NORMAN, *A History of Modern Ireland,* London, 1971, p. 12.
43. BREEN, p. 94.
44. BREEN, p. 104.
45. See *Sunday Times* Insight Team, *Ulster*, London, 1972, p. 159, etc.
46. BREEN, p. 124.
47. BARRY, p. 170. 'Never throughout 1920 and 1921 did GHQ repudiate or reprimand any unit for its aggressiveness or its activities.'
48. BARRY, pp. 84 and 175.
49. TABER, p. 103.
50. BRIAN CROZIER, *The Study of Conflict*, London, 1970, p. 10.
51. CHE GUEVARA, p. 105. 'We sincerely believe that terrorism is of negative value, that it by no means produces the desired effects, that it can turn a people against a revolutionary movement, and that it can bring a loss of lives to its agents out of proportion to what it produces.'
52. BREEN, pp. 161-2. Breen gives 1921 as the date of the meeting but Gandhi was not in London in 1921 but in 1931. Gandhi was 'the most intelligent man and the most implacable foe of Britain whom I have ever met'.
53. BREEN, p. 162.
54. TABER, p. 92.
55. O'MALLEY, p. 193.
56. See 'Insight', *Ulster*, p. 310. For the past 60 years British governments have brought peace by meeting minimum Protestant demands.
57. BARRY, pp. 106-7 and 135.
58. *Collected Works of Mahatma Gandhi,* XVII, 488.

Select bibliography

A   SOURCES

1. COLLECTIONS OF PRIVATE PAPERS:

William Bulfin Papers (National Library of Ireland)
Minutes of Celtic Literary Society (National Library)
George Gavan Duffy Papers (National Library)
J. O. Hannay Papers (Trinity College, Dublin, Library)
Bulmer Hobson Papers (National Library)
A. S. Green Papers (National Library)
William O'Brien (Parliamentarian) Papers (National Library)
William O'Brien (Trade Unionist) Papers (National Library)

P. S. O'Hegarty Papers (Family)
John Redmond Papers (National Library)
John Sweetman Papers (Family).

2. NEWSPAPERS AND PERIODICALS:

    (a) Separatist or advanced nationalist papers
    Shan Van Vocht, 1896–99
    United Irishman, 1899–1906
    Sinn Fein, 1906–10
    Republic, 1906–7
    Peasant, 1907–8
    Irish Nation & Peasant, 1909–10
    Nationality, 1915–9.
    Irish Freedom, 1910–4
    Gaelic American
    Fainne an Lae
    An Bearna Baoghail.

    (b) Other papers
    Cork Evening Echo
    Daily Independent
    Freeman's Journal
    Irish Independent
    Irish Times
    Irish World
    Leader
    Sunday Independent
    United Ireland.

    (c) Periodicals
    Dublin Magazine
    Forum
    New Ireland Review
    North American Review.

3. BIOGRAPHICAL DICTIONARIES, DIRECTORIES AND YEAR BOOKS:

    Annual Registrar, London, 1905–10
    Celtic Who's Who, Dublin, 1921
    Dictionary of National Biography, London, 1927
    Leabhar na hEireann (*The Irish Year Book*, published by the National Council), 1908–20.
    Thom's Irish Almanac and Official Directory, Dublin, 1844—work still in progress

4. MEMOIRS AND SPEECHES:

    Barry, Tom, *Guerilla Days in Ireland*, Tralee (Anvil) 1968

Breen, Dan, *My Fight for Irish Freedom,* Tralee (Anvil) 1964

Brennan, Robert, *Allegiance,* Dublin (Browne & Nolan) 1950

Collins, Michael, *The Path to Freedom,* Cork (Mercier) 1968

Colum, P., *The Road Round Ireland,* New York (Macmillan) 1926

Davitt, M., *The Fall of Feudalism in Ireland,* London (Harper) 1904

Deasy, Liam, *Towards Ireland Free* (ed. John E. Chisholm), Dublin and Cork (Mercier) 1973

Denson, A. (ed.), *Letters from AE,* London (North Western University Press) 1961

FG. F., (ed.), *The Memoirs of Desmond Fitzgerald 1913–16,* London (Routledge & Kegan Paul), 1968

Fremantle, A. (ed.), *Mao Tse-Tung: An Anthology of His Writings,* New York (Mentor) 1971

Gandhi, M. K., *An Autobiography or the Story of My Experiment with Truth,* Ahmadabad (Navajivan Publishing House) 1966

Gandhi, M. K., *The Collected Works of Mahatma Gandhi,* Ahmadabad, (Government of India) 1965

Gogarty, O. St. J., *As I was Going Down Sackville Street,* London (Penguin) 1954

Gogarty, O. St. J., *It Isn't This Time of Year at All!,* London (Macgibbon & Kee) 1954

Griffith, A., *The Home Rule Bill Examined,* Dublin (National Council) 1913

Hobson, Bulmer, *Ireland Yesterday and Tomorrow,* Tralee (Anvil) 1968

Horgan, John J., *Parnell to Pearse,* Dublin (Browne & Nolan)

Kettle, T. M. (ed.), *Irish Orators and Oratory,* Dublin (Talbot) no date

Lyons, G. A., *Some Recollections of Griffith and His Times,* Dublin (Talbot) 1923

MacBride, Maud Gonne, *A Servant of the Queen,* London (Gollancz) 1938

MacSwiney, T., *Principles of Freedom,* 9th ed., Dublin (Irish Book Review) 1964

Mao Tse-Tung, *Selected Military Writings of Mao Tse-Tung,* Peking (Foreign Languages Press) 1966

Mitchel, John, *Jail Journal,* New York 1854 and Dublin (Gill) 1913

Mitchel, John, *The Last Conquest of Ireland (Perhaps),* Dublin (The Irishman Office) 1861

Nehru, J., *An Autobiography,* London (Bodley Head) 1955

O'Brien, W., and Ryan, D., eds., *Devoy's Post Bag, 1871–1928,* Vols. I and II, Dublin (Fallon) 1948 and 1953

O Faolain, S., (ed.), *Autobiography of Theobald Wolfe Tone,* London (Nelson) 1937

O'Malley, Ernie, *On Another Man's Wound*, London (Rich and Cowan) 1936; London (Four Square) 1961

O'Leary, John, *Recollections of Fenians and Fenianism*, London (Downey) 1896

Paul-Dubois, L., *Contemporary Ireland* (trans. T. M. Kettle), Dublin, (Maunsel) 1911

Ryan, Mark, *Fenian Memoirs*, Dublin (Gill) 1945

Sibley, M. Q. (ed.), *The Quiet Battle: Writings on the Theory and Practice of Non-Violent Resistance*, New York (Anchor) 1965

Tolstoi, L., *Writings on Civil Disobedience and Non-Violence*, New York (New American Library) 1968

UNESCO, *All Men are Brothers: Life and Thoughts of Mahatma Gandhi as told in his own words*, Paris (UNESCO) 1958

Wade, Allen, ed., *Yeats, W. B., Letters*, London (Hart-Davis) 1954

Yeats, W. B., *Dramatis Personae 1896–1902*, Dublin (Cuala Press) 1935.

5. POLITICAL PAMPHLETS:

(a) National Council Pamphlets,
Griffith, A., *How Ireland is Taxed*, Dublin, 1907
Griffith, A., *The Sinn Fein Policy*, Dublin, 1905
Lynd, Robert, *The Ethics of Sinn Fein*, Limerick, 1912
O'Sheehan, J., (Seaghan O Siothchain), *Constitutionalism and Sinn Fein*, Dublin, 1907
Sweetman, J., *Purchase of the Irish Railways*, Dublin, 1906
Anonymous, *Ireland and the British Army*, Dublin, no date
Anonymous, *The Police and the Nation*, Dublin, [1907?].

(b) Dungannon Club Pamphlets,
Anonymous, *Irishmen in the British Army*, Belfast, no date
Anonymous, *Manifesto to the Students of Ireland*, Dublin, 1906
Hobson, Bulmer, *Defensive Warfare*, Belfast, 1909 (debate with J. J. O'Neill)
Hobson, Bulmer, *Ireland or Westminster*, Belfast, 1908
Hobson, Bulmer, *Manifesto to the Whole People of Ireland*, Belfast, 1905
Hobson, Bulmer, *The Creed of the Republic*, Belfast, 1907
Hobson, Bulmer, *The Flowing Tide*, Belfast, no date
Lynd, Robert, *The Orangemen and the Nation*, Belfast, 1907.

(c) Unionist Pamphlets,
Outlook, *National Organisations in Ireland*, London, 1907
Irish Unionist Alliance, *Pamphlets on Gaelic Movement and Sinn Fein*, Dublin, no date

(d) Miscellaneous:
Griffith, A., *The Resurrection of Hungary*, Dublin, 1904

Griffith, A., *The Resurrection of Hungary* (containing also *The Sinn Fein Policy and Pitt's Policy*), Dublin, 1918
Pearse, P., *Ghosts*, Dublin, 1913
Sweetman, J., *Liberty*, Dublin, 1908
Sweetman, J., *Nationality*, Dublin, 1909.

6. LITERARY WORKS:

Béaslaí, P., (ed.), *Songs, Ballads and Recitations of Arthur Griffith*, Dublin (Walton's Musical Instrument Galleries), no date
Fogarty, L., *James Fintan Lalor, Patriot and Political Essayist*, Dublin (Talbot) 1919
Griffith, A., (ed.), *Jail Journal*, by John Mitchel, Dublin (Gill) 1913
Griffith, A., (ed.), *Meagher of the Sword*, Dublin (Gill) 1914
Griffith, A., (ed.), *Poems and Ballads of William Rooney*, Dublin (Gill) 1901
Griffith, A., (ed.), *The Felon's Track*, by Michael Doheny, Dublin (Gill) 1914
Griffith, A., (ed.), *Thomas Davis – the Thinker and Teacher*, Dublin (Gill) 1914
Kinsella, T., (ed. and trans.), *The Tain*, Oxford (OUP) 1970
MacManus, S., (ed.), *Prose Writings of William Rooney*, Dublin (Gill) 1909
Maguire, W. J., *Irish Literary Figures*, (Vol. I), Dublin (Metropolitan Publishing Co.) 1945.
Ryan, W. P., *The Plough and the Cross*, Dublin (Irish Nation Office) 1910
Yeats, W. B., *The King of the Great Clock Tower and Other Poems*, Dublin (Cuala Press) 1934.

B   SECONDARY WORKS

1. GENERAL STUDIES:

Hancock, W. H., *Survey of British Commonwealth Affairs*, Vol. I. (Problems of Nationality 1918–36), London (OUP) 1937
Kee, Robert, *The Green Flag: A History of Irish Nationalism*, London (Weidenfeld & Nicolson) 1972
Lecky, William E. H., *A History of Ireland in the Eighteenth Century* (5 vols.), London (Longmans, Green) 1906
Lyons, F. S. L., *Ireland Since the Famine*, London (Routledge & Kegan Paul) 1971
Macaulay, T. B., *The History of England*, (Everyman edition), Vols. II and III

Mansergh, N., *The Irish Question, 1840–1921*, London (Allen & Unwin) 1965

Norman, E. R., *A History of Modern Ireland*, London (Allen Lane) 1971

O'Hegarty, P.S., *A History of Ireland under the Union, 1801–1922*, London (Methuen) 1952

Packenham, Frank, *Peace by Ordeal*, London (Cape) 1935

Strauss, E., *Irish Nationalism and British Democracy*, London (Methuen) 1951.

2. SPECIAL SUBJECTS:

Béaslaí, Piaras, *Michael Collins and the Making of a New Ireland*, London (Harrap) 1926

Bell, J. Bower, *The Secret Army*, London (Anthony Blond) 1970

Bennett, Richard, *The Black and Tans*, London (Four Square)1964

Birmingham, George A., *An Irishman Looks at His World*, London (Hodder & Stoughton) 1919

Brown, T. N., *Irish-American Nationalism*, Philadelphia and New York (Lippincott) 1967

Bury, J. B., *A History of the Freedom of Thought*, London (Home University Library) 1944

Butler, Ewan, *Barry's Flying Column*, London (Les Cooper) 1971

Catlin, George, *In the Path of Mahatma Gandhi*, London (Macdonald) 1948

Clarkson, J. D., *Labour and Nationalism in Ireland*, New York (Columbia University. Studies in History, Economics, and Public Law, Vol. CXX) 1925

Corkery, Daniel, *The Fortunes of the Irish Language*, Dublin (Mercier) 1968

Cronin, Sean, *The McGarrity Papers*, Tralee (Anvil) 1972

Crozier, Brian, *The Study of Conflict*, London (Institute for the Study of Conflict) 1970

Davis, R. P., 'The Irish-Catholic Question and New Zealand Society, 1868–1922', University of Otago, Ph.D. thesis, 1968

de Blacam, A., *What Sinn Fein Stands For*, Dublin & London (Melifont) MCMXXI

Desmond, Shaw, *The Drama of Sinn Fein*, London (Collins) 1923

Edwardes, M., *The Last Years of British India*, London (NEL Mentor), 1963

Fox, R. M., *Green Banners*, London (Secker & Warburg) 1938

Graves, C. Desmond, *Liam Mellows and the Irish Revolution*, London (Lawrence & Wishart) 1971

Gregg, R. B., *Power of Non-Violence*, London (Routledge) 1935

Guevara, Che, *Guerilla Warfare*, London (Penguin) 1970

Hackett, Francis, *Ireland: A Study in Nationalism*, New York (Huebsch) 1918

Hammond, J. L., *Gladstone and the Irish Nation*, London (Longmans) 1938

Henry, R. M., *The Evolution of Sinn Fein*, Dublin (Talbot) 1920

Jeffares, A. N., and Cross, K. C. W., *In Excited Reverie: A Century Tribute to William Butler Yeats, 1865–1939*, London (Macmillan) 1965

Kedourie, E., *Nationalism*, London (Hutchinson University Library) 1966

Kohn, Hans, *Nationalism: Its Meaning and History*, Princeton (Van Nostrand Anvil) 1955

Laffan, Michael, 'The Sinn Fein Party 1916-1921', in *Capuchin Annual*, Dublin (Capuchin Periodicals) 1970

Laffan, Michael, 'The Unification of Sinn Fein in 1917' in *Irish Historical Studies*, XVII, Dublin (University Press) March 1971

List, F., *The National System of Political Economy*, (translated by S. Lloyd), London (Longmans) 1885

Lynch, Diarmuid, *The IRB and the 1916 Rising*, (ed. Florence O'Donoghue), Cork (Mercier) MCMLVII·

Lynd, Robert, *Ireland, a Nation*, London (Richards) 1919

Lynd, Robert, *Home Life in Ireland*, London (Mills & Boon) 1909

Lyons, F. S. L., *The Fall of Parnell, 1890–91*, London (Routledge & Kegan Paul) 1960

Lyons, F. S. L., *The Irish Parliamentary Party, 1890–1910*, London (Faber) 1951

Macardle, D., *The Irish Republic*, Dublin (Irish Press) 1951

Martin, F. X., (ed.), *Leaders and Men of the Easter Rising: Dublin 1916*, London (Methuen) 1967

Mill, J. S., *England and Ireland*, London (Longmans, Green, Reader and Dyer) 1868

Moody, T. W., (ed.), *The Fenian Movement*, Cork (Mercier) 1968

Moody. T. W., 'The New Departure in Irish Politics: 1878–9' in *Essays in British History in Honour of J. E. Todd*, London (Frederick Muller) 1949

Namier, Lewis, *Vanished Supremacies: Essays on European History 1812–1918*, New York (Harper Torch Books) 1963

Ní Mhurchú, Eibhlín, *Siúlach Scéalach*, Dublin (Cló Grianréime) 1968

Nowlan, K. B., (ed.), *The Making of 1916*, Dublin 1969, (Donal McCartney, 'The Sinn Fein Movement', pp. 31–50)

O'Brien, Conor Cruise, *States of Ireland*, London (Hutchinson) 1972

O'Brien, C. C., *Parnell and His Party, 1880–90*, London (OUP) 1957

O'Brien, C. C., (ed.), *The Shaping of Modern Ireland*, London (Routledge & Kegan Paul) 1960

O'Brien, George, *The Four Green Fields*, Dublin & Cork (Talbot) 1936

O'Brien, William, *The Irish Revolution and How it Came About*, London (Allen & Unwin) 1923

O'Hegarty, P. S., *Sinn Fein: an Illumination*, Dublin & London (Maunsel) 1919

O'Hegarty, P. S., *The Victory of Sinn Fein*, Dublin (Talbot) 1924

O Luing, Sean, 'Arthur Griffith, 1871–1922: Thoughts on a Centenary', *Irish Historical Studies*, Vol. LX, No. 238, summer 1971, pp. 127–138

Phillips, W. Alison, *The Revolution in Ireland 1906–1923*, London (Longmans, Green) 1923

Plunkett, Sir Horace, *Ireland in the New Century*, London (John Murray) 1904

Power, Paul F., *Gandhi on World Affairs*, London (Allen & Unwin) 1960

Ryan, Frederick, *Criticism & Courage*, Dublin (Maunsel) 1906

Ryan, W. P., *The Pope's Green Island*, London (Nisbet) 1912

Ryan, W. P., *The Irish Labour Movement*, Dublin (Talbot) 1919

Schilling, F. K., 'William O'Brien and the All-for-Ireland League', Dublin University, B.Litt. thesis, 1956

Scott-James, R. A., *Fifty Years of English Literature, 1900–50*, London (Longmans) 1951

Sunday Times Insight Team, *Ulster*, London (Penguin) 1972

Taber, Robert, *The War of the Flea: A Study of Guerilla Warfare, Theory and Practice*, London (Granada Publishing) 1970

Taylor, A. J. P., *The Habsburg Monarchy*, London (Penguin) 1964

Thornley, D. A., 'The Irish Home Rule Party and Parliamentary Obstruction, 1874–87', *Irish Historical Studies*, XII, March 1960

Wade, E. G. S., and Phillips, G. G., *Constitutional Law*, London (Longmans) 1960

Whyte, J. H., *Church and State in Modern Ireland, 1923–1970*, Dublin (Gill & Macmillan) 1972

Williams, Desmond, (ed.), *The Irish Struggle, 1916–26*, London (Routledge & Kegan Paul) 1966

Wittke, C., *The Irish in America*, Baton Rouge (Louisana State University Press) 1956

Wright, A., *Disturbed Dublin*, London (Longmans) 1914.

3. BIOGRAPHIES:

Bourke, Marcus, *John O'Leary: A Study in Irish Separatism*, Tralee (Anvil) 1967

Bourke, Marcus, *The O'Rahilly*, Tralee (Anvil) 1967

Burdon, R. M., *The Life and Times of Sir Julius Vogel*, Christchurch (Caxton Press) 1948

Chavasse, M., *Terence MacSwiney*, Dublin (Clonmore & Reynolds) 1961

Colum, P., *Arthur Griffith*, London (Browne & Nolan) 1959

Coxhead, Elizabeth, *Daughters of Erin: Five Women of the Irish Renaissance*, London (NEL) 1965

Forester, M., *Michael Collins—The Lost Leader*, London (Sphere) 1972

Fox, R. M., *James Connolly – the Forerunner*, Tralee (The Kerryman) 1946

Gwynn, D. R., *The Life of John Redmond*, London (Harrap) 1932

Gwynn, D. R., *Edward Martyn and the Irish Revival*, London (Jonathan Cape) 1930

Hone, J. M., *W. B. Yeats, 1865–1939*, London (Macmillan) 1942

Hone, J. M., *Thomas Davis*, London (Duckworth) 1934

Hurst, M., *Parnell and Irish Nationalism*, London (Routledge & Kegan Paul) 1968

Irvine, St. J., *Parnell*, London (Ernest Benn) 1925

Kenny, H. E., (*Sean-Ghall*) *Arthur Griffith*, Dublin 1922

Lacouture, J., *Ho Chi Minh*, London (Lane) 1968

Larkin, E., *James Larkin*, London (NEL) 1968

Lavelle, Patricia, *James O'Mara: A Staunch Sinn Feiner, 1873–1948*, Dublin (Clonmore & Reynolds) 1961

Lyons, F. S. L., *John Dillon: A Biography*, London (Routledge & Kegan Paul) 1968

McCay, H., *Padraic Pearse*, Cork (Mercier) 1966

MacDermot, F., *Theobald Wolfe Tone*, London (Macmillan) 1939; Tralee (Anvil) 1969

MacManus, M. J. (ed.), *Thomas Davis and Young Ireland*, Dublin (The Stationery Office) 1945

Marreco, Anne, *The Rebel Countess: The Life and Times of Constance Markievicz*, London (Sphere) 1967

Nanda, B. R., *The Nehrus*, London (Allen & Unwin) 1962

O'Brien, R. B., *Life of Charles Stewart Parnell*, London (Nelson) 1910

O'Connor, Frank, *The Big Fellow: Michael Collins and the Irish Revolution*, London (Corgi) 1969

O Cobhthaigh, D., *Douglas Hyde,* Dublin (Maunsel) 1917

O'Donoghue, Florence, *No Other Law* (the story of Liam Lynch and the Irish Republican Army, 1916–1923), Dublin (Irish Press) 1954

O Luing, Sean, *Art O Griofa,* Dublin (Sairseal & Dill) 1953

O Luing, Sean, *I Die in a Good Cause* (a study of Thomas Ashe), Tralee (Anvil) 1970

Owen, Frank, *Tempestuous Journey, Lloyd George His Life and Times,* London (Hutchinson) 1954

Ryan, Desmond, *Sean Treacy and the Third Tipperary Brigade,* Tralee (Anvil) 1962

Ryan, D., *The Phoenix Flame: A Study of Fenianism and John Devoy,* London (Barker) 1937

Shearman, Hugh, *Not an Inch: A Study of Northern Ireland and Lord Craigavon,* London (Faber & Faber) 1942

Sheehy-Skeffington, F., *Michael Davitt – Revolutionary Agitator and Labour Leader,* London (MacGibbon & Kee) 1965

Tahmankar, D. V., *Lokamanya Tilak: Father of Indian Unrest and Maker of Modern India,* London (Murray) 1956

Tendulkar, D. G., *Mahatma, Life of Mohandas Karamchand Gandhi,* Delhi (Government of India) 1953

Thornley, D. A., *Isaac Butt and Home Rule,* London (MacGibbon & Kee) 1964

Wheeler-Bennett, John W., *John Anderson Viscount Waverley,* London (Macmillan) 1962

White, Terence de Vere, *Kevin O'Higgins,* London (Methuen) 1948; Tralee (Anvil) 1966

Younger, Calton, *A State of Disunion* (Griffith, Collins, Craig and de Valera), London (Fontana) 1972.

Index